The Book of Sin

How to Save the World
A Practical Guide

The Book of Sin

How to Save the World
A Practical Guide

Jerry Hyde

Winchester, UK
Washington, USA

First published by Soul Rocks Books, 2018
Soul Rocks Books is an imprint of John Hunt Publishing Ltd., Laurel House, Station Approach,
Alresford, Hants, SO24 9JH, UK
office1@jhpbooks.net
www.johnhuntpublishing.com
www.soulrocks-books.com

For distributor details and how to order please visit the 'Ordering' section on our website.

ISBN: 978 1 78535 693 3
978 1 78535 694 0 (ebook)
Library of Congress Control Number: 2017940005

A CIP catalogue record for this book is available from the British Library.

Design: Stuart Davies

Printed and bound by CPI Group (UK) Ltd, Croydon, CR0 4YY, UK

We operate a distinctive and ethical publishing philosophy in
all areas of our business, from our global network of authors to
production and worldwide distribution.

Contents

To the past
Pete and Alice Muckley
And the future
Noor and Tara Kubba Hyde and Sam Nathan Saffron

I don't know how generations to come are going to manage
surnames.

He who is without sin among you, let him throw the first stone...
John 8:7

Someday a real rain will come and wash all this scum off the streets.
Taxi Driver

All the Seven Deadly Sins are man's true nature. To be greedy. To be hateful. To have lust. Of course, you have to control them, but if you're made to feel guilty for being human, then you're going to be trapped in a never-ending sin-and-repent cycle that you can't escape from.
Marilyn Manson

I shot a man in Reno, just to watch him die.
Johnny Cash

Sin

sɪn/

Noun.

An immoral act considered to be a transgression against divine law.

'A sin in the eyes of God.'

Synonyms: Immoral act, wrong, wrongdoing, act of evil/ wickedness, transgression, crime, offence, misdeed, misdemeanour, error, lapse, fall from grace.

Verb.

Commit a sin.

'I sinned and brought shame down on us.'

Synonyms: Commit a sin, offend against God, commit an offence, transgress, do wrong, commit a crime, break the law, misbehave, go astray, stray from the straight and narrow, go wrong, fall from grace.

Foreword

22 December 2015
South-East France

Dear Hyde,

What *ARE* 'The Seven Deadly Sins'? I've forgotten, even though I had to memorise them when I was a kid in Catholic school. Lust, Greed, Anger, Gluttony... What else? Oh yeah, *SLOTH*... That's a good one. *ENVY*... That was one, I believe. Well, that's six. What about gullibility, credulousness, wilful ignorance? There's a deadly sin if ever there was one.

Didn't Bosch do a nice painting of the Seven Deadly Sins? I think so. I'll have to go and look for that in a book of his works that I possess.

Five minutes later: Yes, I found it. A crazy circular painting, a sort of dial of the Seven Deadly Sins. The seventh one is *PRIDE*.

What about *DISHONESTY*, deceiving the ignorant and the innocent? What about *CRUELTY*, harming other humans or animals unnecessarily, excessively or simply because you *ENJOY* it?

Obviously, there are *MORE* than seven deadly sins. Excessive *INTOXICATION*—there's a big one. *REVENGE*—a deadly sin. Humans have trouble distinguishing between revenge and justice. Two different things. Maybe revenge falls under the heading of anger—a subcategory.

The whole exercise is an oversimplification. That's what it comes down to. The terms are too broad, but you know people in the old days loved those kinds of simplifications. The seven virtues, the seven keys to power; seven—an archetypal number. I've sailed the seven seas, been to see the Seven Sisters, the seven wonders of the world, the seven sacraments.

1

All those 'Deadly Sins' are part of our nature: Lust, Anger, Greed, etc. I know I'm 'guilty' of all of them, committed them all. Most of them repeatedly. We can't help it. But it's only in excess that they become 'deadly'.

Take *LUST*. 'Lust' is just a judgement put on a hormone-driven animal urge. Without 'Lust' there would be no reproduction. But most of us learn through experience that excessive Lust, just as with excessive Gluttony, can indeed be 'deadly.' So, we try to control these drives: the pursuit of pleasure, the pursuit of wealth, power, glory ('Pride'). Most people I know, myself included, behaved excessively in their youth and then gradually toned it down after many painful consequences. We all can wince at the memory of the stupid things we did. We can all feel remorse for our excesses.

So, there's my two cents about the Seven Deadly Sins.

Robert Crumb

Prologue

We were somewhere around Barstow on the edge of the desert when the drugs began to take hold. I remember saying something like, 'I feel a bit lightheaded; maybe you should drive...' And suddenly there was a terrible roar all around us and the sky was full of what looked like huge bats, all swooping and screeching and diving around the car, which was going about a hundred miles an hour with the top down to Las Vegas...

Hunter S. Thompson, *Fear and Loathing in Las Vegas*

New Year's Day 2016.

I have, of late, been microdosing psychedelic mushrooms each and every morning, to the great enhancement of my spirit and the benefit of my constitution, but I have, *as yet*, seen no giant bats in the skies over Tottenham.

Clouds the colour of gunmetal grey, oh *yes*; crows the colour of the abyss, *aplenty*; carrier bags, orange-and-white of hue by the baker's dozen born high on a clammy wind supernatural in its mildness and sinister in its balminess given that this is a January day, indeed the very *first* January day of this new year of our Lord 2016; but, as yet...

No bats.

The darkness presses its haunted face against my dirty windows pleading to come in, the city tossing uncomfortably in a fitful slumber made barren by pills, weed and cheap alcohol, and all the while a post-apocalyptic quiet hangs over the streets, slick with last night's vomit and the ghosts of already discarded resolutions.

I sit at my old oak desk and reflect on the task ahead. It's late. Outside a storm rages. The single bulb of a 1940s Herbert

Terry angle-poise lamp struggles to penetrate the smoky gloom; cigarette butts are piled high in a *Bates Motel* china ashtray. My emphysemic *MacBook*, with its cataract-clouded screen, returns my gaze with blank disinterest; dull eyes staring back at me through a dirty patina of grime, compacted dust and coffee stains.

This isn't working.

I need more than stale incense and the cold, creeping draft that sneaks invisibly down the back of my neck. I need plantation shutters, an overhead fan, blood-stained sheets and discarded bourbon bottles.

I need *atmosphere*, goddammit, I'm an *artist*.

Something must be done. And so come, come with me now; for it is this very day I have pledged to embark on a journey, a long, mysterious and arduous journey lasting all of 366 days (this being a leap year), during which time I will meditate often and attend the gym three times a week and write each and every day, curtail my overspending on unnecessary shit on eBay and indeed buy *no more guitars*, because surely eleven is enough for any man, and avoid excessive masturbation, tobacco, dairy produce and refined sugar wherever possible, and behave with love and compassion towards my fellow man at all times, and I will *not rest…*

Until we have saved the world.

To do this, we will venture through all nine layers of hell, supping from the cracked chalice of Sin, and leave no stone unturned until we have a complete and *total* understanding of that which has led us astray, corrupting and poisoning our biosphere through war, greed, lust for power, dominance and control, that has brought this once beautiful paradise that we call Earth to the very edges of extinction.

This place that we call home.

Throughout this trial, given that the greatest Sin of them all is considered to be Pride and Vanity, I will neither shave my beard nor cut my hair, and thus resolved I shall—with no thought for my own personal safety and for the good of all mankind— explore, experience, investigate, touch, taste and smell...

Sin.

In all its dark glory.

And it's not until we have savoured *all* that is twisted, abhorrent and evil that we will emerge afresh into a new world, a world of hope, a world of possibility...

A world of our own dreaming.

What's more, it is my suggestion that the very *notion* of Sin that we all live with is out-dated, ladies and gentlemen; that the old codes of guidance and morality no longer serve us; and I contest that if we are indeed to save the world, we need a *new operating system*, a new way. And *that* is the express purpose of this adventure: a call to arms, a clarion cry to your deeper spirit, a demand to throw out the musty rule book and to come up with your own so that by the end of this book you will have explored, as will I, your *own* dark corners, your *own* ethics, your *own* morality, to find your *own* code.

And then go out and live it.

You see, this isn't a *self-help book*.

This is a *do-it-yourself-help book*.

It's not my job to tell you to rebel against society and I'm not going to tell you how to live or what to do or how to do it or even what's right or wrong for you. But stick with the journey (and I gotta tell you right now, I haven't got a clue where it's going to take us), and by the end of the ride you should have a better understanding of how to live *your* life, and how to make the world a better, safer, richer and more peaceful place.

As Osho said, where there is certainty there is no learning. And while I have absolutely no idea how we might save the world, I *had* thought that I knew a thing or two about Sin, but as I begin to explore, even at this early stage, I realise that the whole area... is vast.

But that's exciting, right?

To get on a plane and not know its destination? A magical mystery tour. Let's just hope we end up in the Seychelles rather than Southend. All I know is that we won't rest until we have rescued mankind and found the answer... to what is Sin.

January

In the beginning, God created the heaven and the earth. And the earth was without form, and void; and darkness was upon the face of the deep. And the Spirit of God moved upon the face of the waters.

> The Book of Genesis

And so, before we set forth, let's talk some more about you.

Yeah…

You.

Despite my gossamer-thin promise that if you read this you'll know how to live life by your own rulebook, and indeed save the planet, why would you accompany me on this trek? Why would you choose to leave the comfort of the fireside and venture out into the wasteland in the full knowledge that this journey is at best unpredictable and at worst liable to drive us to the edge of madness or beyond?

Two reasons:

First, the world we live in is fucked. Our terrorist governments and corrupt, self-serving politicians have propagated a vast disparity in the division of wealth; a semi-visible and perpetual World War III rages above and below ground, and we need to find a whole new value system if we are to survive as a species.

Then there's the second reason and that is all about you.

Because, like it or not, *you* are a Sinner.

And look, I know you try your best, OK? I know you're one of the good guys. I know you subscribe to *Avaaz* and you've got a standing order to the World Wildlife Fund. I applaud you for that, I really do.

But way, way back, when you were born, when you were fresh and pure and new, you had no notion of mortal Sin, or even morality; and unless your mother had experienced some kind of trauma when you were in the womb, the chances are you were largely a blank canvas, secure in the innate knowledge that you were loveable.

And you had no concept of Sin.

My belief, after working as some kind of therapist for over two decades now, is that there is essentially only one core wound that any of us have and that all presenting issues are but symptoms of that wound:

Do I belong?
Am I accepted?
And most of all...
Am I loveable?

As soon as you are admonished, bullied or shamed, you run naked in your humiliation from the Garden and do whatever you possibly can to *cover your arse.*

And so it goes on. You develop an inner radar like a soldier on sentry duty, peering into the darkness, eyes on stalks in a fixed 1000-yard stare; hyper-vigilant to any perceived attack, your armour becomes thicker and thicker. But still the messages penetrate, at first from your family: 'big boys don't cry, little girls should never get angry, children should be seen and not heard, you wait until your father gets home, don't be naughty or the sandman will get you, mummy won't love you if you do that, you'll never go to heaven if you do that...'

Then comes school: 'you're too short, too tall, too fat, too thin, you wear glasses, you smell, you have greasy hair, you're stupid, you don't have the right clothes to be in the gang, you're shit at maths...'

As you grow older, maybe you realise that all of this was nonsense. Maybe you get over it or maybe you get some therapy, but inside you're wounded and deep down uncertain as to whether anyone will ever really love you.

And still the messages come: 'you're too slow, too fast, too short, too tall, too bald, too hairy, not sexy enough, too sexual, you're arrogant, you're a failure, you're brash, you're under-confident, too bullish, too weak....'

And by the time you're fully-grown, you're going to have ingested a whole library of data that says, in essence...

You're just *no good*.

And from that position you are very susceptible to the idea that you are a Sinner, not because of what you do or what you *don't* do, but because you inhabit this world; and part of the core of this world's very *structure* is that you, by default, are born morally depraved and therefore must plead for salvation.

How else would you be controllable? By your parents, your state, your church?

Now hold on. Before you throw this book away, this isn't just another conspiracy theory rant. Not yet, anyway.

Wikipedia defines Sin as:

The act of violating God's will. Sin can also be viewed as anything that violates the ideal relationship between an individual and God; or as any diversion from the perceived ideal order for human living.

However, rather than committing a wrongdoing, the original Hebrew word Sin meant 'to miss', to not be present, to be unconscious.

I apologise now if you don't like Osho because there's going to be a fair amount of his twisted genius in this book. He said:

The word 'Sin' is very significant; not in the way Christians interpret it, not according to the dictionaries, because they have been influenced by the religions, but according to its original roots: the word 'Sin' simply means forgetfulness. And that gives a totally new dimension to the word—a beauty. It is nothing for which you can be thrown into hell. It is something that you can manage. It is not concerned with any action in particular; it is concerned with your awareness.

To be aware is to be virtuous. And to remain in unawareness is the only Sin. You may be doing good things without awareness. But those good things are no longer good, because they come out of darkness, unconsciousness, blindness. And as far as awareness is concerned, a man who is full of awareness, alert, cannot do anything wrong. It is intrinsically impossible.

Awareness brings so much clarity, so much perception, so much understanding that it is impossible to do anything that can be harmful to anyone. It is impossible to interfere with somebody's freedom or somebody's life. You can only be a blessing to existence, nothing else. So, to forget that you are a seeker is dangerous. It is falling into Sin. This is the only Sin I accept as Sin.

Did you get that?
Spoiler alert.

The only true Sin…
Is that of unconsciousness.
Boom!

There we have it and I'll tell you right now, *that* may well be the most important point raised in this book, so if you're just skim-reading you can quit here and still have got something profound.

But should you wish to persevere…

We are born *pure*, we are told we are *Sinners*, we desperately *adapt* in order to be *loveable* and thus lose touch with *ourselves*, which makes us *unconscious*, and in so doing…

We become *Sinners.*

What a rip-off.

Of course, the notion of Sin and its hellish consequences have been used as a vehicle for the last 2000 years to control the masses, as well as, I grant you, providing some kind of social guideline in the form of morality. But, as Osho said, 'morality is so that people don't have to think for themselves.'

If you want to *control* people—whether it is to keep them in 'order', to exploit or to manipulate them—the best way is to instil in them a deep sense of guilt, or better still scare the *b'Jesus* out of them.

Keep them fearful.

The war against terror is a contemporary example. By manufacturing or manipulating a scary situation with a semi-visible or questionably real enemy we feel beholden to our governments to protect us.

Even better than terrorism, how about a list of things that you will almost certainly want to indulge in at some time because you're *human*, but—and here's the clever part—if you *do* you will fry for all eternity. That's *all* eternity mind, not just a quick, 'ouch! oh fuck I just burned my forearm on the edge of the oven' kind of moment. No, we're talking about that kind of pain times a thousand for all eternity. Forever. And ever. Unless…

You do as your told.

Convince people of that bullshit from as early an age as possible, preferably while they're young and untarnished like perfect little sponges, and man, you've really got control of them.

That's real power.

Christianity in particular is a religion that blossomed among the slaves of the Roman Empire, people of a servile nature who were sold an ideology of a saviour who died for their Sins.

The Pagan religions of the Romans and Greeks were much more level. I mean, you could even shag a god if you got lucky— there wasn't quite the same hierarchy as there is in Christianity.

There wasn't so much bowing down before a vengeful god.

* * *

A while back it seemed that everyone who came to see me suddenly wanted to talk about sex, and my friends and clients encouraged me to write a book about the sticky subject.

I think it's a good idea. I think it needs to be done. There are so many lies around sex, so many myths. The truth needs to be told.

I have so much experience of working with sex, and so many people who trust me enough to talk to me in great and explicit detail about their own personal experiences, and...

Sex sells.

And so yeah, I could write a whole book on sex, and maybe I will, and maybe I should, but right now it's just not calling me. I simply don't feel evolved enough in that area to do it. But in thinking about it I went to Lust and from there to the other Sins. And so...

Here we are.

Lust

Noun.

1. Strong sexual desire.

'He knew that his lust for her had returned.'

Synonyms: Sexual desire, sexual appetite, sexual longing, sexual passion, lustfulness, ardour, desire, passion.

Verb.

1. Have strong sexual desire for someone.

'He really lusted after me in those days.'

Synonyms: Desire, be consumed with desire for, find sexually attractive, find sexy, crave, covet, want, wish for, long for, yearn for, hunger for, thirst for, ache for, burn for, pant for; informal—have the hots for, letch after/over, fancy, have a thing about/for, drool over, have the horn for.

According to Wikipedia:

> Lust is an emotion or feeling of intense desire in the body. Lust can take any form such as the lust for knowledge, the lust for sex or the lust for power. It can take such mundane forms as the lust for food as distinct from the need for food. Lust is a psychological force producing intense wanting for an object, or circumstance fulfilling the emotion.

OK, that helps a bit. Maybe it's what religion does with Lust that makes it problematic.

In Buddhism, while technically not a religion, it still seems they believe that 'suffering is caused by lust.'

In Hinduism, Lust is considered the greatest enemy to mankind and the gateway to hell.

In Islam, it is frowned upon and seen as the first step towards adultery, rape and other antisocial behaviours.

In Sikhism, Lust is counted among the five cardinal Sins or Sinful propensities, the others being anger, ego, greed and attachment. The uncontrollable expression of sexual Lust is considered evil.

However, *none* of the Pagan religions considered Lust a vice at all, especially the Ancient Roman Bacchantes and the Dionysians; and all things Tantric—art, writings and religious rituals—glorify sex as a route to the divine.

The Christians believe that Lust devalues the eternal attraction of male and female, reducing personal riches of the opposite sex to an object for gratification of sexuality; and the Catholic church considers it to be a disordered desire for sexual pleasure, where sexual pleasure is 'sought for itself, isolated from its procreative and unitive purposes'.

To me, the best interpretation I've come across so far is from Russell Brand, who described his sexual addiction as 'Like being chained to a maniac.'

And yeah, out of control or taken to the point of obsession, Lust can be a problem.

But then, so can anything.

* * *

Gluttony

Noun.

Habitual greed or excess in eating.

'She said plumpness was a sign of gluttony in most cases.'

Synonyms: Greed, greediness, overeating, overconsumption, binge eating, gourmandism, gourmandising, gluttonousness, voraciousness, voracity, wolfishness, insatiability; informal — piggishness, hoggishness, gutsiness; technical polyphagia, hyperphagia; edacity, gulosity, esurience.

The order of the Sins — those considered worst listed last — comes from Dante's *Divine Comedy* and next in line, Gluttony, is defined as the 'wasting of food, either through eating too much food, drink or drugs, misplaced desire for food for its taste, or not giving food to the needy.' Or as Dante saw it, 'excessive love of pleasure.'

Gluttony is clearly a serious issue in today's Western culture. As I understand it, human beings aren't designed to deal with abundance. We've come from millennia of feast or famine. In times of abundance — after a harvest or a successful hunt — people would gather for a ritual feast and once it was done, hunker down and live off the dried and preserved leftovers, sometimes for months at a time.

Nowadays, we live in a time of perpetual feast. Every high street has a multitude of food outlets, supermarkets, convenience stores, cafés and restaurants. Despite the increasing prevalence of food banks, it's hard to actually starve in our culture. My corner shop doesn't even have doors. It's open all day and night, every day of the year.

But our bodies don't know how to deal with this perpetual feast. So we keep eating. And eating. Three meals a day on average, plus God knows how many snacks.

I've done a lot of fasting in my time, either through poverty or spiritual practice, and the thing I've noticed is that we just don't need that much food. The trouble is mealtimes have become part of our social regime and so we eat because it's 'lunch time', not necessarily because we're hungry. It's one of the many ways we've become detuned from ourselves, out of sync, asleep. If you break with traditional mealtimes and only eat when you are genuinely hungry, not only will you almost certainly eat less, but also you'll find that you are much more sensitised to your whole being.

* * *

Greed

Noun.

Intense and selfish desire for something, especially wealth, power or food.

'I don't know why I'm eating more—it's not hunger, it's just greed.'

Synonyms: Avarice, acquisitiveness, covetousness, rapacity, graspingness, cupidity, avidity, possessiveness, materialism; mercenariness, predatoriness; informal money-grubbing, money-grabbing; informal grabbiness; rare Mammonism, pleonexia, gluttony, hunger, ravenousness, voraciousness, voracity, insatiability; gourmandising, gourmandism; intemperance, overeating, overconsumption, self-indulgence; informal swinishness, piggishness, hoggishness, gutsiness; rare edacity, esurience, desire, urge, need, appetite, hunger, craving, longing, yearning, hankering, hungering, thirst, pining; avidity, eagerness, enthusiasm, impatience; itch.

That's a lot of synonyms…

OK, we all get what Greed is. It's when somebody wants more things than the person needs or can use. That'll be guitars for me, then. And denim. I've got me a bad case of Greed for 24 ounce unsanforised, raw Japanese denim.

The problem already facing me with this book is that I wanted to reclaim some of these Sins, I wanted to find the *good* side. Lust isn't too hard a sell, but Gluttony and Greed?

I fear I'm facing defeat in the opening chapter.

* * *

But with Sloth I might be back in the game.

Sloth

Noun.

1. Reluctance to work or make an effort; laziness.

'He should overcome his natural sloth and complacency.'

Synonyms: Laziness, idleness, indolence, slothfulness, inactivity, inertia, sluggishness, apathy, accidie, listlessness, lassitude, passivity, lethargy, languor, torpidity, slowness, heaviness, dullness, shiftlessness; archaic fainéance; rare hebetude.

2. A slow-moving tropical American mammal that hangs upside down from the branches of trees using its long limbs and hooked claws.

It's while lazing around that I have most of my best ideas. The bath is a fertile tub where the muse often visits me, as is the couch that my grandfather made in the 1930s that my family and I have lounged around on ever since.

I'm not saying that I'm not lazy. I am. When it comes to housework, accounts and washing my car, I'd much rather pay someone else to do them. My concern is not that we waste that much time, but that we don't spend enough in peaceful contemplation. We don't sit and wait, we don't tune in, we don't cultivate our intuition, and we're too busy emphasising the value of productivity to the degree that we often sacrifice the kind of inspiration that comes with stillness.

What's more, everything has to be fast these days—high-speed broadband, 4G phones, drones delivering shit from Amazon. We seem to be in a terrible hurry.

But when it comes to productivity I'm a big advocate of doing nothing.

Nothing at all.

Because, to my mind, the best way to hit a creative dead end is to *try*—try really hard to come up with a great idea, bang your head against the wall as you attempt to think outside the box, to be brilliant, to be great, to shine, to prove to the world that you are of value, worth having on board...

To prove that you are not lazy.

I remember my mum sometimes used to say to me at the end of the day during the holidays, 'So, what have you done to justify your existence today?'

I always found that a tricky one to answer and even now, aged 51, I find it hard to lie in bed in the mornings when I don't have to get up. That programming goes deep and who among us can claim to have been raised to do nothing? I was raised to worship the great gods of *Do* and *Think*. To do nothing, to be still, to wait or to contemplate... they were false gods, forbidden gods, pagan gods, gods worshiped by losers and wasters.

I remember when I left school the careers advisor shrugging his shoulders and saying, 'I expect you to be in prison within a year.'

Imagine if, instead, he'd said, 'Right, we've identified you as someone who displays strong dropout capabilities and therefore we figure you're qualified to take stressed-out people, sick of their corporate treadmill lives, into the woods to do nothing for several days until they have a direct experience of the divine, which blesses them with the absolute certainty of what their life's purpose should be.'

Things might have turned out...

Just like *this*.

So Sloth. Not all bad.

* * *

What's next? Oh yeah:

Wrath

Noun.

Extreme anger.

'He hid his pipe for fear of incurring his father's wrath.'

Synonyms: Anger, rage, fury, annoyance, indignation, outrage, pique, spleen, chagrin, vexation, exasperation, dudgeon, high dudgeon, hot temper, bad temper, bad mood, ill humour, irritation, irritability, crossness, displeasure, discontentment, disgruntlement, irascibility, cantankerousness, peevishness, querulousness, crabbiness, testiness, tetchiness, snappishness.

OK, I know Wrath has a bad rap, but let's divide it into two categories—*clean* anger and *dirty* anger.

A weird example of clean anger occurred for me in the elevator at Covent Garden tube a few years ago. It was a Friday evening and I'd popped into Marks & Spencer opposite the station on my way home, where I availed myself of a two-course meal (plus a bottle of wine) for sad, lonely people for a tenner.

The elevator was packed, but I managed to squeeze into a small gap. As the doors were closing, a group of about five wide boys in town on the piss muscled their way in, pushing aggressively into the crowd to a typical flurry of muted English tuts.

Beside me stood a young black guy, a typical London office worker on his way home at the end of a long week, minding his own business, doing no harm. I don't remember him making any noticeable response to being barged into; he just looked at the ground.

The wide boys decided they were going to have some fun. They started poking him and sneering, 'You gonna cry, are you? You gonna cry?'

I felt an immediate volcanic heat rising from my chest and, grasping my bottle of rosé like a club, through Dirty Harry teeth, I hissed, 'Leave. Him. Alone.'

They looked at me. I looked at them. Everyone else looked at the floor with sudden and immediate fascination.

'You fucking heard me.'

The elevator reached the bottom and the crowd bolted from the claustrophobic warzone, but I stood my ground, rosé held high, burning down the wankers with death-stare eyes, as if to say, 'We like black people in this town, right. So, fuck off back to whatever provincial shithole you come from before I wrap this bottle of delightfully elegant and fruity wine with its enticing aroma of strawberries and cream, and a crisp finish, around your thick, shiny, shaven skulls, you inbred, racist twats.'

While all the time, a tiny voice inside my head was going, 'Please, Jerry, please don't do this. Please just walk away.' Much the same as the time I told a couple of corrupt Moroccan cops to go fuck themselves and the voice was going, 'Please, Jerry, please don't do this. You're gonna get raped in some Marrakech hellhole. Just give them the money and walk.'

But, interestingly, on both occasions, they just went, 'Alright, mate, alright,' and backed off.

Leaving me feeling like the *boss*.

But then we have *dirty* anger.

A few days after the rosé incident, I was driving my kids to school through Muswell Hill. They were thirsty and pleading for water, so I slammed the car into the curb without indicating and jumped out, while the driver behind me leaned on his horn. Unperturbed in the knowledge that I could take on anyone, I gave him the finger and, next thing you know, this beast of a man is out of his vehicle and bounding down the road towards me like an enraged silverback.

I reached for my rosé. It wasn't there.

And so I did what any sensible coward would do and ran for the safety of my car and locked all the doors. Silverback wasn't deterred; he pounded on the window, his spit smearing down the glass as I drove away, my little girls asking, 'What does "cunt" mean, Daddy?'

Looking back on it, I realise the difference. In Covent Garden, The Force was strong within me. I felt clear and true to my beliefs, and that translated into a pure energy that created an impregnable boundary around me.

In Muswell Hill, I was all over the place, stressed and driving badly. And when the shit hit the fan, I abandoned all sense of hardness and self-composure and ran for the hills. Giving him the finger was my version of dirty anger and I got the impression that the man who came bounding down the road after me hadn't spent too much time reflecting on the many possible ways of expressing his, either.

Wrath. It's a mixed bag.

* * *

Envy

Noun.

1. A feeling of discontented or resentful longing aroused by someone else's possessions, qualities, or luck.

'She felt a twinge of envy for the people on board.'

Synonyms: Jealousy, enviousness, covetousness, desire.

Verb.

1. Desire to have a quality, possession, or other desirable thing belonging to (someone else).

'He envied people who did not have to work at the weekends.'

Synonyms: Be envious of, be jealous of.

Bertrand Russell said that envy was one of the most potent causes of unhappiness. I feel that envy has its uses, however. It's like a signpost to what we truly want for ourselves. I envy that person's job, family, car, status… it shows us what we most desire.

I'd tweak what Bertrand says to be more in line with Osho and suggest that *comparison* is what causes envy and jealousy, and is therefore the root of the most potent cause of unhappiness. When we compare—which we are all conditioned to do from an early age—it's very much an integral part of our educative ethos; we come out better or worse than the other and therefore *separate*. At best, it's a shallow victory; at worst, a total defeat.

Osho said:

From the very beginning you are being told to compare yourself with others. This is the greatest disease; it is like a cancer that goes on destroying your very soul.

Jealousy is comparison.

Comparison is a very foolish attitude, because each person is unique and incomparable. I am just myself and you are just yourself. There is nobody else in the world to be compared with. There has never been any individual like you before and there will never be again. Once this understanding settles in you, jealousy disappears. You are just yourself, and you need not be like anybody else, either.

Everybody is jealous of everybody else. And out of jealousy we create such hell, and out of jealousy we become very mean.

Or more simply perhaps, in the words of Keith Moon, 'I am the greatest Keith Moon-type drummer in the world.'

And therein lies the answer to true happiness.

* * *

Pride

Noun.

1. Be especially proud of (a particular quality or skill).
2. Excessive pride in one's appearance, qualities, abilities, achievements, etc.; character or quality of being vain; conceit.
3. Something about which one is vain or excessively proud.
4. Lack of real value; hollowness; worthlessness: the vanity of a selfish life.

'The faces of the children's parents glowed with pride.'

Really? That's the *worst* Sin?

OK, so one of the *main* concerns here seems to be this idea of excess. To be *excessively proud*. I'm guessing that this is an English notion, the idea that we might be *too much*. Too much pride, self-love, even confidence is definitely seen as a terribly poor show in the UK. I've written about this before. Despite some serious reservations about some aspects of US culture—or perhaps more specifically, US politics and foreign policy—the one thing I really admire about the US is the fact that they aren't phobic about 'boasting'. Sure, to our eyes they can be brash; but they have a dream—that you can better yourself. We don't have that in the UK.

It's considered to be bad taste.

I woke early this morning to the startling news that David Bowie had died in the night. It's hard to imagine a world without Bowie—he's *always* been here. But had he adhered to the moral code stating that pride is the worst sin of all, that's the world we'd have lived in. Bowie free. Watching his iconic performance of Ziggy Stardust at Hammersmith on YouTube, I'm guessing he wasn't too encumbered with a fear of showing off or using his beauty to promote his art.

Like a lot of great wisdom, I found this among the photos of kittens and selfies on Facebook:

> When in doubt, listen to David Bowie. In 1968, Bowie was a gay, ginger, bonk-eyed, snaggle-toothed FREAK walking around South London in a dress, being shouted at by thugs. Four years later, he was still exactly that, but everyone else wanted to be like him too. If David Bowie can make being David Bowie cool, you can make being you cool. PLUS, unlike David Bowie, you get to listen to David Bowie for inspiration. So, you're one up on him really. YOU'RE ALREADY ONE AHEAD OF DAVID BOWIE.

Was David Bowie guilty of 'the vanity of having led a selfish life'? Who gives a shit? He left the world a better place for his existence and that, to me, is a job well done.

* * *

So, there you have them. The Seven Deadly Sins.

But why seven? Why not six? Or eight?

As Robert Crumb pointed out:

The seven virtues, the seven keys to power; seven — an archetypal number. I've sailed the seven seas, been to see the Seven Sisters, the seven wonders of the world, the seven sacraments.

Seven, it seems, is a fairly hefty number. Cosmically speaking.

Used 735 times in the Bible, seven is the foundation of God's word.

It's considered the number of completeness and perfection.

There are seven days in a week and God's Sabbath is on the seventh.

The Bible was originally divided into seven major parts.

There are seven men in the Old Testament who are specifically mentioned as men of God.

Jesus is quoted as giving seven parables.

In *The Book of Revelation*, there are seven churches, seven seals, seven trumpet plagues, seven thunders and the seven last plagues.

There are seven annual Holy Days.

Jesus performed seven miracles on the Sabbath.

There are seven colours in the rainbow.

Seven continents.

There are seven hills of Rome.

Seven was considered the number of gods in Ancient Egypt.

There are seven pure notes in the diatonic scale; seven inches is the diameter of a 45rpm record; there are seven musicians in a septet and seven basic swaras in Indian Carnatic music.

7-Eleven is a chain of convenience stores.

In Hinduism, there are seven worlds in the universe, seven seas in the world and seven gurus called Sapta Rishis.

In Islam, the ritual pilgrimages of Hajj and Umrah require seven walks between the Al-Safa and Al-Marwah mountains, and Muslims on a pilgrimage to Mecca walk seven times around the cuboid building at the centre of Islam's most sacred mosque.

There are seven levels to heaven and seven doors to hell, and the number of big Sins or vices is...

Yup.

Seven.

In Judaism, Shiv`a is another pronunciation of the Hebrew word for seven and is the number of days of mourning; hence, one sits shiva.

Seven blessings are recited during a Jewish wedding ceremony and the bride and groom are feted with seven days of festive meals after their wedding.

Japanese mythology has the seven lucky gods of good fortune.

The Buddha walked seven steps at his birth and his mother died seven days later.

The number of dwarfs was seven.

In the Vedic system, there are seven chakras.

The Irish hero, Cúchulainn, has seven fingers on each hand, seven toes on each foot and seven pupils in each eye.

The seventh son of a seventh son is a vampire. Fact.

The ancient world had seven wonders.

Yul Brynner, Steve McQueen, Horst Buchholz, Charles Bronson, Robert Vaughn, James Coburn and Brad Dexter were magnificent, and there were seven of them, as were there samurai.

In numerology seven is the seeker, the thinker and the searcher of truth.

In Chinese culture, seven represents the combination of Yin, Yang and Five Elements (Metal, Wood, Water, Fire and Earth). This combination is considered as harmony.

I live in Seven Sisters and the street number of my building is 28, which is not only divisible by seven but which, if you add the two and the eight together, you get ten; take away three and you get seven, and seven is the number of espressos I used to drink in a day before it nearly killed me.

None of which really, *really* explains *why* there are *seven* Sins, but that's what we've got so that's what we'll work with.

* * *

Concerned that having looked at the Big Seven I may already have run out of Sinful ground to cover, and the next 11 chapters might be woefully short and thin on content, I decided to go and pick the brains of old friend and caustic Essex artist, Grayson Perry.

If you don't know Grayson, he's famous for being mentioned in *The Ladybird Book of the Hipster*, but he also won the Turner Prize for his pots and he's exhibited at a few places like the Tate, the Stedelijk, the Australian Museum of Contemporary Art, the Saatchi Gallery, the National Portrait Gallery, the British Museum, and he's done some telly and stuff.

He greets me at the door of his Islington studio with a warm hug. We sit in the middle of what strikes me as quite a modest space for the UK's most loved artist. Somehow, I was expecting something more cavernous, perhaps with a legion of gorgeous young hermaphrodites and eunuchs doing the boring bits on his latest masterpieces.

We spend over an hour discussing masculinity, the subject of his next TV show, book and live tour. I feel comfortable and at ease with the topic. It is, after all, the area where I have the most experience. He is well prepared and knowledgeable, and yet still humble and curious, and seems softer than when I knew him in the past.

Eventually, we exhaust his list of carefully thought-out questions and I fumble my way into Sin with far less focus.

Grayson takes the lead…

'The word *Sin* immediately sets up a kind of idea that it comes from a biblical idea, and therefore it's associated with religiousness and the Bible; and then it's got overtones of a sort of burlesque *naughtiness*, y'know what I mean? 'Sin, oooh I'm sinful!' It's like, 'Ummm… oooh Sinful chocolates,' y'know? Like girls go, 'Oooh, these are Sinful chocolates,' y'know? 'Oooh, that's a bit naughty!'

'So, Sin for me is kind of domesticated bad behaviour.

'It's not a dark, terrible thing. It's not what ISIS is up to. It's something now that is quite like a pet that's a little bit naughty. It's a middle-class sex shop like *Coco de Mer*. It's a bollock-tickling stick.'

He grins and finishes with a flourish. 'Sin has lost its teeth.'

And I think, *oh fuck, he's right, it's as I've already wondered. I've picked a musty, old, out-dated and irrelevant subject to write a book about,* but I'm not ready to pack up and go home yet, so I try to get him back on board.

'I came at it with the attitude, "right, Seven Deadly Sins. I'm gonna debunk all that. I'm gonna take 'em back. I'm gonna write about what's so terrible about Lust and this and that." But the more I get into it, I think, *actually no. Some of these things are really dreadful.* Maybe I'm less a rebel than I thought I was. Maybe I'm much more of a…' I hesitate as the word takes shape in my mouth. 'Conformist?'

Grayson's voice goes up an octave. 'But you're a therapist. You're a moral person.'

And I think, 'Whoa… I've never been called that before.'

'I think we all have little Sins,' Grayson says, smiling, 'that we do on a day-to-day basis, like bad manners and little deceptions and hypocrisies that we all go through, and maybe eating a bit too much and drinking a bit too much. Whereas there's a whole other level of misdemeanour that I don't think Sin covers any more because, as I said, Sin's had its teeth pulled.

'Sin feels like a leisure conversation rather than a world political dilemma.'

'I think that's part of the question,' I reply. 'I mean, it's changing shape every day for me as I look at it more and more, but do we still have a moral code?'

'I think we've got a moral code and it's developing. And, of course, we've got the luxury of talking about it from the rich, politically developed West, where we've probably ironed out most of our really hideous traditions. But there are other places where they still believe in witchcraft or whatever and stuff that's distorted, but we've still got criminals. I think the biggest Sin is probably masculinity!'

His cutthroat Sid James laugh ricochets around the high roof of the studio.

'95 per cent of our prisoners are men. I actually talked to several young guys in police cells and I said, "Why do you think you're here?" And they go, "Well, y'know, my parents were bad, y'know, and I just didn't get on very well at school and there's no jobs round here and I'm bored, y'know..." I said, "That's interesting, but didn't the girls grow up on the same estate? Didn't the girls go to the same school? Didn't the girls have the same parents?"'

He lowers his voice to a near whisper.

'They're not in *here*.'

He lets that sink in, more for himself than for me, it seems.

'There's a different structure to bad behaviour than Sin. Sin sounds like a... it's almost like a...'

'Well, it's an *archaic* word,' I interject. Fuck knows why, I thought I was on *my* side...

'*Yeah*, it's an archaic system. Nowadays, we look at the problems of the world in a much more sophisticated way. And so it's all interconnected. Gluttony, Greed and Lust... they're all part of a recipe that's in different proportions in all things.'

'Maybe that's it, then?' I suggest. 'I'm thinking maybe it was easier when people had that structure of the Seven Deadly Sins or the Ten Commandments.'

'I think Sin brings up the notion of self-control,' he proffers. 'Like not having that next beer, that next chocolate, that next wank. But I don't have it off with other women, *not* because I'm restraining Lust but because I want to be in a relationship with my wife, Philippa.'

'So, if the *good* side of Sin is exercising self-control,' I suggest, 'I'm also interested in what the downside is. Are there things that you don't allow yourself to do because of some kind of programming? I think it's interesting that we both acknowledge that Sin is an outdated word, but it's not an outdated thing in terms of our programming.'

'Well, you could probably write a modern set of Sins, couldn't you?'

'That's ultimately where I'd like to get to.'

'Yeah, you might say that emotional repression is a Sin, or shyness is a Sin. And things that we think of that are mentally unhealthy are Sins, because you're gonna act them out in other ways, so you look at the root of the things that might turn into Sins.

'I'm working on a book called *The Descent of Man,* which has made me really think about the shadow side of my own masculinity. Y'know, I used to be the world's worst road rager. I used to spit, hurl and kick cars on my motorbike, and then one day I had Philippa on the back. We were coming through Hackney and on the Harley I had at the time the light on the speedo was always on, even when the headlights weren't on, so I thought the lights were on. This guy pulled out on me and he was a big black guy.'

His voice drops to a whisper.

'*Really* big. I was fucking incandescent. Shouting at him, pointing at him, I might have even spat at him, and he just got out of that car, got a big spanner and said, "*Your fucking headlights weren't on.*" And he just pushed me and Phil and the bike over. I have never road raged since, because it was like, "*Whoa, OK, I've got you.*"

'But, yeah, I used to be really, really bad… off-the-hook bad.

'And growing up with the family I did, the angry man was the real demon and so to have it in myself wasn't comfortable.'

'That was the most painful thing for me,' I nod. 'Amid all the delights of becoming a parent was opening my mouth and my parents coming out, and realising how much of them I had in me. That's what I'd attribute as being one of the main causes of my adultery. I just never thought I'd do it, cos I was so adamant that I'd never be like my dad, so when I did it I think I was probably more shocked than anyone.'

'I think that embracing the dark side is best done at leisure,' he cackles. 'You don't want to find out about it in the heat of the moment. Most people do and that's the problem.'

'Yeah, when you're lying on the ground and there's a guy with a spanner in his hand.'

Three hours passed. Outside it was dark and quiet. He showed me out with a hug and a sneak preview of a piece that's half-finished in one of the giant kilns: a 5-foot-high penis-shaped pot, and it's clear that, as for me with Sin, this middle-aged transvestite genius is still trying to work a thing or two out about his own masculinity.

The conversation continues even to the door.

'My dad's still alive out there somewhere,' I turned to him.

'Yeah.' It was hard to see in the street light what his expression was, but it's almost as if he slumped. 'So's mine.'

* * *

Grayson raised an important point: Sin really *has* lost its teeth and if we're going to learn anything new on this escapade, we're going to have to come at it from a different angle and dig much deeper.

But before we abandon all the old-fashioned notions of Sin (not that the Seven Deadly Sins are *that* old—they're not even in the Bible; they weren't cobbled together until as late as AD 590 by Pope Gregory)—we had better take a look at that other hideous list: the Ten Commandments.

What the Hell… I never much liked February, anyway.

* * *

February

> Abandon all hope ye who enter here is scrawled in blood red lettering on the side of the Chemical Bank near the corner of Eleventh and First and is in print large enough to be seen from the backseat of the cab as it lurches forward in the traffic leaving Wall Street and just as Timothy Price notices the words a bus pulls up, the advertisement for *Les Miserables* on its side blocking his view, but Price who is with Pierce & Pierce and twenty-six doesn't seem to care because he tells the driver he will give him five dollars to turn up the radio, 'Be My Baby' on WYNN, and the driver, black, not American, does so.
>
> Brett Easton Ellis, *American Psycho*

An enviably brilliant opening to an enviably brilliant book, written by perhaps the bravest living man in literature.

If you haven't read it...

Don't.

It's one of my all-time favourite books: utter genius, blacker than black, beyond black, darker than black... it's really black. I mean depraved black, sick and twisted black, nauseatingly black, dropped by its first publisher because of public outcry kind of black.

It's a terribly dark novel.

I laughed my arse off most of the way through it, the kind of laugh like when you have to stifle a grin when someone tells you their mum just died. You know that one? (You do that, right? It's not just me?)

The lead character, Patrick Bateman, is the ultimate superficial, sociopathic monster of consumer culture, driven by nothing other than greed and hate: a shallow, vicious and loathsome predator dredged from the deepest, darkest corners of Ellis' hideously fucked-up psyche.

Which is what makes him a literary hero.

I mean, I'm pretty frank, OK. I'll tell you about some shadowy shit in my inner workings, but *American Psycho*... It's the sickest thing I've *ever* read. It's like Ellis just plumbed his own inner sewer of horror, and then went out and shared it with the world.

It's the *ultimate* shadow piece.

Just last year in 2016, we had the terrorist attacks on Paris. I remember when it happened, part of me thought, *one hundred and thirty dead? Pussies.*

Which is not me being insensitive to just how awful the events of that night truly were. It's just...

I could have done worse.

For years, I felt horribly ashamed for having fantasies of opening up with a Bren gun and some hand grenades on Oxford Street during rush hour, but then I started to take the risk to share my fantasy with other people and discovered that I wasn't alone.

Now, either a) I happen to attract a certain kind of 'sleeper' serial killer and it's all about to go off, or b) it's not *that* uncommon to have dark fantasies.

I lay in the bath reading the reports on the Paris attacks the morning after and found myself thumbing the following Facebook post, wondering how much hate I'd get in response:

Don't be shocked about Paris.

Don't post messages asking how this could have happened. Ask yourself which part of YOU could have pulled the trigger, could have detonated the explosive vest, could have planned to perpetrate the massacre and justified your actions in your own head.

I dare you.

This is nothing new.

Massacre, mass murder, genocide... It's part of our human

history. It's what we do to each other. And when we do what we do (more often in countries far away so that it gets little media attention), we go, 'Oh yeah, I heard about that.' And then go about our day.

So...

If you really wanna spare a thought for our sisters and brothers in Paris, make sure that thought goes deep into the darker corners of your soul, to your own prejudice and hatred and righteous indignation.

And yeah, I know you're not like that. You're a nice person, one of the good guys, otherwise you wouldn't be on my friend list, but the only way these kinds of behaviours are EVER gonna stop is if people take responsibility for their own shit. That's how we make the world a safer, more peaceful place. Not by pointing the finger and blaming but by looking inwards.

I could go on. And on. And on...

See, that's what I think Brett Easton Ellis was doing. He was *owning* his shit. He was making public his shadow side and therefore taming his demons. He was saying, 'This is how evil I can be, but in coming clean, in shining a light on it, it has no power over me.'

It was an act of consciousness.

The book was published in 1991 to a huge public outcry that went as far as Ellis receiving death threats. In Australia, it was sold shrink-wrapped. This is the same country whose British ancestors buried Aboriginal babies in lines up to their necks in the ground and then competed to see who could kick the heads off the furthest; who gang-raped the mothers and then tortured them to death by inserting sharp objects into their vaginas; who tied the fathers' hands behind their backs, cut their penises and testicles off, and made them run around screaming until they bled to death.

Shrink-wrap that.

American Psycho is a very disturbing book, not just because of its content, but because it confronts us with our own human potential for pure evil.

Something Grayson said to me was that most people who appear evil are just *really* fucked up. They're fucked-up individuals. But when you get human beings acting out their shadow side en masse then that's true evil. And we Brits have perpetrated some of the worst atrocities in history. Right up until the twentieth century, we were using a method of execution known as 'blowing from a gun'.

Can you guess what that meant?

The prisoner is generally tied to a gun with the upper part of the small of his back resting against the muzzle. When the gun is fired, his head is seen to go straight up into the air some forty or fifty feet; the arms fly off right and left, high up in the air, and fall at, perhaps, a hundred yards distance; the legs drop to the ground beneath the muzzle of the gun; and the body is literally blown away altogether, not a vestige being seen.

The method was last employed in Afghanistan in 1930 against eleven Panjshiri rebels.

Yeah, that's right…

Nineteen-fucking-thirty

Even more recently in 2015, North Korea's leader Kim Jong-un had his defence chief, Hyon Yong-Chol, executed using a *four-barrelled anti-aircraft gun* loaded with 14.5mm calibre rounds at a firing range in front of hundreds of people. Kim Jong-un is rumoured to have dispatched others who have incurred his displeasure with flamethrowers, poison and ravenous dogs for offences ranging from corruption to watching South Korean soap operas.

For the British, in the mass reprisals following the Indian Mutiny, blowing from a gun, it seemed, wasn't quite nasty enough, so they deepened it with a religious dimension. The Hindu and Muslim sepoys about to be dispatched were made to strip and smear their bodies in beef or pork fat before being tied to the front of cannons and blown apart. By blowing the body to pieces, the victim lost all hope of entering paradise.

Human beings can be right bastards to each other, especially in the name of God.

* * *

Surely killing is one of the *greatest* Sins, even though it doesn't appear in the Big Seven. We've already established that the Seven Deadly Sins don't appear in the Bible, but they have been an important tool in Christianity for the last 1500 years or so. Most religions have some kind of similar code, apart from the cool ones like Buddhism, Native American Spirituality and Left Hand Tantra. Is it a coincidence that these are the spiritual practices you will find represented in New Age shops selling dreamcatchers and rose quartz Buddhas?

I think not.

Do I have a point?

Not that I'm aware of.

What *does* appear in the Bible is the list that we know as the Ten Commandments, the purpose of which, according to St Paul, was to point out Sin.

> There is no way of coming to that knowledge of sin, which is necessary to repentance, and therefore to peace and pardon, but by trying our hearts and lives by the law.
>
> Romans 7:7-13

But even as I approached this, I could feel myself getting all pumped up and defensive.

'We don't need no stinkin' Commandments...'

That teenage hangover *fuck-you* bravado that postures as the rebel but in truth is just hurt. I always felt that about those characters that James Dean and Brando played. We may have raised them to that status of uber-cool legends, but the truth is they were just damaged and lonely outcasts who gave us damaged and lonely outcasts something to identify with—a place to belong, a uniform.

'What are you rebelling against, Johnny?'

If Brando had answered the question truthfully, instead of sneering, 'Whadda ya got?' he might have said:

The people who judged and abused me when I was growing up, the school system that baffled me, a society whose values and beliefs don't fit my own, thus leaving me feeling unwanted and without purpose or value, the people on the inside for whom life looks so easy, and for whom rewards and opportunities just seem to fall in their laps, where every door of opportunity seems closed to me.

Something like that.

Doesn't sound so rock 'n' roll though, does it?

* * *

I was all ready to shoot the Commandments down in flames, but as I looked around the Internet at the essence of what these archaic teachings actually meant, I realised... they're pretty cool.

I'm gonna end up a priest by the end of this book, aren't I?

What I discovered is:

The First Commandment, 'Thou shalt have no other gods before me,' is about loyalty.

The Second, 'Thou shalt not make unto thee any graven

image, or any likeness of any thing that is in heaven above, or that is in the earth beneath, or that is in the water under the earth,' is about worship.

The Third Commandment, 'Thou shalt not take the name of the Lord thy God in vain; for the Lord will not hold him guiltless that taketh his name in vain,' is about respect.

The Fourth Commandment, 'Remember the Sabbath day, to keep it holy,' is about the importance of the sanctity of relationships.

The Fifth, 'Honour thy father and thy mother,' is about respect for our elders.

Number Six, 'Thou shalt not kill,' is about respect for all life.

The Seventh, 'Thou shalt not commit adultery,' is about purity in relationships.

The Eighth Commandment, 'Thou shalt not steal,' is about honesty.

The Ninth, 'Thou shalt not bear false witness against thy neighbour,' is about truthfulness.

And, last but not least, 'Thou shalt not covet thy neighbour's ox 'n' shit,' is about contentment.

So, if that adds up to a code that encourages us to be loyal, practise some kind of worship, be respectful, to value our relationships, to respect our elders and all life, to be pure in our relationships, be honest and truthful, and to be content with what we've got...

I think my work here might be done.

But if I dig the Ten Commandments, what does that mean? I have to convert to Judaism? What's in the small print? I mean, I'm not anti-Semitic, OK? It's just the *cock* thing. I'm almost fifty-two and I've grown rather attached to my foreskin.

I think we need to delve deeper before I commit.

* * *

So, let's start with the first one:

Loyalty

Loi-uh l-tee.

Noun, plural loyalties.

1. The state or quality of being loyal; faithfulness to commitments or obligations.

2. Faithful adherence to a sovereign, government, leader, cause, etc.

3. An example or instance of faithfulness, adherence, or the like: 'a man with fierce loyalties.'

From Wikipedia:

'Loyalty is faithfulness and a devotion to a person, country, group or cause.'

Loyalty is something that I've not always maintained in my life and yet, life is contradictory and I'm sometimes a hypocrite, because it's also a quality that I pride myself in having. I was totally loyal to my wife for fifteen years and then I cheated on her. I would die for my children and yet I left them. To the men in my life, I am completely devoted. To the women, less so.

Loyalty is a quality that matters to most of us. Treason still carries the death penalty in the UK. As does killing swans, which just strikes me as weird.

Unless you're a swan.

So, what does being loyal entail? I'd say it means never shaming or embarrassing someone you love, especially in front of other people; it means keeping confidences, not using private information as gossip or talking about people behind their backs; it means keeping your word, being truthful and reliable; it means thinking about other people's needs and being considerate; it means not burning royal shipyards; it means not cheating on those you love or betraying those close to you.

It means you're real, congruent and transparent, and people can rely on you to do the shit you said you'd do. It means behaving like a dog, not a metaphorical 'bad' dog, but an actual dog — one that's always there for you and forgives whatever you do and loves you and will rip the throat out of anyone that so much as looks like they're going to hurt you (*that* bit's metaphorical).

* * *

Worship

Wur-ship.

Noun.

1. Reverent honour and homage paid to God or a sacred personage, or to any object regarded as sacred.

2. Formal or ceremonious rendering of such honour and homage: 'They attended worship this morning.'

3. The object of adoring reverence or regard.

Verb (used with object).

1. Worshiped, worshiping or (especially British) worshipped, worshipping — to feel an adoring reverence or regard for (any person or thing).

Verb (used without object).

1. Worshiped, worshiping or (especially British) worshipped, worshipping — to render religious reverence and homage, as to a deity, to attend services of divine worship or to feel an adoring reverence or regard.

Wikipedia:

Worship is an act of religious devotion usually directed towards a deity. An act of worship may be performed individually, in an informal or formal group, or by a designated leader.

Like Sin, to many people worship is an archaic notion, in this godless West, anyway. I've stood in ancient Indian temples and watched in awe the Hindu prayer rituals known as Pūjā, which are performed at the *same* time of day using the *same* sacred artefacts that have been used in the *same* way—anointed with milk, and smudged with sacred herbs and incense—for thousands of years.

Worship is not a notion. You can smell it. You can taste it. You can feel it. Go into any church or temple and I *defy* you not to feel it.

Strangely, and not dissimilarly, I've felt it on the fields of the Somme, standing there at dusk as the mist creeps into the ancient shell holes. You can feel the power of not just what *happened* there, but of all the people who have made the pilgrimage in the 100 years that have passed since those terrible events: the mothers, fathers, widows and children who have come just to be close to where their loved ones were slaughtered, and whose tears have watered the grass beneath your feet, whose very emotion has infused the soil and the air and the trees through their collective acts of devotion.

The monuments and graveyards that trace the old battle lines of the Western Front are all places of worship, with their identical Portland stone grave markers, their Lutyens' monuments and their Kipling inscriptions.

But what *is* the energy of these temples and these places of death? What is held captive in the atmosphere of these shrines?

I would say love.

It's that mixture of joy and sorrow, pleasure and pain, suffering and ecstasy. A place of contradiction, where the heart bursts open and feelings collide to create the electricity that hangs in the air long after the wedding, the funeral, the battle, the honouring of heroes long passed.

It's the essence of love that we leave behind when emotions run deep. If true evil only really happens when humans behave en masse, then the electricity of worship is created by repetition, by the focused devotion of the collective.

One old soldier from the Accrington Pals—friends from the same Lancashire town, who grew up together, joined up together, trained together, fought together and were massacred together—described how he would return, by motorbike, to the same spot each year on the anniversary of the battle, well into old age, just to stand on the spot where he and his friends went over the top at dawn on 1 July 1916.

That is worship.

Worship can take any form you like. It can be changing your baby's nappy. It can be sending your lover a beautiful bunch of flowers. It can be dusting your house. Devotion enriches life; it removes us from the rush, the bustle and the hurry. Worship takes time.

But as the Buddha said, 'The trouble is, you think you have time.'

Life is too short to fill with important meetings, deals and conferences. Steal a bit of time back for you. Bring a bit of worship into your world, a bit of reverence, a moment of quiet stillness.

Make room for the magic.

* * *

Respect

Ri-spekt.

Noun.

1. A particular detail or point (usually preceded by in): to differ in some respect.

2. Esteem for or a sense of the worth or excellence of a person, a personal quality or ability, or something considered as a manifestation of a personal quality or ability.

3. The condition of being esteemed or honoured—to be held

in respect.

Verb (used with object).

4. To hold in esteem or honour—I cannot respect a cheat.

5. To show regard or consideration for—to respect someone's rights.

6. To refrain from intruding upon or interfering with—to respect a person's privacy.

Wikipedia:

Respect is a positive feeling of admiration or deference for a person or other entity (such as a nation or a religion), and also specific actions and conduct representative of that esteem.

By the way, if anyone here is in advertising or marketing... kill yourself. You are the ruiner of all things good. You are Satan's spawn filling the world with bile and garbage. You are fucked and you are fucking us. Kill yourself. It's the only way to save your fucking soul. Kill yourself.

Bill Hicks

Bill Hicks is actually a very good role model for *not* respecting. Which is an interesting angle that I wasn't expecting to explore. But fuck it; let's go there.

Because I'm a huge fan of respect, I'd put it up there alongside love in the importance stakes. I mean, what *use* is love if it isn't paired with respect? Is there even such a thing as love *without* respect? Doesn't that shift more into the realm of pity?

Respect is the cornerstone of my work. I cannot work with someone until I have their respect. How could they trust me? And I cannot do my job unless I have respect for my client. The oft-difficult challenges I make and feedback I give are only possible within an atmosphere of mutual respect.

But lack of respect can be a beautiful thing.

Take this wonderful tweet response by Scottish comedian Frankie Boyle to Richard Branson:

@richardbranson
It's time for bold leadership and conservation for the #Arctic
@frankieboyle
You own an airline you mad cunt

That's pure poetry. It's one of those slap-in-the-face reality checks where you go, 'Oh wow, that's just so right.'

I think comedians are the modern-day philosophers, the Socrates and Aristotles of our time. They are the tricksters, the fools, the jesters—traditionally, the second most powerful character in the court in that they were the only ones allowed to ridicule the king and not be executed.

The fool lifts the veil of authority, devoid of decorum, acting irreverently, unmasking the unpleasant aspects of power.

That's a hefty role—unmasking the unpleasant aspects of power.

And my God did Bill Hicks go for the jugular with that one. But way before Bill, the Native Americans had already learned the value of the fool.

The Lakota Indians' sacred clown was the Heyókȟa, a position of great responsibility and tribal importance. Their power came from their lack of concern for taboos, rules, regulations, social norms or boundaries and their job was to stir things up when people became too comfortable or complacent. The point being that with the right kind of *disrespect*, people can be woken up.

Respect has to be earned and where it is not, disrespect is the only path open to us. The world is in crisis and one of the reasons for this is the absence of good, honest, congruent and trustworthy leadership.

And so, I would say respect, *appropriate* respect for ourselves, for each other and our planet is the only hope the human race has. Respect underpins humanity and if we let these monsters take charge through our own apathy, we will simply not survive. It is the Bill Hicks of this world, the George Carlins, the Eddie Izzards, the Frankie Boyles, the Russell Brands, the *Heyók@as* who are the ones to trust, to show the way. They are the heroes, the dependable ones, the bringers of light and truth.

* * *

Sanctity

saŋ(k)tɪti.

Noun.

1. The state or quality of being holy, sacred, or saintly.

Synonyms: holiness, godliness, sacredness, blessedness, saintliness, sanctitude, spirituality, piety, piousness, devoutness, devotion, righteousness, goodness, virtue, virtuousness, purity.

2. Ultimate importance and inviolability, as in 'the sanctity of human life.'

Synonyms: sacrosanctity, ultimate importance, inviolability.

Wikipedia has nothing to say on the matter. Given my track record in intimate relationships, you could say that I'm not exactly qualified to comment. Then again, maybe it's given me a degree of expertise.

My grandparents were happily married for just under seventy years. They set the bar pretty high. I remember when I was about twelve talking to a kid I knew whose parents had divorced. I was fascinated. I'd not met anyone like that before. Now, more than 50 per cent of marriages end in the courts. It has become normal, and each child now has a selection of parents and step-parents, not to mention siblings.

So, I would say that the sanctity of relationships is something that, once again, we in the West have lost touch with. In the early Nineties, I travelled in pre-Internet India, when the portals to the Great White West were few for the people of the subcontinent, and so every train ride and bus journey included a series of complex interviews and interrogations from our fellow travel companions. I learned a lot from these discourses; in particular, the lack of choice that the Indians had compared to Westerners. And while the suffering and deprivation of much of the Indian population is very real, they somehow seemed less... *neurotic*.

Which I would put down to their lack of choice.

Their caste system denotes that someone can work on a factory floor their entire life and yet some 18 year old of a *higher* caste can be promoted over their head without question.

They are told *who* to marry and many of those I encountered appeared happy with this system; of course, that may have just been the relief that their spouse hadn't turned out to be a total arsehole.

To us, the notion of arranged marriage may seem abhorrent, but while we point a judgemental finger at cultures that don't use *romantic love* as the primary criterion for choosing a partner (which still makes up the majority of the world's population), it's worth remembering that...

Our system simply isn't working.

I'm not saying that we should all stay together. My parents stayed together 'for the sake of the children' and I dearly wish they hadn't. But we need to pause and take a breath before pushing the detonator. Most of the couples I work with, say 80 per cent, make it if they pause long enough to ride out the storm.

There's one person who illustrates much of the world's problems when it comes to the sanctity of relationships and his name...

Roosh V.

Wikipedia has something to say about *this* particular antifeminist, neo-masculinist, pencil-dick, misogynist throwback, mummy's boy demon of hate:

> Daryush Valizadeh (born June 14, 1979), also known as Roosh Valizadeh, Roosh V and Roosh Vorek, is an American writer and pickup artist known for his controversial writings on the seduction community and antifeminism. He is a leader of a movement that he terms 'neomasculinity'.
>
> Roosh writes on his personal blog and also owns the *Return of Kings* website. His writings have received widespread criticism, including accusations of misogyny and promotion of rape.

What Roosh and his frightened followers are doing is dividing men and women further—even the use of the word 'return' implies a reversion to old ways, outmoded gender roles that no longer serve our species. We are in a time of huge social transition, where men have lost their way, and women are confused and disappointed at the lack of good, honest, transparent and *present* men. A time where suicide is one of the largest killers of adult males and women still struggle for equal rights—the last thing we need is Roosh dragging us back to the Stone Age.

Return of the Kings?

Oh, do fuck off.

* * *

Respect for our elders:

Elder

Eld·er.

Adjective.

1. Greater than another in age or seniority.

2. Archaic Superior to another or others, as in rank.

Noun.

1. An older person.
2. An older, influential member of a family, tribe, or community.

Wikipedia:

An elder is someone with a degree of seniority or authority.

OK, this is a good 'un. So, let's begin again by turning 'respect for our elders' on its head.

When I first became a parent, I didn't have a clue how to do it. I mean, I could change a nappy and fill a bottle and all that, but that felt like going through the motions.

I couldn't find the way to have a relationship with this small person. I knew that I didn't want to be the authoritarian bully that my own father had been, but... how to fill that void?

Among all the parenting guides that suddenly filled our house, a friend gave me a rather beautiful book called *The Other Side of Eden* by Hugh Brody—an anthropological study of the origins, history and future prospects for hunter-gatherer tribal people. And it was a depiction of a belief system held by the Inuit of the Canadian Arctic that taught me everything I ever needed to know about how to be a dad.

The Inuit do not have a hierarchical system relating to children in the way that we do. They do not look down on their children, because they believe that their offspring are their elders reincarnated and therefore apportion them the respect owing of their ancestors.

There's your road map. Remember—life is simple.

We complicate it.

Role models are important and people to look up to are essential, and that can be as simple as a family member or friend, as well as public figures. My grandparents were my saviours, but as more and more of us are having children later in life, there's a very real danger that grandparents may well become extinct, which makes the need for a new generation of trustworthy elders even more essential.

The African saying, 'it takes a village to raise a child', is not only true, but also explains so many of our social problems. With the death of community came the death of village elders, people who we knew and could therefore make a personally informed decision when electing them. Now, politicians are distant figures whom most of us are unlikely even to meet, let alone know.

Beyoncé may seem a strange choice of elder to bring into our convoluted story at this point. But I feel that her recent, and sadly controversial, performance at the Super Bowl, where she used the global half-time stage to showcase her political message about racism and police brutality, makes her a modern-day role model. *The Guardian's* Barbara Ellen raises the question: 'How did one of the globe's consummate mainstream superstars manage to reposition herself as a lightning rod for radical politicised black America?'

The answer is simple: the girl's not afraid to risk her prefab pop position to sing about what really matters—black lives. While she could so easily hide away, and live in luxurious and relative peace, Beyoncé is using her fame to speak out against racism and injustice that time and again is perpetrated by people who should be considered elders—those charged with maintaining the peace but who instead commit acts of murder and violence while hiding behind their badges of office. As Wikipedia says, an elder is someone with *a degree of seniority or authority*.

So… stop shooting innocent black people. Fuck it; let's go hog-crazy. Stop shooting *guilty* black people.

Just stop shooting black people.

A culture that cannot trust those allotted the position of elder can only produce a rotten society where civilisation putrefies and freedom burns on a funeral pyre of fear and hatred.

* * *

Thou shalt not kill.

Kill

Verb (used with object).

1. To deprive of life in any manner; cause the death of; slay. Synonyms: slaughter, massacre, butcher; hang, electrocute, behead, guillotine, strangle, garrotte; assassinate.

2. To destroy; do away with; extinguish.

3. To destroy or neutralise the active qualities of.

Verb (used without object).

4. To inflict or cause death.

5. To commit murder.

Wikipedia:

Kill may refer to: The act of causing the death of a living organism, homicide, one human killing another.

OK, plenty to say on this one.

Let's look at some stats. I thought I'd be clever and hit you with some shocking numbers. Like the fact that an estimated 203 *million* people died as a result of warfare in the twentieth century.

But you probably heard that, right? If I asked you, you'd probably go, 'Yeah, yeah, I heard that...'

So, then I thought, I know, I'll give you the figures that show how in all the wars leading *up* to the twentieth century, fewer than 203 million people died. That, despite our notion of ourselves as civilised, in the last 100 years *more* people died in conflict than in all the thousands of years leading up to it.

I assumed that was the case.

But I was wrong. Very wrong. It seems we really *like* killing.

In the Mongol Conquests between 1206 and 1324, 70 million people died. What's more, my friend, the artist John Graham, explained to me that:

The estimated world population at that time was roughly 450 million. Over one-sixth of all human beings died in that conflict. In today's numbers, that's one billion souls—about the present population of Europe.

The Three Kingdoms War in China resulted in the deaths of 40 million people between AD 184 and 280.

The Qing dynasty conquest of Ming Dynasty of 1616 to 1662 cost a mere 25 million lives.

The Taiping Rebellion that lasted from 1850 to 1864 snuffed out 100 million souls, a figure that 'may be underestimated'. Sloppy admin from the Chinese. That's *five times more* than the Great War, by the way. And I don't know about you, but I've never heard of it.

Over the 200 years between 1492 and 1691, 138 *million* North and South American Indians were slaughtered.

Kind of gets a bit *numbing*, doesn't it?

Dungan Revolt, China, 1862 to 1877, 21 mil... never 'eard of it. Conquests of Tamerlane—20 mil; Thirty Years War—12; Napoleonic Wars—6; French Wars of Religion—4; Shaka's conquests—2; and the Japanese invasions of Korea of 1592 to 1598 only managed to account for 1 million dead, which isn't really a proper war, is it?

And that's just a few that I've listed, because numbers get *boring*.

And all this, even though the Bible says, thou shalt *not* do it.

So, I Googled, 'What does 203 million people *look* like?' Because I simply can't get my head around that one.

Didn't come up with much.

Apparently, 100 million pennies will make two cubes, one

12-by-12-by-12 feet, the other seven-by-seven-by-seven feet. My fridge freezer, I'm assured, can hold about 1 million pennies. So, that's 203 fridge freezers full of pennies... in the last century.

More than a Beko free-standing fridge freezer with water dispenser's worth have died in the conflict in Iraq since 2003, while the war in Darfur has accounted for an under-counter larder fridge, and the Afghan conflict a 17-litre compact mini fridge.

And you see how it's got me taking the piss just writing about these figures? I've strayed into the area of bad taste. It's the only way I can handle it. But the truth is, every single one of those pennies was once a little boy or girl.

As I sit in the safety of my home in front of the warm, comforting glow of my laptop, Saudi Arabia is preparing to send in an Ice King RZ109AP2 50cm under-counter freezer's worth of ground troops to Syria to combat ISIS, while intelligence reports suggest Turkey is also preparing to invade. With a terrifying array of rival superpowers wading into the chaotic conflict on opposing sides, the consequences are unthinkable should their forces clash with Russians or Iranians already on the ground.

> I'm glad mushrooms are against the law, because I took them one time and you know what happened to me? I laid in a field of green grass for four hours going, 'My God! I love everything.' Yeah, now if that isn't a hazard to our country... how are we gonna justify arms dealing when we realise that we're all one?

Bill Hicks, where are you when we need you most?

Thing is, when it comes to killing, seems there's a lot of small print. The Hebrew Bible, for example, makes exceptions:

> A number of sins were considered to be worthy of the death penalty including murder, incest, bearing false witness on

a capital charge, adultery, idolatry, having sexual relations with a member of the same sex.

The Holy Quran says in 17:33, 'You shall not kill any person— for God has made life sacred,' ummm... except in the course of justice. It gets more specific in 9:5:

And when the forbidden months have passed, kill the idolaters wherever you find them and take them prisoners, and beleaguer them, and lie in wait for them at every place of ambush. But if they repent and observe Prayer and pay the Zakat, then leave their way free. Surely, Allah is Most Forgiving, Merciful...

Fair enough.

There is no indication in the New Testament that it is unjust, immoral or inappropriate for secular civil governments to execute those guilty of shedding innocent blood, while the Catholic Church states:

Assuming that the guilty party's identity and responsibility have been fully determined, the traditional teaching of the Church does not exclude recourse to the death penalty, if this is the only possible way of effectively defending human lives against the unjust aggressor.

At least 1722 people were sentenced to death in fifty-eight countries in 2012. This is a decrease from 2011, when at least 1923 people were known to have been sentenced in sixty-three countries worldwide.

Now, before we move on from this horrific subject, spare a thought for the 150 billion farmed animals that are killed every year by humans. More than 3000 animals die every *second* in slaughterhouses around the world. This does not include fish and other sea creatures whose deaths are measured in tonnes.

Slaughterhouses pay their staff according to the number of animals killed in a day. The EU Scientific Veterinary Committee estimate that around 5 to 10 per cent of cattle are not stunned effectively. These animals experience the pain of being shot in the head and then having their throats cut while still conscious. It's estimated that up to 4 million insufficiently stunned sheep suffer a similar fate.

Some 1.7 million birds a year die before they even reach the abattoir from heart failure, dislocation of the hip and having their skulls crushed when the drawers on the transporter are closed. Male chickens, that comprise half of all that hatch, are ground up alive.

Most other animals are stunned before having their throats slit, but abattoir vet Gabriele Meurer was quoted as saying:

> They are all upset, some very frightened and some move violently. The animals are never given time to calm down. Sometimes the slaughterman misses, wounding the animal terribly instead of stunning it. It may happen that the second shot cannot be done immediately and the animal is suffering for quite some time.

Most pigs are electrically stunned, but inaccurate placement of the electric tongs is a big problem. Video footage has shown pigs regaining consciousness as they bleed to death. The other 25 per cent of pigs (over 2 million a year) are stunned with CO_2 gas. It takes pigs up to thirty seconds to lose consciousness, during which time they squeal, hyperventilate and try to escape.

Each year, more than 100 million animals, including mice, rats, frogs, dogs, cats, rabbits, hamsters, guinea pigs, monkeys, fish and birds are killed in US laboratories alone for biology lessons, medical training, curiosity-driven experimentation, and chemical, drug, food and cosmetics testing.

Don't even start me on super-rich trophy hunters with their Donny Osmond teeth posing in front of their 'kills'.

OK, I can't take any more of this.

Like I said, read the small print.

* * *

Number Seven: 'Thou shalt not commit adultery.' Can't argue with that. Did it. Wasn't nice. Don't advise it.

* * *

The Eighth Commandment: 'Thou shalt not steal,' is about honesty.

On-uh-stee.

Noun, plural honesties.

1. The quality or fact of being honest; uprightness and fairness.

2. Truthfulness, sincerity, or frankness.

3. Freedom from deceit or fraud.

Wikipedia:

Honesty refers to a facet of moral character and connotes positive and virtuous attributes such as integrity, truthfulness, and straightforwardness, including straightforwardness of conduct, along with the absence of lying, cheating, theft, etc. Furthermore, honesty means being trustworthy, loyal, fair and sincere.

Welcome to Lawrence Square. Bellway Homes is proud to announce an exciting new development of apartments— including live/work units—and three- and four-bedroom townhouses in Tottenham.

Innovatively designed for twenty-first century living, this striking new development offers a range of high-specification properties, including apartments, live/work units and townhouses. Residents can also take advantage of some on-site parking, electric car charging points and a private gym.

Lawrence Square is perfectly positioned for those who want to make the most of city living, with surrounding boroughs and Central London close at hand. Tottenham is a unique place to live, work and play. This up-and-coming, lively and colourful area currently offers an array of independent retailers, supermarkets and local eateries along its bustling high road. These local amenities will continue to flourish as part of the area's continued regeneration. From the high road, residents can find the historic Tottenham ward of Bruce Grove, which offers a relaxed setting, with a selection of cafés, independent stores and delicatessens.

On Sunday, 7 August 2011, I awoke to a flurry of texts from friends checking to see if I was all right.

Why wouldn't I be all right?

Looking out of my bedroom window, I could see *slightly* more smoke than usual hanging over the borough and there had been perhaps more police helicopter activity in the night than usual; but sirens and choppers on a Saturday evening—or any evening—are an integral part of the rich and varied soundtrack of my district.

But switching on the TV, I soon became aware that I was at the epicentre of a wave of violence and 'public disorder' that was sweeping my little corner of the world, and was soon to spread across the country.

It's interesting to look back at my Facebook feed from that time: 'I love the smell of Tottenham in the morning...'

Then later, following a walk through the tense aftermath: 'They burned the fucking Aldi, man! They looted Halfords but not Lidl. Votin' with your feet, Tottenham!'

Two days later, I wrote:

Woken up by sirens again. Weird and interesting time to be in London. With Diana, it allowed out everyone's suppressed grief; this time it's rage, violence and greed... ain't nothin' political about this one, just seems like consumerism gone mad. Thatcher's evil spawn go shopping. There's not a JD Sports in the land that is safe.

And later the same day: 'Shocking scenes in Tottenham this morning. I actually saw several people *paying* for things in my local corner shop. *What is going on*?!'

And my final commentary before it all quietened down:

I'm very worried about this situation, cos there's a real danger that we might *miss the fucking point*! We're fed and bred on greed and consumption. Of *course* it's kicked off, everything has a shadow and this is it. *These riots*, while awful and weird, *are honest*. They show what's just below the surface, all the time, and I really hope that it wakes people up, cos if we just judge it as 'thuggery' then we avoid looking at ourselves and how we all buy into this shit.

And that's when it all started to go tits-up for the area, and it was only a matter of time before Bellway Homes showed up like a manky old buzzard picking over the chicken bone carcass of the neighbourhood.

Poor old Bellway. I searched around on the Internet and I couldn't actually find any dirt on them, which is a shame. I was looking forward to having a go at those bastards, but it seems they're a reputable building company with a clean track record. It would have suited me much better if they'd a history of dodgy dealings, but you can't have everything. No, they're just a bunch of regular, normal liars.

How so? I hear you ask.

Well, I came to this conclusion having watched the promotional video for the Lawrence Square development, which is at the *other* end of my road. It's replacing a bunch of hideous old 1950s municipal office buildings that in turn had been built on old bombsites.

This video shows the beautiful glass balconies and minimalist stainless steel interiors, intercut with exterior shots of the vibrant and colourful street life that is Tottenham.

Except… they're not *in* Tottenham.

No, they're in Brick Lane and Columbia Road, uber-fashionable Shoreditch, which is several miles from here: flower shops and 'street food'; hipsters and Banksy graffiti; huge beards and happy cyclists; and warm, frothy, artisan frappe mocha latte. A long way from the fried chicken shacks and strange shops selling yams, phone cards and Rasta hats that make up my locale.

A while back I saw a very hip young couple—she wore cashmere, he was in Paul Smith and Cutler and Gross—standing on my street corner opposite the permanent traveller site that neighbours my building with its ceramic horse heads and caravans and children with Mohawks and attitudes to match. The yuppies were pouring over their shiny Bellway brochure and I have to say they looked… nervous. Like, the penny was dropping but they couldn't quite marry up what their eyes were telling them. That they'd been…

Conned.

SoTo. That's where I live now. *SoTo.*

South Tottenham. Can you believe that?

* * *

'Thou shalt not bear false witness against thy neighbour.'

Is about truthfulness.

Truth

Trooth.

Noun, plural truths.

1. The true or actual state of a matter.

2. Conformity with fact or reality; verity.

3. A verified or indisputable fact, proposition, principle, or the like.

4. The state or character of being true.

5. Actuality or actual existence.

6. An obvious or accepted fact; truism; platitude.

7. Honesty; integrity; truthfulness.

Wikipedia:

> Truthfulness may refer to: Honesty — a moral character of a human being, related to telling the truth. Accuracy — the propensity of information to be correct.

Barclays Bank's credo is: 'Respect, integrity, service, excellence and stewardship.'

Bwaaaaaha-ha-ha-ha-ha-ha-ha-ha-ha…

Sorry, just blew coffee through my nose. Where was I?

Barclays Bank (I'm referring to the British multinational banking and financial services company, not the cockney rhyming slang for masturbation) has total assets of 242 *trillion* US dollars, making it the seventh largest of any bank worldwide.

In 2012, Boston Red Sox supporter, Republican and advisor to Boris Johnson, Bob 'the unacceptable face of banking' Diamond was Chief Executive of the Barclays Group, for which he received an annual bonus of 6.5 million pounds on top of his 63 million basic salary.

In June of that year, the FSA imposed its biggest fine ever on

Barclays: 290 million pounds in total, for 'serious, widespread breaches of City rules relating to the Libor and Euribor rates.' What this means in lay terms is that the bank had fixed interest rates and had been found to have lied, both to make a profit and to make the bank look more secure during the financial crisis. 'Libor' stands for London Interbank Offered Rate, which is the average of interest rates estimated by each of the leading banks in London that it would be charged were it to borrow from other banks.

Despite evidence that the instruction to lower Libor rates had come directly from Diamond, he refused to resign until widespread anger finally forced him to step down in July 2012, albeit with a paltry 2-million pound compensation cheque.

Diamond was succeeded by Oxford graduate Antony Jenkins, who announced, 'I will not tolerate any circumstances in which our clients are lied to or misled, and any instances I discover will be dealt with severely.'

Bwaaaaaha-ha-ha-ha-ha-ha-ha-ha-ha...

Oh man, it's coffee city round here right now.

Anyway, Jenkins had giant Perspex signs erected all around the company's Canary Wharf headquarters bearing the aforementioned slogan: 'respect, integrity, service, excellence and stewardship'; and the lifts showed slickly edited videos of the wonderful charitable deeds that the bank and its staff were involved in.

Since then, at least eight of its current and former top executives, including Diamond, have been interviewed under caution by the Serious Fraud Office. The company has also faced disciplinary action and penalties for cheating clients on the gold bullion market, and rigging energy prices in California. (Just one example of one of the 'bad banks' that brought the global economy to the brink of collapse in 2008, since which financial institutions around the world have paid 150 billion pounds in fines and penalties for wrongdoing.)

In 2015, Jenkins was fired, with Barclays stating, 'A new set of skills is required at the top in order to boost revenue growth.' Apparently, 242 trillion just isn't cutting it.

Of course, I'm just using Barclays as one example of a corrupt, lying, cheating corporation, but whole books have been written about the rottenness of the global banking system. I guess I could cut and paste this section into the part about Greed. The list goes on and on.

But banks aren't the only lying, dishonest cornerstones of our society. Over the last few years, the UK has been rocked with allegations and evidence of paedophile rings in Westminster and the BBC, involving high-level members of government and the entertainment world.

But it's not all bad.

Wikileaks' Julian Assange, winner of the Sydney Peace Foundation Gold Medal for Peace with Justice (which is held by just three other people — Nelson Mandela, the Dalai Lama and Buddhist spiritual leader, Daisaku Ikeda), is currently residing in Ecuador's London Embassy having sought asylum there following US investigations with a view to prosecuting him under the Espionage Act of 1917.

Assange became the focus of the FBI and other US investigative agencies following the publication of secret information, news leaks and classified media from anonymous sources. Wikileaks revealed that the US government and military form a 'vast lying machine' that perpetrates mass murder throughout the world.

Another hero of our times is former CIA employee Edward Snowden, also charged under the Espionage Act for revealing thousands of classified NSA documents that illuminated previously unknown details of a global surveillance apparatus run by the US' NSA, and the existence and functions of classified surveillance programs, which had previously been denied by the US government.

Snowden's revelations showed that US courts had approved

direct access to Americans' Google and Yahoo accounts, and the recording of millions of phone calls daily in both the US and France, plus the surveillance of Xbox Live users, UNICEF and *Médecins du Monde*, as well as the EU chief, the Israeli prime minister and German Chancellor Angela Merkel, plus tracking the online sexual activity of people they termed 'radicalisers' in order to discredit them.

The budget for these operations was 52 billion dollars for 2013 alone.

Snowden fled the US that same year for Hong Kong, where he handed over the documents to reporters from *The Guardian* before flying to Russia, where he received asylum.

While the US has failed in all attempts to extradite him, Edward Snowden was awarded *The Guardian's* Person of the Year 2013, the German Whistle Blower Prize, the Sam Adams Award, the Ridenhour Truth-Telling Prize, the Right Livelihood Award and the IQ Award.

For telling the truth.

Me? I don't give too much of a shit who's watching me. The infantile, attention-seeking, petulant part of me bought an Arabic scarf, an idiot's guide to the Quran and a large hunting knife on Amazon when I heard Muslims were being targeted based on their online purchases. And I live next to a mosque and my children are part Iraqi, so I'm probably on some watch list already.

I'm no stranger to the war against terror. In the late Eighties, in the era of the IRA and the 'ring of steel' around the City of London, my friends and I had an unfashionable rock 'n' roll band. We decided to rent a quiet little country cottage on Salisbury Plain to get some peace and quiet, to write and record music. Unfortunately, our lead guitarist, Nigel, a soft-spoken Irishman with a broad Belfast accent, made the booking.

We'd been there but a day, when a man in white overalls knocked on the door and said he'd come to fix the washing machine. Remember, this place was in the middle of *nowhere*.

A couple of hours later, a man wearing tweed with an immaculately trimmed moustache knocked on the door looking for his 'lost dog'.

Next came a call from my girlfriend. Her parents had been interrogated by plain clothes 'people' who wanted to know what our car (registered at their address for insurance purposes) was doing being driven by 'suspected terrorists'.

We thought this was all terribly funny and flattering, but Nigel was freaked. He'd grown up in the troubles and knew this could end badly.

Nothing further happened until late that night when, during a recording session, I began to experience severe interference through the headphones while sitting at the mixing desk.

'Someone's feeding back,' I shouted.

The band stopped playing but the noise continued—a dull throbbing that grew increasingly louder. Above me, small china figurines started to slide across a shelf as the vibrations grew more intense.

The whole cottage began to shake as it became apparent that the feedback was in fact a huge twin-bladed Chinook helicopter.

'This is what they do back home,' Nigel cried. 'And when the Provos make a run for it they shoot them down.'

Slowly the noise subsided, but we'd had enough. Piling all our gear into our cars, we disappeared into the mist without a shot being fired.

Later, it emerged that a stash of guns and plastic explosives had been found under a hedge not long before our arrival, but no one ever approached us directly.

I look back on this now and laugh. In fact, I laughed at the time, but I *was* terribly stoned.

But is Glaswegian decorator Harry Stanley laughing? Shot dead in 1999 by police while walking home from a Hackney pub, carrying a table leg, following reports of 'an Irishman with a gun wrapped in a bag'?

Is Jean Charles da Silva e de Menezes — assassinated by armed officers in the fervour that followed the 2005 July bombings in London — snickering in his grave?

The war against terror is a book in itself. Many suspect, myself included, that the war itself has been largely a construct, or at least exaggerated, for a number of reasons, not least of all to fund the arms trade, but perhaps more so to make us feel that we need the protection of our governments. This is not to try to discredit or disrespect the very real victims of the terrorist attacks that we have seen over the last two decades or more but, as ever, there is more than meets the eye.

If nothing else, the multitudes of conspiracy theories that populate the Internet go only to prove that we, the people, have lost trust in those responsible for running our society.

The very real questions surrounding the detail of the 9/11 attacks prove that we have not forgotten the assassination of John F. Kennedy, where the CIA deliberately withheld information from the Warren Commission, and officers were instructed to give only 'passive, reactive and selective' assistance to the commission, in order to keep the commission focused on 'what the Agency believed at the time was the "best truth"' — that Lee Harvey Oswald had acted alone in killing the President.

Nor have we forgotten the Gulf of Tonkin incident, where it was proved that the US had purposely falsified claims that North Vietnamese torpedo boats had attacked USS *Maddox* in order to legitimise an escalation of the war.

So, if the page goes blank after this section, you can reach me at Guantanamo Bay Detention Camp, Caimanera, Cuba 95100.

Note: this location may have restricted access or private roads.

* * *

And, last but not least, the Tenth Commandment: 'Thou shalt not covet thy neighbour's ox.'

Is about contentment.

Contentment

kuh n-tent-muh nt.

Noun.

1. The state of being contented; satisfaction; ease of mind.

2. Archaic. The act of making contentedly satisfied.

Wikipedia:

Contentment is hypothetically a mental or emotional state of satisfaction maybe drawn from being at ease in one's situation, body and mind. Colloquially speaking, contentment could be a state of having accepted one's situation and is a form of happiness.

I know little on this subject.

Deepak Chopra made a very interesting observation in *The Path to Love.* He said that the quality that we humans most value in ourselves as a species is our ability to struggle. Give us a mountain, we'll climb it; give us a war, we'll fight it.

Give peace a chance...

We don't know what to do with it.

Contentment. It's not part of our culture. Everything is sold to us with the promise of contentment, which never delivers. Faster broadband, a bigger TV, a new partner, a house...

I've yet to meet a *successful* person. Yet, I am blessed to work with a diverse assortment of highly talented people. But whenever asked if they consider themselves successful, the answer is always no. Not *yet*. Not *until* something is achieved — the award, the bank balance, the relationship, etc.

It's always in the future.

Wikipedia goes on to say:

> The source of all mentally-created dissatisfaction appears to stem from the ability to compare and contrast experiences and then inferring thereby that one's life state is less than ideal.

We already began to look at Osho's views on comparison. Here, he expands on the same theme:

> Each individual is unique, and comparison is not possible. I am just myself and you are just yourself. There is nobody else in the world to be compared with. Do you compare a marigold with a rose flower? You don't compare. Do you compare a mango with an apple? You don't compare. You know they are different—comparison is not possible.
>
> Man is not a species. Each man is unique. There has never been any individual like you before and there will never be again. You are utterly unique. This is your privilege, your prerogative, life's blessing—that it has made you unique.

That's a beautiful statement—'there has never been any individual like you before and there will never be again.'

Lao Tzu, said, 'Be content with what you have; rejoice in the way things are. When you realise there is nothing lacking, the whole world belongs to you.'

But I'm clutching at straws, cutting and pasting quotes about a condition that eludes me.

Simply because I push it away in favour of the familiar, the known. Familiar, we could argue, is the enemy of contentment. In the therapy world, they use the analogy of a hole in the ground outside your house. You go out one day and you fall in the hole. The next day you do the same. The third day you go out, see the hole and fall in it anyway. And the next. And the next. Because it's *familiar*. It's what you know.

I see many people who don't even know they're in a hole. For all of us, our childhoods are normal; it's all we ever knew until shown otherwise. It wasn't until I was seventeen while staying with another family that I became aware that they hugged each other routinely. I'd not known this before, so living without touch was normal.

Someone told me recently that in infant intensive care units it is routine to cuddle babies for twenty minutes each day. Statistics show that if this is not done, mortality rates are much higher. So, I now understand that touch isn't a luxury, it's a basic human need, like oxygen, food and water.

Contentment is extremely rare. As a fleeting experience, it is not uncommon, but as a state of being, few people have attained this level.

According to Buddhism, most of us live in a condition known as Dukkha, or suffering, brought on by the physical and mental experience of ageing, illness and dying, and the anxiety and stress of trying to hold on to things that are constantly changing.

Slowly, these ideas are creeping more and more into the fabric of our Western culture. Mindfulness is now available on the National Health Service in the UK. Even Tottenham is changing.

Next to one of the fried chicken shops at the end of my road I noticed a small yoga studio. I fear I may have made myself *persona non-grata* when I pranced in with the announcement, 'Wow, Tottenham really is becoming gentrified!' which evidently caused the proprietor some degree of Dukkha, judging by her reaction.

* * *

It's the end of February, and this road trip is still taking many twists and turns. Stylistically, my beard and hair have made the transition from hipster to homeless, my vanity is despairing and the bathroom mirror has become my nemesis. And so, before this month perishes forever, let's briefly return to Dante's 'abandon all hope ye who enter here', the words scrawled above the gateway to hell and, you may be unsurprised to learn, above the door to my practice room.

And no, it's not part of my Gonzo approach to keep my clients fucked up and therefore guarantee me a fat income. To me, it has Buddhist connotations; it has similar meaning to phrases like *letting go* or *surrendering*.

And while it may seem counter-intuitive to the therapeutic process, abandoning hope is a major step on the road to freedom and contentment.

Perhaps all of us who have ever been wounded live with a deep, semi-conscious longing that one day someone will come along who will make everything OK. Go deeper still and you'll usually find that the yearning is for our parents to become the parents that we really wanted.

We live in agonising hope.

I've got good news and bad news…

The bad news is that the cavalry is never going to come.

The good news is that the cavalry is never going to come.

Which is not to say you can't have friends and allies along the way—they're essential, as are the enemies (perhaps the greatest helpers of them all)—but no one is coming to rescue you.

You've got to face your own demons; they're yours and no one else's.

But once you abandon all hope of being saved and you mourn that realisation accordingly in your own good time, you will discover the most delicious freedom. The freedom afforded to only those who have faced their fears and crawled out the other side, bleeding but whole; the freedom afforded to those who may now call themselves adult, having cut the cord and abandoned the illusion that a saviour was required.

Only those brave souls who've traversed the fire of false hope can walk with true sovereignty, heads held high, the monarchs of their own destiny.

The clock is ticking, time is passing and we still have so much to do if we are to save the world. March beckons and with it...

The Nine Circles of Hell.

* * *

March

At one point midway on our path in life,
I came around and found myself now searching
Through a dark wood, the right way blurred and lost.
How hard it is to say what that wood was,
A wilderness, savage, brute, harsh and wild.
Only to think of it renews my fear!
So bitter, that thought, that death is hardly more so.
But since my theme will be the good I found there,
I mean to speak of other things I saw.
I do not know, I cannot rightly say,
How first I came to be here—so full of sleep,
That moment, abandoning the true way on.

Dante Alighieri, Inferno

When I was a kid, I remember staying up late to watch a programme that had caught my eye called *The Divine Comedy*.

It wasn't funny.

I think I lasted about five minutes before I turned it off and it's taken me until now to return to Dante's masterpiece.

Dante's *Inferno* is one of those works that somehow exists in the consciousness of many of us regardless of whether we ever read it or not; a bit like Shakespeare, it's just in the *fabric* of our existence. Likewise, you don't need to have read Dickens to describe something as Dickensian—we all get what it means.

You remember that film *Anacondas: The Hunt for the Blood Orchid*?

No, no you don't. Because there's a reason why some stories seep into our souls and others pass us by. It is said that there are only seven basic plots in storytelling: *Overcoming the Monster, Rags to Riches, The Quest, Voyage and Return, Comedy, Tragedy* and *Rebirth*, all of which we relate to on an archetypal level.

Well, it doesn't get much more basic than *Anacondas*—a story about scientists searching the jungle for a mystical orchid who are attacked by giant snakes. I mean, I could just about cobble together *some* kind of archetypal resonance with my own world in Tottenham, but it'd be a stretch.

Inferno, on the other hand, is the story of a man who strayed from his true path and finds himself lost in the dark forest of mid-life, and has to pass through Hell in order to find himself again, which is one of those occasions when you read it and go, 'Shit, someone's been stalking me.'

In this case, a time-travelling fourteenth-century Italian poet.

We know this story from the inside; it speaks to us of our own journey. It has deep resonance, much like that other great timeless tale, the Grail myth, which is about the search for compassion and self-acceptance.

Star Wars. Apocalypse Now. The Wizard of Oz.

Bunch of misfits make an arduous journey to confront a shadowy figure who lives in a far-off world protected by minions, representing the inner journey to our own shadow side.

A good storyteller simply embellishes what we already know in our hearts, dark or otherwise. So, we all know the *Inferno*, but when it comes to symbolic embellishment, Dante is the king.

Dante's hell is depicted as a huge underground funnel with nine concentric circles leading to its frozen core. Yeah, that's right—you heard me. Frozen. Dante's version of Hell is fairly flame-free; this being because fire is a source of light, representing good; but what we have here is as dark as it gets, a place devoid of life. A hollow, empty void. A realm of nothingness, despair and confusion. Like Slough in winter.

Dante is shepherded through the underworld by the poet, Virgil, who takes him first to Limbo, where the Uncommitted dwell—the souls of those people who in life did nothing, neither for good nor evil.

Ambivalence, to me, is one of the greatest sins and one that is rife in our world. I went to one of Russell Brand's little warm-up soirees recently and he made a comment that illustrates what I'm talking about perfectly: 'Members of our government, past and present, have been fucking and murdering small children. I tell people that and they go, 'oh yeah. I heard that.''

For a while, I made regular posts on social media about the Westminster paedophile ring, but I found it harder and harder to find any news reports of the case. I guess people just don't care that much. And I get it. It's hard, right? I mean, there's so much shit in the world, how can we care about it all? It's just when I hear of someone being kicked to death outside Sainsbury's on a Saturday afternoon while people walk by without intervening that I begin to despair.

Ambivalence... is a Sin.

Don't just stand by and watch.

Don't let Trump slip and slide and hate his way into power.

Don't let Cameron fuck pigs... and *us*.

Don't let Roosh V hold 'neo-masculinity' rallies.

Don't ignore the plight of refugees or forget that they are *people*; don't turn a blind eye to the rise of the far right, the Ku Klux Klan, Britain First or UKIP; don't ignore the homeless; don't ignore the US or China or Saudi Arabia or Iran or North Korea or the *UK's* violation of human rights; don't ignore the crucifixion of teenagers, the beheading of Filipina housemaids or the stoning of adulterous women; don't forget that Black Lives Matter and the extrajudicial killings of black people by police is murder and nothing else; don't pretend that unprecedented suicide rates among men and, in particular, war veterans doesn't matter; don't ignore the fact that World War III isn't something that might happen but is something that started on 11 September 2001, if not before; don't ignore the 30,000 gun-related deaths in the US each year; don't ignore Guantanamo; don't ignore global warming—it's real; don't forgive corrupt bankers, paedophile MPs or child-raping celebs; don't think that *it* will never happen to you, whatever *it* is, and that if *it* happens in another country, it doesn't matter.

Just give a shit.

* * *

Moving through the pre-Hell of Limbo, Dante comes to the First Circle, the domain of those guilty of vice—incontinence, violence and fraud.

So, we've covered, to a degree, violence (although there's certainly more to be said) and fraud; but it's *incontinence* that interests me and that, I can assure you, is the first time I've ever made that statement.

You see, when we speak of incontinence, it's not to say that there's a place in Hell for old people who couldn't help weeing themselves. It refers more to the weakness in controlling our desires and natural urges.

Natural urges?

Surely if they're natural then…

I just had to sit and ponder on that one awhile.

OK, so self-control is useful up to a point, but I'd go for self-awareness over self-control any day. Self-control smacks of pain and denial to me—repression, suppression and rigidity. Self-*awareness*, on the other hand, is a state of consciousness, whereby the impulses associated with the id or reptile brain are *managed*—equally contained and utilised depending on the situation. I'd understand if you argued that they're the same thing and maybe you'd be right. It's just that self-control for me doesn't necessarily require consciousness and isn't as solid. I have a terrible relationship with tobacco and rely on self-control not to smoke, but I still haven't reached the bottom of what it is that compels me to indulge, and so I'm constantly on and off the wagon. I've not attained the degree of consciousness to set myself completely free.

I think the real danger is when we suppress our natural urges to the point where they get so backed up they explode. Killing sprees, binge eating, rape, child abuse... *war*.

Society demands that we deny our natural urges, and so we learn to conform and behave. But Jung observed that 'sometimes you have to do something unforgiveable just to be able to go on living,' which clearly and deliberately clashes with the mainstream... beautifully. I guess this is the human dilemma: be accepted or be true to yourself. We do go on and on about authenticity, but few have the balls to actually live it.

Jung's contemporary, Otto Gross, boiled it down to one easy statement: 'If there is one thing I've learned in my short life, it's this: never repress anything.'

Access *all* that you are. Own it. Savour it. Enjoy it. Gain mastery over yourself without fear or self-deceit. Or suffer the true living hell of wrestling your demons in a fight to the death that you're ultimately doomed to lose.

Just sayin'...

* * *

The Second Circle of Hell is a place of complete darkness, where the terrible noise of a fierce storm is accompanied by the moaning and shrieking of spirits doomed by carnal Lust, who are cursed to be whirled and swept by a relentless wind for all eternity.

Dante was exploring the difficult relationship between Love and Lust, but I feel that if he were writing today, his view would almost certainly have been dominated by pornography.

Playboy writer, Damon Brown, once wrote: 'If we invent a machine, the first thing we are going to do—after making a profit—is use it to watch porn.'

The way things are going, porn will account for a vast overcrowding of Level 2 in the not too distant future. Back in 2009, Montreal researcher Simon Louis Lajeunesse was forced to abandon a study into how pornography affects men because he couldn't find a single guy in his twenties who hadn't seen porn. I'd be surprised if that statistic hadn't dropped since then to boys of fifteen or sixteen, so prevalent is porn on smartphones being passed around the playground.

The genie is out of the bottle.

You could say that pornography, a word first introduced to the Oxford English Dictionary in 1857, has been through five significant phases.

The Venus of Willendorf, the oldest statue depicting a naked human form, was carved 25,000 years ago.

In 1524, the first book of erotic engravings was published.

In 1839, the daguerreotype was introduced and very quickly people began producing 'dirty' images.

In 1896, Thomas Edison's *The Kiss* was the first erotic film to be produced and soon after, the culture of 'Stag Films' emerged.

But the really big leap came with the arrival of the Internet in 1991 and three years later the first ever porn site. By 2012, Xvideos was getting 4.4 billion page views per month, second only to Google and Facebook.

For me, Lust is often driven by unhappiness. It's an attempt to find some kind of soothing experience while in pain and I doubt I'm the only one who responds in this way. In fact, I know I'm not.

I managed to watch part of a TED talk on porn by a guy called Ran Gavrieli and before my infantile attention span drew me elsewhere, he made a statement that I liked: 'Porn is filmed prostitution.'

Which I guess, now I think about it, is a no-brainer. People having sex… for money.

Most of the guys I've talked to (and one woman) who have paid for sex have done so when deeply unhappy. I'm not making excuses. It's an observation that most people seem to reach for porn or pay for sex as an anaesthetic. They don't tend to go,

'Wow, I feel *fantastic*. I think I'll log onto www.soapytitwank. com.' (I just checked that domain and it *is* available for transfer from Synergy Wholesale PTY Ltd.) No, when people feel good, the isolation of porn doesn't usually appeal, let alone that of prostitution.

Both these industries rely on unhappiness to get punters in the door and so there is a cycle of pain from the workers to the users, with the pimps and pornographers exploiting both ends of the chain.

I don't use porn. Part of me wishes I did. I kind of like the idea of such hostile self-sufficiency. It would extend my pathological hermit-like existence even further; give me a pill for food and a website for sex, and I could retire from the human race altogether and buy an ex-MOD bunker to hide in for when Trump drops the big one. But I dunno. I just find it so jaw-droppingly *dull* and on the odd occasion when I'm miserable enough to go there, I last about thirty seconds before I remember that it just makes me feel worse watching other people doing what I'd like to be doing. I might as well watch a movie of people eating cake when I'm really hungry.

It's not a turn-on.

To me, pornography is spending all your money and not educating the people, and spending it instead on weapons. That's pornographic. That's totally filthy.

Bill Hicks

* * *

Dante comes next to the Third Circle, where the gluttonous sinners suffer under a cold and filthy rain—Gluttony not only being overindulgence in food and drink, but also other kinds of addiction.

Addiction, at its worst, is possession: a life in servitude to the demon of uncontrollable need, craving and desperate hunger; a foul place of disease and decay, where mothers will sell their children for an all-too-brief respite from the monkey that tears the meat from their withered backs.

I've watched in dismay my hands rolling yet another joint that I simply *do not want to smoke* — expertly binding together the papers, mixing and blending the warm, pungent hashish with the soft and comforting tobacco while all the while looking on like a stranger at my own kidnapped and hog-tied soul.

That was long ago, but still the demon grips me in a multitude of colourful and malevolent ways, from eBay to sugar, tobacco, expensive rum, love or derivatives thereof, adrenalin, intensity, work… The list, like my addictions, is apparently quite limitless.

Addiction, I am told, is a disease for which there is no cure, but one that must be fought each and every day with prayer, self-discipline and commitment to a twelve-step programme or the like. And who am I to disagree?

Whichever way you approach it, addiction is tough. Dante's vortex-like image of Hell describes it well: just as you think you've got it licked, you spiral down even further into the heart of the beast and there are many, many more than nine circles involved.

I'm not sure in my case I'd call it a disease, although for sure there may be genetics involved. I can't avoid the fact that both my parents are addicts, but to me a disease is a purely negative thing and my own addiction has its plus sides. The way that I'm compulsively approaching this book is addictive; I get a buzz from it when I satisfy the hunger to write, and sometimes I overdose and everything in my life seems to be about Sin.

All addicts are control freaks with obsessive-compulsive traits and given that I accept that this is a management system rather than something I seek (or even want) to cure, then harnessing that incredible energy is the name of the game. In that sense, my addiction is like this powerful beast that needs taming. Let it run wild and it causes chaos and destruction, gain mastery over its incredible strength and it becomes a formidable ally.

Of course, in some areas this creature stills bites me when I get too close. But treated with a degree of respect, and provided I maintain my own sense of authority, it serves me well. Take my eye off the ball for even a second and I'm screwed, though. So yes — dangerous it will always be.

It's perhaps a risky strategy to try to dance with the demon. The twelve-step programme promotes total abstinence and to most this is the only way. I knew I couldn't do that. I didn't want to live in fear of falling off the wagon, so six months after my last joint I made sure to skin up a fat one. I hated it. Which was the best possible outcome. I felt free and I've never looked nervously over my shoulder since.

Know thyself in whichever way works for you. That is the only *real* treatment for addiction. Know your weaknesses and trigger points, the situations to avoid, the oblique ways in which it'll sneak up on you when you least expect it.

I love Brando's out-take from *Apocalypse Now*:

It takes bravery. The deepest bullets are not to be feared. Phosphorous, napalm are nothing to be feared. But to look inwards, to see that twisted mind that lies beneath the surface of all humans, and to say, 'yes, I accept you. I even love you because you're a part of me, you're an extension of me.'

And, of course, he's *so* right. It's not enough to like ourselves for being sensitive, kind or poetic. We *have* to love our darkness if it's going to stand any chance of transformation; even our hatred, our murderousness, selfishness, cruelty, our addiction. It all needs Love. And just the tiniest glimmer of light shines a long, *long* way.

* * *

Virgil guides Dante to the Fourth Circle, where the greedy people and reckless spenders roll heavy weights in endless circles. Greed, in this instance, represents those whose attitude toward material goods deviated to the point where they lost their individuality and have been rendered 'unrecognisable'.

Lost their individuality? Don't get me started.

Oh, go on, then.

Wikipedia again:

Dunbar's number is a suggested cognitive limit to the number of people with whom one can maintain stable social relationships. These are relationships in which an individual knows who each person is and how each person relates to every other person. This number was first proposed in the 1990s by British anthropologist Robin Dunbar, who found a correlation between primate brain size and average social group size.

By using the average human brain size and extrapolating from the results of primates, he proposed that humans can only comfortably maintain 150 stable relationships. Proponents assert that numbers larger than this generally require more restrictive rules, laws and enforced norms to maintain a stable, cohesive group. It has been proposed to lie between 100 and 250, with a commonly used value of one 150.

Yeah, I've always been suspicious of people with 3500 Facebook friends.

And, seeing as we're looking at how we might save the world, that 150 is going to feature in this book. Humans began to inhabit cities almost 10,000 years ago and that, you could say, was the birth of 'the masses', and perhaps the beginning of many of the problems that threaten our very existence now.

But we've gone way, way beyond the 150 mark and individuality is now an unusual quirk rather than the norm.

Skipping forward ten millennia and in 2015, 74.5 million iPhones were sold during the first quarter of the company's fiscal year. As a modern family, my two daughters, their stepbrother, my ex-wife, her fiancé and myself all have iPhones. Although we attempt to express our individuality through different cases and screensavers, we are essentially an *iPhonically* bland family.

The top three bestselling cars of 2015 in the UK were the oh-so vanilla Ford Fiesta, the Vauxhall Corsa and the Ford Fucking Focus. Tesco were the biggest retailers, JD Sports celebrated a record 80 per cent profit rise, Apple posted a quarterly revenue of 51.5 billion USD, while the Westfield Corporation (which Grayson Perry described as 'a Death Star of consumerism') has a current and future development programme worth approximately 10.5 billion USD, including 'iconic projects in some of the world's leading cities' in Milan, Italy, London and at the World Trade Center in New York.

Donald Trump—billionaire property developer, reality TV star, amateur have-a-go politician and all-round threat to our survival—used a press conference to shift away from his scary presidential campaign for a moment to sell his own brand of wine, vodka, steaks, bottled water and the *Trump* magazine. But perhaps the most bizarre thing worth noting with Trump is that time and again we read statements from US citizens saying that they're going to vote for him because he's an 'individual'.

'He doesn't dress like a politician, he doesn't act like a politician,' says US Navy veteran Denny Gajowiak. 'Maybe that's a good thing, maybe we need someone who is a little rough around the edges to go in there and kick some ass.'

Now that's scary when we're *so* hungry for a bit of individuality that we'll vote for Satan.

It's a fine line though, isn't it? The desire to be ourselves against the desire to belong. And this is where the marketing people step in, with the knowledge that the fear of exile and isolation will get us to part with our cash quicker than most things. I saw a tragic billboard advert in Kathmandu—a beautiful Nepali woman with her skin Photoshopped, or bleached, wearing Western dress, laughing as she looked over her shoulder at a brown woman wearing traditional garb. The caption read, 'Don't get left behind.'

That's just sinister, don't you think? Using shame and ridicule to tap into people's insecurities, with the suggestion that if you don't wear a certain brand you'll not belong.

Jung believed that to be individual one had to develop consciousness, so as not be defined by collective norms. He defined an individual not as an isolated or separate person but as a pre-eminent member of the collective.

One of my all-time favourite quotes is from Cecil Beaton, who spat:

> Be daring, be different, be anything that will assert integrity of purpose and imaginative vision against the play-it-safers, the creatures of the commonplace, the slaves of the ordinary.

Now, that's a clarion call to anyone seeking self-actualisation. To be a true individual requires *acceptance* and *integration* of all aspects of our personalities; it's only then that we find the solidity within ourselves to break the chains of conformity and live a life of genuine freedom. It doesn't matter what phone you have or what jeans you wear (as long as they're Japanese raw denim). What matters is what's *inside*.

Abraham Maslow believed that the development of individuality was central to self-actualisation, where a person becomes aware of their potential and chooses to aspire for what they think is right with *self-confidence* and *self-respect*, even if it requires them to break with social conventions.

Materialism is perhaps the biggest drug of our times. There's irony here because so much of the hunger for material things comes as an attempt to fill the painful void left by the collapse of *community* as a way of life. And so, as we've become more isolated as opposed to individuated, our need for self-soothing behaviours has increased. Shopping at the click of a button is an amazing way to seek instant, same-day delivery gratification, which brings us back to addiction again.

The other huge modern dependency is screen addiction. Whether it be computer, phone, tablet or phablet even, it seems we must all check our social media compulsively, to see what is *going on* and where we *fit in*. Facebook, LinkedIn, Twitter — they all feed the same desperate need for community, for tribe, the myth of the *global village*, and I'm as guilty of this as the next person.

But I've got a feeling that the more we become conscious and individuated, the need for these portals to 'belonging' will diminish as people learn that true acceptance comes as a result of self-definition and fearless personal expression.

Someone sent me a video of Sting talking about his ayahuasca experiences recently. Inevitably, the conversation came around to the question: So if this stuff is so profoundly healing, why is it illegal?

'I don't think authority, whether it be Government or the established Church, really wants you to have direct access to this kind of connection,' he explained. 'Because their power-based lies are keeping you in the dark, are keeping you disconnected or alienated from that kind of experience and so, whether it's conscious or unconscious, their instinct is to prevent this from happening, they want to control everything.'

You don't have to take drugs to be individual. You don't have to do anything other than listen to yourself and know that you're loveable, no matter what. Who was it said, 'All you need is love?' I can't remember, but it's a good 'un.

And that statement alone might just save the world.

* * *

The Fifth Circle is the domain of the Wrathful. But this is not the kind of anger that we've explored earlier in this book, no. This is a particular kind of rage, one turned inwards, cancerous and deadly, potent yet impotent at the same time; for this is the place of the most dreaded of beasts.

This is the place of the Sulkers.

And I'm not talking about some God-awful, chirpy-cheeky, Scouse beat group from the Sixties. I'm talking about the part that lives within us all—the silent, simmering, passive aggressive, 'You'll be sorry when I'm gone,' part that dominates and oppresses with clenched jaw and avoidant eyes, all leaden atmosphere and withheld emotions, sullen and bitter to the end.

The US Department of Justice sponsored a National Crime Victimization Study in 2007, which found that men commit 75.6 per cent of all murders.

I disagree with this finding.

I would say that sulky little boys in men's bodies commit 75.6 per cent of all murders.

Sulky little boys are the most dangerous creatures on Earth.

Adult human beings are, by and large, stable, caring, responsible creatures. It's when we lose our adult form that we act out with irrational violence and retribution.

In Dante's super-creative vision of Hell, the Sulkers, resentfully silent in life, are forced to recite hymns while submerged in a river of mud, so that their words come out only as gurgles.

As a man who works with a lot of men, I've come to understand that sulking is something that we excel in. Not to say that women aren't also experts at being withdrawn and unreachable when hurt. But because of gender conditioning we men are more often less equipped to extricate ourselves from the sticky swamp of infantile self-loathing and wounded, silent venom, hence why we are so much more prone to killing.

Women are more inclined to commune, to gather, to congregate, to share and bond. Men isolate, especially when wounded. They take to the shed or go fishing or just retreat into an inner world. Dante doesn't mention the gender balance in the river of mud, but my money's on it being mostly male.

You don't need me to spell out to you the worthlessness of sulking. It's a dangerous trait, one that risks explosion if maintained and compressed for too long. And anger turned inward leads to depression, anxiety, digestive complaints, skin conditions, divorce, loneliness and, in extremes... suicide, which we will explore in more detail all too soon.

* * *

In the Sixth Circle Heretics, who say 'the soul dies with the body', are trapped in flaming tombs. Heresy is defined as 'opinion or doctrine at variance with the orthodox or accepted doctrine, especially of a church or religious system.'

BRIAN
I'm not the Messiah! Will you please listen? I am not the Messiah, do you understand?! Honestly!

GIRL
Only the true Messiah denies His divinity.

BRIAN
What?! Well, what sort of chance does that give me? All right! I am the Messiah!

FOLLOWERS
He is! He is the Messiah!

BRIAN
Now, fuck off!

Silence

ARTHUR
How shall we fuck off, O Lord?

I first saw *Monty Python's Life of Brian* on its release when I was fifteen on one of my first solo excursions to London. It's hard now to appreciate the uproar that accompanied this work of genius that documents the life and times of Brian Cohen, a Jewish man born next door to Jesus Christ, and subsequently mistaken for the Messiah.

The controversy began when the original backers, EMI Films, pulled out of the project two days before production was due to start filming in Tunisia.

Terry Gilliam said, 'They pulled out on the Thursday. The crew was supposed to be leaving on the Saturday. Disastrous. It was because they read the script... finally.'

Long-term *Python* fan George Harrison remortgaged his house for 3 million pounds and set up Handmade Films to produce the movie. On its release, thirty-nine local authorities in the UK banned it from being shown, while Ireland and Norway banned it outright. This didn't stop it from becoming a box office success, becoming the fourth highest grossing film in the UK in 1979. In 2009, it was announced that a thirty-year-old ban of the film in the Welsh town of Aberystwyth had finally been lifted.

Director Terry Jones said of the film, 'It isn't blasphemous because it doesn't touch on belief at all. It is heretical, because it touches on dogma and the interpretation of belief, rather than belief itself.' Heresy is rather out of fashion in the Christian world these days, but in the Middle Ages it spawned the Inquisition, a somewhat disregarded genocide. It began in 1231 and accounted for several million deaths until the very last execution, which wasn't until *1826*.

Currently, we still see the issue raised in the name of Islam, where heresy, or apostasy (the conscious abandonment of Islam in word or through deed), is punishable by death. In November 2015, the death sentence imposed on Palestinian artist Ashraf Fayadh, accused of renouncing Islam, was met with huge international outcry. *The Guardian* reported:

> Fayadh's supporters believe he is being punished by hardliners for posting a video online showing the religious police in Abha lashing a man in public. Some Saudis think this was revenge by the morality police.

In February 2016, the sentence was reduced on appeal to an eight-year prison term, with 800 lashes to be carried out on sixteen separate occasions. He was also ordered to repent through an announcement in official media.

Fayadh's lawyer argued his conviction was seriously flawed, because information regarding the poet's mental health was withheld from the original trial. A panel of judges revoked the death sentence but upheld the conviction for apostasy.

Author Irvine Welsh said, 'When this twisted barbarism is thought of as a compromise, it's way past time Western governments stopped dealing with this pervert regime.'

And what of the anonymous apostates who languish on death row waiting their turn in 'chop chop square' (the nickname given to the place of public killing in Saudi)?

The fact is, although the crime still carries the death sentence, execution is rare. The last case in Iran was Hossein Soodmand in 1990, a man who'd converted from Islam to Christianity in 1960 when he was 13 years old and who was ultimately hanged thirty years later by the Iranian authorities for that decision. In Saudi, it's one or two per decade. But there is an alarming rise in the persecution of apostates within the ranks of ISIS, who have decided that archaeology equates to heresy.

Islamic State is known for destroying artefacts it views

as idolatrous, and the belief that the curating of antiquities is apostasy and therefore punishable by death. However, while it publicises its destruction of archaeological sites, it keeps quiet about how much plundered antiquities help finance its activities. Stolen artefacts make up a significant stream of the group's multimillion-dollar revenues.

In August 2015, 82-year-old antiquities scholar, Khaled al-Asaad, was beheaded in the Syrian city of Palmyra. His mutilated body was hung on a column in a main square because he apparently refused to reveal where valuable pre-Islamic artefacts had been moved for safekeeping. The inscription on a board in front of the desecrated corpse accused him of managing Palmyra's collection of 'idols'.

Oh yeah... I heard about that.

* * *

The next circle, the Seventh, is comprised of three smaller circles that address Violence—one for Violence against persons and their goods, another for Violence against themselves (suicides), and the final circle for Violence against God, Art and Nature.

So, we've explored Violence against people, and we've considered ISIS' Violence against God and Art, and we've looked at Violent methods of farming animals. But what of suicide?

I'm a busy and successful psychotherapist with over twenty years of clinical practice. I'm also sometimes depressed and occasionally still have suicidal feelings. But I know that unless I became terminally ill, I will never kill myself. But I still feel it. For example, recently my eldest daughter became unwell with a mystery affliction. My very first thought when she entered hospital was that if she died, I would join her.

But the point I'm making here is that this is what I consider to be my qualification for working with suicidal people. I know what it feels like and I stay alive to those feelings. They give me an edge.

Every therapist fears losing a client to suicide. My one came when I'd been practising for twelve weeks. I had neither the experience nor the skill to recognise just how close to the edge he was. His family buried him in unconsecrated ground, because suicide is a Sin.

And I would never be so crass to suggest that this young man's death was worth it, because it wasn't. But because of what I learned through that experience, I've not lost another one since. No way. I'm hyper vigilant. At the first whiff of suicide, I'm all over it like a rash. And I'll let you into a little secret. There's *nothing* I won't stoop to in order to keep someone alive.

My favourite trick is manipulation. The *minute* I see that someone is suicidal, I immediately make a hard contract with them. If they really decide that they want to die, they are to come to me and do an ending session. Once they've done that, I tell them they are free to do whatever they want. But as long as they are working with me, they are forbidden to kill themselves. I lay it on thick. 'I don't want anyone else's blood on my hands,' I say.

And it works. A little bit of emotional blackmail. A little bit of accountability. Fuck it, I don't care, because I know that if they can just weather the storm and get through this patch, that the day will come when they can face life again and feel so, *so* glad that they didn't kill themselves.

Suicide is a modern-day plague. It's a reflection on the world that we live in that so many people are choosing to jump ship. I could write a whole book on the impact of the loss of community. We've become isolated and this is what I blame the bulk of the world's problems on.

Without community, there is no accountability, so of course people are thoughtlessly raping the world. It's someone else's problem. If when we threw garbage away it mounted up on our own village green, we'd pretty quickly come up with a better way of disposing of it than landfills and polluting the oceans. With

7 billion people mostly living separate, disconnected lives then crime—in which I include the wanton destruction of our planet, of which I am an active participant—violence, sexual abuse and ultimately war become not only possible, but also epidemic.

* * *

The Eighth Circle of Hell is the place of the Fraudulent— panderers, seducers, flatterers, sorcerers, astrologers, false prophets, corrupt politicians, hypocrites, thieves, fraudulent advisers, evil counsellors, falsifiers, alchemists, counterfeiters, perjurers and impostors. It's a fairly jam-packed corner of Hell. But am I the only one who reads that list and goes, 'Ooops?' Shit, I'm in more trouble than I thought.

On 22 March, ISIS bombed Brussels. The death toll this time being 31, including 2 of the suicide bombers, with up to 230 people reported injured. Trump immediately pounced on the atrocity to fuel his hate-filled campaign-trail rhetoric, calling for the reintroduction of waterboarding and, rather chillingly, for 'much worse...' He abandoned us to our own dark imaginings, filling the gaps with nightmarish visions of Gestapo-esque proportions, given The Donald's twisted and evil psyche.

But does Trump really belong in the domain of corrupt politicians, a place where the guilty are immersed in a lake of boiling pitch, representing the sticky fingers and dark secrets of their dubious deals? I'm not sure. Not because I've done an abrupt U-turn and suddenly decided that The Donald is above judgement, and that his integrity is without question, but because of the very real question, *is he actually a politician?*

To me, he's a savvy and ruthless market trader who's spotted a vacuum in terms of world leadership. In that void he has erected a soap box from which to sell his dubious and sleazy wares.

But perhaps scarier than this despotic Walnut Whip-haired

fuck is the fact that a great many people actually support him. As we've already seen, they like him because 'he doesn't dress like a politician, he doesn't act like a politician,' in this US already fluffed into an ecstatic fervour by George Double-Yuh fifteen years ago. A US that feels most alive and potent when manning the walls of the Alamo in the war against terror. And Trumpster Cogburn, his fat fingers buried to the knuckles in organised crime, litigation and more than a few Eastern European women, is leading the charge with the cry, 'Fill your hand, you son of a bitch!' Also, the promise to 'Make America great again,' without actually referencing a time when the US was *ever* great, whatever great means.

Trump's team, meanwhile, have painstakingly constructed this fetid Trojan Horse of a false idol in the notion that The Donald is a man who 'tells it like it is'. He has no regard for convention or political correctness, appealing to a mob tumescent at the idea of a good ol' boy taking the reins, twirling six shooters and spitting tobacco phlegm at filthy Mexicans, alimony-hungry whores and suicide-bombing sand niggers.

It's an act of utter PR genius if you think about it: to take someone as morally bankrupt as Trump and sell him on the basis that he may be a lot of things, but at least he's not... Fraudulent. Then again, it's worth remembering that we live in a world where Adolf Hitler was *TIME* magazine's Person of the Year in 1938, as was Joseph Stalin in 1939 *and* 1942, followed by Nikita Khrushchev in 1957 and Ayatollah Khomeini in 1979.

The awful truth is that it's a rare person who isn't fraudulent in some way or other. I wonder if the only truly honest people are the newborns, the aged and the insane. You don't have to spend long in the maternity ward, where the screams of infancy fly free and exuberant, as yet unchained by appropriateness and good manners; the old people's home to hear naked truth spluttered from a toothless mouth beyond the constraint of etiquette or nicety; or the psychiatric ward to bear witness to the unfettered animal sexuality and the raw, weeping viscera of emotional despair.

The youthful easily become fraudulent, all too soon stretched on the rack of social expectation, pulled out of shape by fashion, beauty and the pressure of peers, their true essence sacrificed on an altar spattered with entrails and gore to the great god of acceptance, uniformity and belonging.

And every time we wonder, What would the neighbours think?

We've sold out.

We've abandoned ourselves for fear of ostracisation, that should we express our actual truth we will be exiled or humiliated by the mob.

As I write this, I'm approaching my fifty-second birthday. If there is *one* quality in myself that I prize above all others, it's my ability to simply not give a fuck. This is not to say that I don't care if I hurt someone, I really do, but I rarely constrain my words or opinions out of fear that I might offend. I'm not prepared to wait for the care home or the asylum before I let loose and within that attitude I've discovered an amazing sense of freedom.

And, strangely, people seem to *like* me all the more for it.

Don't get me wrong; I make no claim to pure authenticity. My persona, painstakingly built over half a century, is a Frankenstein's monster of mockney accent, rock 'n' roll tattoos, Japanese denim and swaggering rebellion. I still bullshit my way through life, albeit in a much subtler way than in my youth, promoting the 'brand of Jerry' through well-constructed (and sometimes stolen) one-liners, Facebook posts designed to be ever so slightly shocking or risqué, and selfies that strive to convince the world that my *fuck-you* construct has substance and form.

The whole Gonzo therapist package is a construct. The ink, wallet chain, skulls, incense, guitars, and Dylan and Hunter S. Thompson posters that adorn the walls of my practice room...

it's *all* designed to convince prospective punters and reassure existing clients that I'm on their side. I'm not working for *The Man*. I'm cool. I can be trusted. I'm not like *the others* and I'm just a little bit strange.

There's nothing more satisfying to me than when a newbie steps over the *Fuck Off* doormat into my workspace for the first time and goes, 'Wow. This isn't what I was expecting.'

That's when I know that the seduction is working.

But the point is, my manipulation isn't designed to harm or *exploit*. I'm using my persona to sell a product, which I believe is to the benefit of the prospective buyer. This is no dud car or malfunctioning gadget that I'm trying to shift.

This is a creative use of a part of myself that I know is palatable to the kind of people that I enjoy working with. But it's only one aspect of the multifaceted person that I and all human beings are. Gurdjieff stated that we all have multiple personalities that increase and multiply on a daily basis, there is no end to our many different sides, and to *know thyself* is perhaps the greatest challenge that any individual can face.

* * *

The Ninth Circle is for those guilty of Treachery—betrayal of family ties; betrayal of community ties; betrayal of guests; and betrayal of liege lords.

Liege lords? That's an interesting term from the times of serfdom and homage. A time of even greater hierarchy. Or perhaps not. As we approach an era where 100-year mortgages become a likelihood, we risk entering a time of thinly veiled slavery, our liege lords the building societies and banks in place of shamans, chieftains or inspirational figureheads.

A question I often ask people is: So who are the role models in society? To which I'm usually rewarded with yet another blank face. The fact is, as The Donald is taking full advantage of, there are no potent leaders who spring to mind and it is our liege lords who have betrayed us.

It would be lovely to put a positive spin on this and say, 'Surely this is because we are becoming more autonomous, more self-governing. It's a symptom of our decreasing need to be told what to do by *The Man*?'

But I don't think we're there yet.

Maybe by the end of this book.

As I've already mentioned, the Ninth Circle of Hell is not a place of fire and brimstone. It is a frozen place, a realm of cold and ice. It is all too representative of the society we've all created without heart or community, a place where people respond, 'Oh yeah... I heard about that.'

In the UK, Margaret Thatcher is famous for her 'No such thing as society' quote, which apologists have claimed is taken out of context. And perhaps it is, but it doesn't take away from the fact that she was a cold-hearted, cruel and tyrannical leader. Although as our liege lords, Blair and Bush Junior and Senior now stand beside her for history to judge, even Maggie doesn't look *all* that bad by comparison.

In these jumpy, hair-trigger days of 'The War on Terror'® you're in danger of being shot dead on the spot for mumbling *Allah Akbar* in the wrong company. As a stupid, irresponsible and troubled young man, I cheated what would now be almost certain death in an ill-planned and ill-advised attack on Thatcher and all she stood for with an improvised explosive device, or homemade, single-shot, non-automated, handheld drainpipe rocket launcher (HSSNAHDRL for short), to be more precise. I forget whose idea it was. It *may* have been mine.

The HSSNAHDRL, a basic but nonetheless effective weapon, was fashioned from a 3.5-foot length of black plastic downpipe, liberated from a neighbour's house, with an 18-inch 'loading slot' cut from the rear end, sealed with an oversized, uncooked Maris Piper baking potato and side-mounted in the passenger window of a blue 1974 Citroen 2CV.

With the HSSNAHDRL loaded with an 8-ounce *Astra Fireworks Sky-Bomb* and the promise of 'a mighty take-off followed by a very loud bang with giant red coconut ring surrounding a four-starred golden pistil centre', my three companions and I set off in the dead of night from our housing coop hideout in East London. Our mission? To send a message to Thatcher that… actually, I'm not sure that our message was all *that* thought out, but we were going to send a message, anyway.

Approaching the House of Commons at speed, I levelled the HSSNAHDRL in the general direction of the seat of power from my position in the rear of the 2CV as my accomplice, Will, ignited the *Sky-Bomb* with shaking tobacco-stained fingers. With the launcher pointed out of the window, the rocket ignited with a fearsome rush of flame and smoke, frying the Maris Piper as it burst from the eager, gaping mouth of retribution on its unstoppable trajectory towards Margaret and all that she stood for.

Except that none of us would-be-Hashishine had an O level in physics between us. With the HSSNAHDRL pointed almost directly into the wind, the *Sky-Bomb* was blown straight back into the speeding vehicle. Here, it screamed and ricocheted around the interior, belching Dante-esque sulphur and flame like some kind of stricken Luftwaffe dive-bomber as we hurtled anonymously through Parliament Square, past the baffled eyes of two dozy and perplexed policemen on duty by the Commons gates.

Before they'd had time to compute the pathetic and ludicrous spectacle that blazed harsh and bright before them, we were gone. Racing down the Embankment with nothing but a plume of acrid smoke to betray our idiotic presence, inside the car I finally managed to trap the *Sky-Bomb* beneath one of my blue suede brothel creepers, melting the crepe sole in the process and singeing all the hair from my lower leg.

Consoling ourselves with a bag of chips, we limped back to Wanstead. Thatcher, our liege lord extraordinaire, remained in power for a further six years.

And thus is history made.

* * *

And so ends March and our journey through the Nine Levels of Dante's Hell. What will April bring and how can we follow this torturous escapade? I dread to think, but as I write these words, the dark, fluid Eastern notes that emanate from the dirty, blistered fingers of a Stratocaster-hugging wild man in the corner of my room tell me...

It's all going to get rather pagan.

* * *

April

APRIL is the cruellest month, breeding
Lilacs out of the dead land, mixing
Memory and desire, stirring
Dull roots with spring rain.

T.S. Eliot, 'The Waste Land'

It takes a whole village to raise a child.

Igbo and Yoruba Proverb

We are not the good guys.

John Pilger

Shivam O'Brien—spiritual seeker, chieftain of the great Spirit Horse Community (to which we will return in detail later), poet, storyteller and wandering Irish bard—at a little over 6 foot is more or less my height (perhaps an inch taller, perhaps an inch shorter). To describe him as unkempt would be kind, unless he's in his ceremonial robes, in which case he looks like a tribal king.

Hunched in the dark recesses of my living room beside a rotten kilim sack containing all his worldly possessions, teasing sounds from a Stratocaster more Hindu Kush than Delta blues, Shiv presents a wild and timeless figure beyond the constraints of any era or society that your average, decent law-abiding citizen would recognise as normal or correct.

Parsifal-like in his demeanour Shivam, too, is on a single-handed mission to save the world, or as he puts it, 'to reinvent culture'. While I never really got my head around what he means by that, I know that he works around the clock with demonic frenzy to bring light and goodness and beauty with his every breath, and that's good enough for me or any man. Laying down the guitar he launches, in his soft Galway brogue, into a breathless diatribe on Catholicism, ancient land-dwelling peoples and *Sin*—a field in which he has not inconsiderable expertise.

'If you wanna control people, you've got Purgatory and Hell and a few other nasty places. Adults would send the kids off to confession; you'd never see *them* down on their knees, but it was considered good for the kids.

'I could never think of anything bad that I'd done. But these fucking bastards, sitting there in their boxes, would give you five Hail Marys or something. They'd never say, "Ah that doesn't matter, you're alright, you're a good boy." It'd just be five Hail Marys and an Our Father. And so you'd say the prayers and it was like a total inoculation against reality, not a scrap of inner reflection or enquiry.

'So that's Irish Catholicism for you, but it's also got a bit of medieval Europe in it, too. We have the problem, we have the solution and we control you.

'Now that game is up, but it's kind of interesting to reflect on what a thorough and awful machine it was, cos it's got hundreds and hundreds of years of Europe's history in it.

'When I was about twelve I started questioning it and by the time I was fifteen I'd decided that the Hindu view of the world was far more interesting, and the Catholic thing was kind of childish. I thought I'd outgrown it, but then when I got to my mid-twenties, although I didn't believe in it, my subconscious did. For a time, every night as I was falling asleep I'd have these Hieronymus Bosch demons behind my eyelids. I thought I was going crazy. It would happen night after night after night.

'By then I'd done two trips to India and was living with a woman. I was living the hippy lifestyle: smoking dope, taking acid, doing meditation. I was out there. I'd read everything by then, every major religion and crazy thing. I was free, *felt* free, but that other vast subterranean part of my being was still trying to work it out.

'So, I was doing therapy at the time and I mentioned to the therapist, "When I fall asleep I get these demons on my eyelids. I don't believe in them, but why are they there every night?"

'His response: "So what Sins are you committing?"

'He was an English guy and he knew I was an Irish Catholic, of course. We were a couple of years into therapy by now and so I said, "Everything's a Sin. Living is a Sin. Everything I was brought up with; you're not supposed to do anything where I come from."

'"So, what did they tell you? What was the teaching?" he said.

'What flashed up for me was that everything was punishable by Hell and I believed it. And so, I thought, *What else am I doing now other than not going to Church?* And the answer was having sex. Having sex was so not allowed in my childhood that it didn't even exist. Nobody had sex. There was no such thing. Children came from cabbages, nobody ever took their clothes off, everyone was always dressed from the day they were born to the day they died—there wasn't anything bad about it, because it didn't exist. That's how bad it was.

'But I wasn't ready to admit that I'd believed that at a certain stage in my life, so I said, "What's that got to do with me? Sin's got nothing to do with me now."

'"What was the punishment for not going to Mass?" he asked. "What was the punishment for having sex?"

'"The same punishment for everything—you'd go to Hell. You'd go to Hell and be tortured by demons forever."

'So, when I went home, my girlfriend was there and we had this raucous fuck. And there was something different about it... the sex was *sexier*. And there were no more demons after that. Ever.

'But it showed me that all that Catholic stuff goes *in*. And I don't mind being on record with this and saying they should all be lined up against a wall and shot with their own shit.

'What the Catholic Church does to young minds...

'Is a Sin.

'If there's such a thing as Sin anywhere—and to Sin means to destroy nature, to be anti-life—it's the Sin against the innocence of childhood.

'I don't think there's true recovery from an Irish Catholic upbringing. It gives you a damaged personality, forever.'

He pauses as if to digest his own statement before shifting down a gear.

'The word pagan is great—with them you're dealing with a ritual culture. Pagan means "people of the land" if you're doing it etymologically, but if you're using that word from a Christian standpoint like when I was growing up, it meant something awful. We couldn't even imagine how bad these pagans were. The worst thing you could be was a pagan who didn't believe in the Catholic God; but what it really means is people of the land, people of the earth, and if you go to the older religions when we were all pagan, they don't have a moral code, there isn't an idea of heaven or that if you curtail your nature in some way you'll get to this other place where you don't have to deal with the suffering, the animal dangerous dark side of life or somewhere that's freer or more everlasting or eternal. Pagan virtues, and pagan Sin, if you like, are all about nature, how things really work. They're living in the real world, the natural world, where tigers eat antelopes, and there's nothing Sinful about it.

'Extolling virtues like compassion isn't a big thing in paganism. We are seen as animals, as part of the earth. We can't pretend to be loving, kind and compassionate, because we kill animals and destroy forests to make a couple of acres to grow food. We know ourselves as the good and bad people that we are; there is no get-out clause from thanking God. We're dealing with a knowledgeable, informed, close-to-the-earth people, who know that the blood is on their hands when they've killed something. If you're eating meat, you've probably seen the animal being killed.

'People living close to the earth know what's going on. They know that they're part of nature. They know very well that they will kill to live. But if you move away from that you can kid yourself that you're not a part of it, which is especially true of people living in industrial societies, who decide to be vegan because they "never harm anything", while they turn on their hot tap or sit in their concrete flat. But people close to the earth know very well the damage they do. They know you can't have a field of wheat without stealing an ecosystem that was teeming with life.

'So, the old pagan idea is that nature is the goddess and the human impact on that can't be ignored. But it's not as if it's a moral thing, like nature is "good" and you're "bad" for damaging it. It's that this is our mother; this is how things grow; this is how life came about; this is something to be honoured; this is where our food comes from; this is what sustains us; this is our source, our origin.

'The pagans have a reverence for the great intelligence that we came from. That's the root religion, the natural religion of natural people and natural community, and there's something to be trusted about it.

'It doesn't have morality.

'It has *reality*.'

And *boom*! there it is. I could finish this book right here and now with that one statement—'reality, not morality.'

But you can't stop Shivam talking that easily.

'We need a new definition of Sin. We have to redecide what it is. It's not like now we've moved out of that medieval way of thinking that there isn't Sin, or that we're innocent. There are a lot of very well-educated people in the Western world who are very consciously destroying this natural environment that we live in and condemning their descendants; whether it's in one generation or two, we're going to live in some kind of a slum. It's going to be a wasteland. And they're doing it with full knowledge.

'But we don't really have a language any more that is as powerful as "we're Sinning". There's no sense that we will be called to justice. We don't believe in a day of reckoning. They don't have a sense of being called to account. It's like, "We can do what the fuck we want; there are no values."

'People don't have a feeling that they've Sinned any more. In my father's day, the priest would shame people from the pulpit. He'd say stuff like, "Mary was seen riding on the handlebars of John's bicycle at three o'clock in the morning," and "What kind of behaviour is that for moral people?" The priest was there monitoring what people were doing. But now that's dead and it's never gonna happen again. So, does that mean there's no shame? Does it mean that without Sin there is no shame?

'We're living in a pretty shameless society. You drink from a plastic bottle and you put it in the bin and they put it in a bigger bin and what are you gonna do with it then? Nobody knows what to do with this stuff, but no one feels ashamed; and I think there's a real danger in a society that has no concept of Sin. Not that people should be *shamed*, that's a different thing, but if people have no sense of shame, then no matter how much you destroy the earth or lie to yourself about what a good person you are and you don't self-enquire, you end up with a society that's shameless. And then because there are no socially held values, we're in a free-for-all, which in a way is a fantastic creative space, but it's dangerous and destructive and out of control.'

He finishes with a flourish.

'There's no shame.'

* * *

That's a hell of a statement—the world is actually *worse off* without shame. I'd never considered that, but then a lot of the really great wisdom can be shocking. It *has* to be to wake you up.

And you know, there's some weird and freaky shit out there in the world. I recently stumbled across the Georgia Guidestones. Hear of them? I hadn't. But they have an interesting and at times challenging prescription as to how to save the world.

In June 1979, a well-dressed, articulate stranger, using the pseudonym R.C. Christian, who claimed to represent a mysterious collective describing themselves as 'A small group of Americans who seek the Age of Reason,' walked into the offices of the Elberton Granite Finishing Company in Elbert County, Georgia. He commissioned them to build a structure of six granite slabs weighing 237,746 pounds. The monument, which stands on one of the highest hilltops in Elbert County, is 19-foot 3-inches tall, with one slab standing in the centre and four arranged around it. A capstone lays on top of the five slabs, which are astronomically aligned, the four outer stones to the lunar declination cycle. The centre slab has a hole drilled at an angle from one side to the other, through which can be seen the North Star, and a slot carved through it, which is aligned with the sun's solstices and equinoxes. The capstone has an aperture that allows a ray of sun to pass through at noon each day, shining a beam on the centre stone indicating the day of the year.

An additional stone tablet, which is set in the ground a short distance to the west of the structure, provides some notes on the history and purpose of the Guidestones, which are inscribed with ten guidelines in eight modern languages. A shorter message is inscribed at the top of the structure in four ancient language scripts: Babylonian, Classical Greek, Sanskrit and Egyptian hieroglyphs.

The guidelines, which some have dubbed 'Ten Commandments of the Antichrist', are as follows:

1. Maintain humanity under 500 million, in perpetual balance with nature
2. Guide reproduction wisely—improving fitness and

diversity
3. Unite humanity with a living new language
4. Rule passion—faith—tradition—and all things with tempered reason
5. Protect people and nations with fair laws and just courts
6. Let all nations rule internally resolving external disputes in a world court
7. Avoid petty laws and useless officials
8. Balance personal rights with social duties
9. Prize truth—beauty—love—seeking harmony with the infinite
10. Be not a cancer on the earth—Leave room for nature— Leave room for nature

The first—'Maintain humanity under 500 million, in perpetual balance with nature'—is what brought the Georgia Guidestones to mind when I was talking of tribes of 150. Now, there's clearly a massive problem in the simple fact that our population has spiralled wildly out of control. In my lifetime alone, it has gone from 3 to 7 billion and there's no real sign of it slowing. As Bill Hicks said, 'We're a virus with shoes.' But there's a problem with guideline Number One...

It requires the extermination of nine-tenths of the world's population.

The vibe of genocide or global culling has obviously spooked a lot of people. There are dozens of sites debunking the Guidestones or linking them to 'the occult' or 'illuminati', mostly because these generic clichés are what people fall back on when they don't understand something 'weird'. But then, anything inexplicable usually gets people going. So, I looked closer at the people responsible for the Guidestones and I'm not sure they're *so* bad.

They produced a pamphlet titled the 'Georgia Guidestones Guidebook' that has the statement on the cover: 'When man reawakens, let him behold the Georgia Guidestones.'

So, they're interested in awakening consciousness? *Aargh!!* Evil *bastards*.

Inside it gets worse:

> We, the sponsors of The Georgia Guidestones, are a small group of Americans who wish to focus attention on problems central to the present quandary of humanity...
>
> It is very probable that humanity now possesses the knowledge needed to establish an effective world government. In some way that knowledge must be widely seeded in the consciousness of all mankind. Very soon the hearts of our human family must be touched and warmed so we will welcome a global rule of reason.

OK, is that scary to you? In the light of the demons in control right now, I dunno... it sounds quite *nice*.

> The group consciousness of our race is blind, perverse and easily distracted by trivia when it should be focused on fundamentals.

Hell yeah.

> Human reason is now awakening to its strength. It is the most powerful agency yet released in the unfolding of life on our planet. We must make humanity aware that acceptance of compassionate, enlightened reason will let us control our destiny within the limits inherent in our nature.

My God! their evil knows no bounds.

> It is difficult to seed wisdom in closed human minds. Cultural inertias are not easily overcome.

I *love* these guys.

> Unfolding world events and the sad record of our race dramatize the shortcomings of traditional agencies in governing human affairs.

You get that bit? 'The *shortcomings* of *traditional agencies* in governing human affairs?'

> The approaching crisis may make mankind willing to accept a system of world law which will stress the responsibility of individual nations in regulating internal affairs, and which will assist them in the peaceful management of international frictions.
> With such a system we could eliminate war, we could provide every person an opportunity to seek a life of purpose and fulfilment.

Ahhh, it's that *last* bit that scares people, the *elimination of war*...

> There are alternatives to Armageddon. They are attainable. But they will not happen without coordinated efforts by millions of dedicated people in all nations of the earth.

See! 's what I've been saying, innit!

> Human beings are special creatures. We are shepherds for all earthly life. In this world, we play a central role in an eternal struggle between good and evil—between the forces which build and those which would destroy.
> We are the major agency through which good and evil qualities of the spirit become actors in our world. Without us there is very little of love, mercy or compassion. Yet we can also be agents of hate, and cruelty and cold indifference. Only

we can consciously work to improve this imperfect world. It is not enough for us to merely drift with the current.

Uh-huh. Yeah, right on.

Controlling our reproduction is urgently needed. It will require major changes in our attitudes and customs. Unfortunately, the inertia of human custom can be extreme. This is especially true when those for whom custom is a dominant force are uninformed of the need for change.

Now this is where it gets sticky. It's like telling people that their cars are destroying the Earth — they generally don't care because they like the autonomy of driving their own vehicle. I've two kids and I don't like the idea of anyone restricting my choices, but someone better come up with a better idea fast, because if I live another thirty years, by the time I go we're gonna be pushing 12 billion. That's four times as many as when I arrived.

That...

Is unsustainable.

* * *

So how do the other 'Commandments' stand up?

Number Two: 'Guide reproduction wisely — improving fitness and diversity.'

China just ended its 35-year one-child-per-family policy because, despite the fact that it avoided 400 million births, it has left the country facing a demographic crisis, with close to 30 million men unlikely ever to find a wife, and a shrinking labour pool.

So, that didn't work. Extremes rarely do. But consciousness is *good*. Have children with consciousness; let it be *considered*, don't just shit out five or six unwanted kids because you got pissed or careless or you need the benefits or because you've got so much fucking money that it just doesn't *matter*.

The improving fitness and diversity bit? OK, I understand how that sounds a little Third Reich in its ethos, but if you step back and look at it in purely practical terms, it's actually very valid.

Something we need to look at urgently if we are to improve fitness is refined sugar. As child and adult obesity rises off the scale, the 'food' industries infiltrate more and more of their products — 80 per cent in the US — with refined sugar, a substance that has absolutely no nutritional value and is highly dangerous, toxic and addictive. The average American consumes between 150 and 170 pounds of refined sugar per year.

Refined sugar is a potent mood-altering drug that contains no fibre, no minerals, no proteins, no fats, no enzymes; it's void of all nutrients and consequently, without the nutrients needed to metabolise sugar, the body cannot rid itself of toxic residues. These residues accumulate in the brain and nervous system, speeding up cellular death, while the bloodstream becomes overloaded with waste products.

That's not a problem, though.

You just substitute products containing refined sugar for ones with artificial sweetener, like saccharin, aspartame, neotame and sucralose, right?

Saccharin can cause headaches, breathing difficulties, diarrhoea and skin problems.

Sucralose is a synthetic chemical now known to reduce the amount of good bacteria in your gut by 50 per cent, to increase the pH level in your intestines while *stimulating* your appetite, *increasing* carbohydrate cravings, and *encouraging* fat storage and weight gain.

OK, so maybe try aspartame, then?

Independent studies have linked aspartame with depression, headaches and weight gain. In liquid form, aspartame breaks down into methyl alcohol, or methanol, which is then converted into formaldehyde, a known carcinogen that causes retinal damage, interferes with DNA replication and may cause birth defects.

OK, so fuck that. Avoid at all costs. Choose products with neotame instead.

Neotame, a potent and dangerous neurotoxin, is much, *much* worse. It's like aspartame on steroids, in that it's the *same* formula with all the same concerns, but with something called 3-dimethylbutyl added. 3-dimethylbutyl is a substance listed on the US Environmental Protection Agency's most hazardous chemical list. Categorised as both highly flammable and an irritant, it carries risk statements for handling, including irritation to skin, eyes and respiratory system.

Yum.

As for diversity, it seems highly likely to me that our mysterious Mr J.C. Christian was familiar with Friedrich Wilhelm Nietzsche.

The Nazis appropriated much of Nietzsche's philosophy, giving rise to the misunderstanding that he was racist or anti-Semitic. This couldn't be further from the case; while you *could* quite rightly accuse him of being anti-multiculturalist, Nietzsche deplored racism and went as far as to say: 'The homogenising of European man is the greatest process that cannot be obstructed: one should even hasten it.'

If we are to follow the Georgia Guidestones, then the homogenisation of humanity seems to me the best way to improve diversity. In a world that seems increasingly dominated by far-right, hate-filled extremists, every mixed-race couple that I see represents a little ray of light for humanity, a positive drop in the dilution of the black-white and everything-in-between divide.

Now I'm aware that there are people who will take exception to this. But I'm not trying to take away from your cultural pride, heritage or ancestry. I'm suggesting that the more humanity meets and joins in loving union in such a way that produces children of all colours, races, creeds and diversities, the more we move toward peace and a world blind to the divides of hatred, suspicion, intolerance and difference.

And even as I write this I notice a tingling of fear that I will be seen as more Hitler than John Lennon. Because it's a contentious subject to say the least. I just hope that in the future we will have interbred to such a point that there will be no such thing as a white *supremacist*, because there won't be such a thing as a white *person*.

There will just be people, people who are no longer elevated or crushed or even defined by the colour of their skin.

You may say that I'm a dreamer, but I'm not the only one.

Actually, I never liked that song, and that house looked like they'd just moved in, just the big white carpet and piano… but you get my point.

* * *

So, we're halfway through April. It's pissing down outside and we're only at Number Three: 'Unite humanity with a living new language.'

What does that mean, then? Similar thing, surely? Homogenise our communication so that we can all understand one another. They tried that with Esperanto, which is apparently the most widely spoken constructed language in the world with over 2 million speakers. Esperanto, which translates as 'one who hopes', was created in 1887 by Polish ophthalmologist, L.L. Zamenhof.

His goal was 'to create an easy-to-learn, politically neutral language that would transcend nationality and foster peace and international understanding between people with different languages.'

Well, you can see why that didn't catch on. Or as they say in

Esperanto, *bone vi povas vidi kial tio ne popularîĝis.*

Remember back when we were looking at that elusive thing called contentment? I was talking about Deepak Chopra's contention that the quality we humans most value in ourselves as a species is our ability to struggle. Give us a mountain, we'll climb it; give us a war, we'll fight it.

John Lennon begged, 'All we are saying is give peace a chance.' But I don't think he'd read Chopra. Personally, I preferred, 'Everybody's got something to hide except for me and my monkey.' About which Lennon said, 'Everything is clear and open when you're in love,' but even love is war-like for so many of us. We don't have a common language in our relationships, let alone globally. Maybe the stone should read, 'Unite each other with a living new language' and work out from there.

It always shocked me—all that shit that we were taught at school, yet when we got out I knew little or nothing about how to communicate. I was still in a cell of my own construction, trapped behind emotionally defended walls a foot thick. And perhaps that's what is missing with Esperanto. Perhaps we need more than vowels and consonants. Perhaps we need some actual, human *meaning*.

None of us is ever going to master the art of living peacefully until we are willing to be transparent, to wear our vulnerability on the outside for everyone to see, without fear of shame or humiliation. This isn't going to happen in a world that's busy arming itself against...

Itself.

But how can we be *together* unless we learn the art of intimacy? And what *is* intimacy? Surely, it's more than a mere buzzword designed to sell weekend workshops in Muswell Hill with promise of chocolates and mystery?

Time to turn once again to Osho:

I do not teach any 'should.' All shoulds make the human

mind sick. People should be taught the beauty of *isness*, the tremendous splendour of nature. The trees don't know any Ten Commandments, the birds don't know any Holy Scriptures. It is only man who has created a problem for himself. Condemning your own nature, you become split, you become schizophrenic.

You have so many faces.

Inside, you think one thing; outside, you express something else. You are not one organic whole. Relax and destroy the split that society has created in you. Say only that which you mean. Act according to your own spontaneity, never bothering about consequences. It is a small life, and it should not be spoiled in thinking about consequences here and hereafter.

One should live totally, intensely, joyously and just like an open book, available for anybody to read it.

If you are simple, loving, open, intimate, you create a paradise around you. If you are closed, constantly on the defensive, always worried that somebody may come to know your thoughts, your dreams, your perversions, you are living in hell. Hell is within you and so is paradise. They are not geographical places, they are your spiritual spaces.

Here's a whole different language worth mastering, one that is *simple*, *loving*, *open*, *intimate*. It's not about words, it's about intention; and, after all, 85 per cent of communication is non-verbal.

Now *that* is magic.

* * *

Number Four: 'Rule passion—faith—tradition—and all things with tempered reason.'

Ha-ha-ha-ha-ha-ha-ha-ha-ha-ha-haaa…

Sorry.

It's just… Trump? Blair? Cameron? Syria? ISIS? Obama? Putin? Where's the tempered reason in *that*?

Kurtz: Did they say why, Willard? Why they want to terminate my command?

Willard: I was sent on a classified mission, sir.

Kurtz: It's no longer classified, is it? Did they tell you?

Willard: They told me that you had gone totally insane, and that your methods were unsound.

Kurtz: Are my methods unsound?

Willard: I don't see any method at all, sir.

* * *

Number Five: 'Protect people and nations with fair laws and just courts.'

No society in history has imprisoned as many of its citizens as the US.

Of all prisoners in the world, 25 per cent are American.

One in nine black men in the US are behind bars; there are more 17-year-old black people in jail than in college.

Prisoners make 93 per cent of domestically produced paints. They make 36 per cent of home appliances and 21 per cent of office furniture.

So, what this means is that much of the produce in the US, in 2016, is manufactured by black people, who work against their will for no money.

You know what that used to be called.

Skip back a few decades to June 1944. Across the sea in Europe, Allied troops were ten days into the invasion of France, but in South Carolina another black person was going to *Old Sparky*.

A couple of young white girls had been found brutally murdered, beaten over the head with a railway spike and dumped in a waterlogged ditch. George Stinney Jr lived close by where the dead girls were found. Following his arrest, police claimed he confessed to killing Betty June Binnicker, eleven, and Mary Emma Thames, eight, admitting he wanted to have sex with Betty.

Understandably, feelings ran high in the community. Stinney was rushed to trial and after a two-hour hearing and a ten-minute jury deliberation, he was convicted of murder on 24 April and sentenced to die by electrocution.

Justice had been served.

Apart from the fact that Stinney's sister, Aime, said she was with him at the alleged time of the crime, watching their family's cow graze near some railroad tracks by their house when the two girls rode over on their bicycles.

'Could you tell us where we could find some maypops?' Aime remembered them asking. 'We said, "No," and they went on about their business.'

There is no written record of Stinney's confession.

His defence lawyer, a local political figure, didn't challenge the three police officers who testified that Stinney had confessed to the murders, despite this being the only evidence against him and despite the prosecution's presentation of two different versions of his verbal confession.

Stinney's trial had an all-white jury. Stinney's counsel did not call any witnesses, did not cross-examine witnesses and offered little or no defence. There was no physical evidence linking Stinney to the murders. The court allowed discussion of the 'possibility' of rape, despite an absence of evidence in the medical examiner's report.

There is no transcript of the trial.

No appeal was filed.

And so, in due course, the execution was carried out at the Central Correctional Institution in Columbia on 16 June 1944 at 7:30 p.m.

There's one other important detail to this case that should be noted.

George Stinney Jr was 14 years old.

George Stinney Jr was a little *boy*.

Shame on you, America.

Shame on you, with your lynch mobs, your burning crosses, your strange fruit, your evil fat-fingered bureaucrats, your burr-haired cops, your bullwhips, your chain gangs and your pearly white mansions.

Shame on you.

'Why would they kill me for something I didn't do?' Stinney asked his cellmate, Wilford Hunter, shortly before he died.

The boy was so small compared to the usual adult prisoners that law officers had difficulty securing him to the frame holding the electrodes. He had to sit on books to reach the headpiece. The adult-sized death mask did not fit him and as he was hit with the first surge of electricity, it slipped off to reveal his tear-stained face to the crowd.

According to George Frierson, a local historian who grew up in the town, the real murderer made a deathbed confession to the killings. Coming from a well-known, prominent white family, the rumoured culprit had family members who'd served on the initial coroner's inquest jury, which had recommended that Stinney be prosecuted.

For seventy years Stinney's family campaigned tirelessly for a retrial, but maintained that they never wanted a pardon.

'There's a difference: a pardon is forgiving someone for something they did,' Norma Robinson, George Stinney's niece, told the press. 'That wasn't an option for my mother, my aunt or my uncle. We weren't asking forgiveness.'

Rather than approving a new trial, on 17 December 2014, Judge Carmen Mullen vacated Stinney's conviction. A vacated judgement makes a previous legal judgment legally void. Mullen ruled that he had not received a fair trial, as he was not effectively defended and his Sixth Amendment right had been violated.

She also found that the execution of a 14 year old constituted 'cruel and unusual punishment. No one can justify a 14 year old child charged, tried, convicted and executed in some 80 days,' concluding that, 'in essence, not much was done for this child when his life lay in the balance.'

'It is my professional opinion,' child forensic psychiatrist Amanda Sales testified, 'to a reasonable degree of medical certainty, that the confession given by George Stinney Jr. on or about March 24, 1944, is best characterized as a coerced, compliant, false confession. It is not reliable.'

It's not. It's not reliable.

Killing children never is.

It's a fucking sin.

* * *

Number Six: 'Let all nations rule internally resolving external disputes in a world court.'

I'm not even sure I understand what that means. So, I had a look around the Internet and found an e-book called *The Resistance Manifesto* by someone called Mark Dice, who explains Number Six like this: 'This chilling Commandment overtly suggests The New World Order's world court should oversee all matters. Resolving the external disputes involves the global reach of the governing powers.'

The Resistance Manifesto is a huge, 440-page work, which

Mark apparently wrote in 2005 after being laid off from his job in a mattress store. During his time of unemployment, he prayed to God for guidance, and 'his thirst for truth and his curiosity of how the world works led him to discover the sinister plans of powerful secret societies and their effects on the world.'

Upon making this discovery, Mark created *The Resistance* to… er… *resist* the evil web that threatens to engulf our world. Apparently, after first releasing *The Resistance Manifesto* in 2005, Mark used 'almost every breath that he had, and every ounce of energy to get the word out about the 9/11 attacks and The New World Order, and the saving grace of Jesus Christ.'

Mark became known for repeatedly calling radio shows and forcing the hosts to talk about subjects they didn't want to discuss. He followed this with a second campaign, where he gatecrashed the classes of college campuses around Southern California to bring the truth to students.

The Resistance Manifesto has plenty to say on the Georgia Guidestones. What is clear to Mark is that they have a deep satanic origin and message, and have the telltale signs of *The New World Order* written all over them. He's of the belief that, 'the Commandments are overall chilling for people of any faith.'

Mark has solved the puzzle of who's behind the stones—it's a perverted sect of Christianity known as the *Order of the Rose Cross*, a gnostic secret society connected to the other illuminated secret orders.

But looking at it a little more objectively, it seems to me that the Sixth Commandment is suggesting that we communicate. Work together. Get along with our fellow man. Am I missing something here? Isn't it just saying sort your own crap out internally and if there's a problem with a neighbour, work it out in an international court rather than bombing the shit out of each other?

* * *

Moving swiftly on to Number Seven: 'Avoid petty laws and useless officials.'

I like that one. Back to Keef, innit: 'We are not old men, we are not interested in your petty morals.'

Chester Council recently unveiled plans to introduce a Public Space Protection Order, which outlined new regulations:

Persons within the area will not ingest, inject, smoke or otherwise use intoxicating substances. Intoxicating substances being defined as substances with the capacity to stimulate or depress the central nervous system. No person shall urinate or defecate in any public place; this does not include public toilets. Persons within the area will not make any verbal, non-verbal or written request—including the placing of hats or containers, or by performance or artistry—for money, donations or goods.

I'm glad they went easy on public toilets.

The council failed to see the funny side when street artists affixed plaques to park benches in the area in protest against the 'draconian' proposals, with statements such as, 'This bench is dedicated to the men who lost the will to live while following their partners around the shoe shops of Chester.'

Another read: 'This bench is reserved for the young, beautiful and affluent. If you are old, ugly or poor please sit elsewhere.'

Maria Byrne, head of place operations for Chester Council, confirmed that the Council had removed the five plaques in all, saying people could be 'offended' by them:

We have removed the plaques from five benches and although they may appear humorous, some people may find them offensive. It has cost the Council taxpayer money for officers to locate and remove them. If anyone knows who is responsible we would like to hear from them.

At the risk of yet again being seen as anti-US, they have some fantastic laws over there. And these are all *genuine*:

You may not have an ice cream cone in your back pocket at any time.

It is illegal to wear a fake moustache that causes laughter in church.

It is considered an offense to push a live moose out of a moving airplane.

Owners of flamingos may not let their pet into barbershops.

Donkeys cannot sleep in bathtubs.

You may not have more than two dildos in a house.

Anyone caught stealing soap must wash himself with it until it is all used up.

It is illegal for men and women over the age of 18 to have less than one missing tooth visible when smiling.

It is a misdemeanour to shoot at any kind of game from a moving vehicle, unless the target is a whale.

In order for a pickle to officially be considered a pickle, it must bounce.

Unmarried women are prohibited from parachuting on Sunday or they shall risk arrest, fine, and/or jailing.

If an elephant is left tied to a parking meter, the parking fee has to be paid just as it would for a vehicle.

Having sexual relations with a porcupine is illegal.

It is illegal for a man to give his sweetheart a box of candy weighing less than 50 pounds.

Residents may not fish from a giraffe's back.

And my personal favourite:

Moustaches are illegal if the bearer has a tendency to habitually kiss other humans.

* * *

Number Eight: 'Balance personal rights with social duties.'
Mark Dice's take on that one is that it means:

In a socialist New World Order, individuals will have to give up personal rights in order to support their 'social duties' of contributing large amounts of their earnings and labour to the system.

I don't quite see it like that, but then again, I *am* on mushrooms.

I kind of went for a more radical interpretation, that it—bear with me here—meant something crazier, like we should maybe, I dunno, balance our *personal* rights with our *social* duties. No? Like, we should maybe live with awareness and consideration for our fellow man rather than in selfish bubbles.

The operative word for me was *balance*.

I mean, I'm the first to leap at a conspiracy theory. I love 'em. If you told me George Bush Senior dusted off his flight jacket and personally flew one of those jets into the World Trade Center, you'd have me, but…

I *like* guideline Number Eight and it doesn't hook my fear that we're being governed by shape-shifting alien lizard people too badly. It sounds like give and take, push and pull, a directive for harmony and fairness, all rowing together, etc.

It sounds like community.

Like something that 150 people might do rather well.

Together.

* * *

Number Nine: 'Prize truth—beauty—love—seeking harmony with the infinite.'

Let's see what Mark has to say about that one:

While saying to prize truth, the words God Almighty or Jesus are not mentioned. Instead, one is instructed to 'seek harmony with the infinite'. What exactly is the infinite? Does it mean Lucifer?

Wow, he's really got a bug up his ass about losing that mattress-selling job. Surely in this context, infinite means your god in whatever shape it takes? Does it have to mean evil incarnate? The great beast? The mighty destroyer? The horned one?

Come on, Mark. Can't it mean something... nice?

Prize truth — beauty and love. How can you find darkness in that? Isn't the fact that we lost touch with those values one of the main problems in this lonely world? As Shivam said, the people who lived with those values, the people of the land, the pagan people, the people who would scare the shit out of Mark, those people died out; those people were suppressed or massacred in the name of other idols, other gods like commerce and power, influence and wealth.

Prize truth — tell that to Blair, to Cameron, to Obama, to Trump.

Prize beauty — tell that to ISIS or IS or ISIL or IGIL or Daesh or Daish or whatever-the-fuck-they're-called this week.

Prize love. Prize love. Prize...

Love.

* * *

And so, to the last of the satanic Georgia Guidestone Commandments: 'Be not a cancer on the earth — Leave room for nature — Leave room for nature.'

See what they've done there? They've repeated it *twice*, just to make the point. They didn't have to. It takes a lot to carve words out of granite. But no, they wanted to stress that one. They didn't want any room for confusion or misunderstanding.

And as Guidestone Commandments go, it's a good 'un.

The Guidestones have been in existence since 1980. You'd think that'd be enough time for people to have taken them on? But no, it seems things are getting worse.

In the Democratic Republic of Congo—a Central African country gripped by conflicts that have killed more than 5.4 million people since 1998—16.9 per cent of all children between the ages of 5 and 14 are forced to work in the mining industry, digging for minerals used in our smartphones (and the laptop I'm writing on) like cobalt, copper and coltan. The UN calls mining one of the worst forms of child labour owing to the dangers inherent in the industry.

The same militia groups from Uganda, Rwanda and Burundi responsible for the slaughter of 800,000 people in the 1994 Rwandan Genocide operate the mines that supply the US tech industry, often conscripting children who are paid just 1 US dollar and fed one meal a day.

'The conditions were inhuman. The armed groups saw themselves as outside the law. There were a lot of thefts and sometimes rapes because no one could control them,' miners reported. 'There were no rules, and sometimes miners died of fatigue. There were also deaths because the pits were deep and there was flooding.'

The UN described US companies who purchase the exploited minerals as 'the engines of the conflict in the Congo.'

Meanwhile in China, where 95 per cent of the rare earth minerals used in smartphones and laptops get produced, the CEO of Foxconn—the chief manufacturer of iPhones and iPads—is worth at least 5.9 billion US dollars, while employees can expect to earn just 17 dollars a day, working a seventy-hour week.

Pay and working conditions at the company are so unbearable that 24,000 people—that's 5 *per cent* of the entire workforce—quit every month. The tech manufacturer has had to install suicide nets at its plants and factory dormitories (where its *300,000* to *400,000* workers live) after a rash of suicides, to prevent them jumping to their deaths. Employees have also been forced to sign contracts forbidding them from killing themselves.

Be not a cancer?

Ugh.

Mongolia holds 70 per cent of the world's reserves of rare earth minerals, the shameless mining of which produces waste that gushes out of pipes in Baotou—a region of Mongolia bordering Northern China—into artificial toxic lakes, some of which span more than 5 miles in diameter.

Be *not* a cancer.

Leave room for nature. Leave *room*.

* * *

May

God is dead. God remains dead. And we have killed him. How shall we comfort ourselves, the murderers of all murderers? What was holiest and mightiest of all that the world has yet owned has bled to death under our knives: who will wipe this blood off us? What water is there for us to clean ourselves? What festivals of atonement, what sacred games shall we have to invent? Is not the greatness of this deed too great for us? Must we ourselves not become gods simply to appear worthy of it?

Nietzsche, *The Gay Science*

Modern morality and manners suppress all natural instincts, keep people ignorant of the facts of nature and make them fighting drunk on bogey tales.

Aleister Crowley

Libertine

Lɪbəti:n,-tɪn,-tʌɪn

Noun.

1. A person, especially a man, who freely indulges in sensual pleasures without regard to moral principles.

From Wikipedia:

A libertine is one devoid of most moral or sexual restraints, which are seen as unnecessary or undesirable, especially one who ignores or even spurns accepted morals and forms of behaviour sanctified by the larger society. Libertinism is described as an extreme form of hedonism. Libertines put value on physical pleasures, meaning those experienced through the senses.

There's a reason I'm writing this book. I just haven't figured out what it is yet.

As I compose these words, a third of 2016 has passed already and so I look back at the intentions set when first I rode out into this Sinful wasteland:

> Something must be done. And so come, come with me now; for it is this very day I have pledged to embark on a journey, a long, mysterious and arduous journey lasting all of 366 days (this being a leap year), during which time I will meditate often and attend the gym three times a week and write each and every day, curtail my overspending on unnecessary shit on eBay and indeed buy *no more guitars*, because surely eleven is enough for any man, and avoid excessive masturbation, tobacco, dairy produce and refined sugar wherever possible, and behave with love and compassion towards my fellow man at all times, and I will *not rest*...
>
> Until we have saved the world.

It seems so long ago already. Of these promises, how many have I honoured?

Meditation?

Nah.

I have meditated like some grovelling toad as and when I've felt the need for some kind of divine guidance, in times of pain and torment, which I'm relieved to say have been few and far between so far in this chaotic Year of the Monkey. But, otherwise, I've shamelessly neglected my practice.

I cancelled my gym membership.

I have written... a lot.

I have curtailed my eBay expenditure and excessive masturbation. Not done *so* well with dairy produce. Done OK with refined sugar. Have I behaved with love and compassion toward my fellow man at all times?

Mostly.

True to my word, I have neither shaved my beard nor cut my hair. That's been an interesting one—there's a lot of unexpected freedom in going wild. I hadn't realised just how trapped I was in conventional ideas of what is attractive.

Meat. No, I've not eaten meat; although fish have died so that I may live.

Which just leaves tobacco.

* * *

The Tibetans consider tobacco a demon. I find that notion helpful and not at all far from the truth. Each time I fall from the wagon and succumb to the delusion that I love smoking, it's because I've been seduced by the voice in my head that's convinced me to return to the coughing, wheezing, poisoned slave existence of nicotine addiction. And then once it's got its claws into my system, it'll go as far as actually waking me up in the morning in order to get its filthy desires quenched.

And so, I fight it like the possessing entity that it is. And I quieten it for a few months, a few years even. But all the while it lurks in the shadows, waiting for a moment of weakness when, like a vampire, it pounces to draw the life force from my veins.

When I was a baby, I recall a demon and an angel sliding through my bedroom wall. My first *ever* memory is of the archetypal figures of good and evil sliding through my bedroom wall and standing by my bed.

Both were female; the demon—short and dark—moved towards me. I felt excited and scared in equal measures.

The angel—tall and blond—barred the demon's way. I felt disappointed.

Dream, delusion, fantasy, visitation? Whichever it was, it's stayed with me ever since and you could say I'm still trying to work out my allegiance.

I guess I'm not alone, given the fact that while, as Nietzsche said, God is *dead*, the Devil it seems...

Is still very much *alive*.

* * *

Sometime between AD 14 and 37, during the lifetime of Christ and the reign of Tiberius, news of the death of the great goat god, Pan, was met with groans and laments when it reached the shores of Palodes in Southern Albania.

The poet and mythologist Robert Graves suggested that the sailors who first reported Pan's demise had actually misheard the information, which was born by divine voices from on high — a notoriously unreliable news source. Graves himself had been reported dead on the Somme in August 1916, his obituary appearing in *The Times* while he lay in a casualty clearing station somewhere behind the lines, and so one can understand why this might be a touchy subject for the old bard.

I'm with Graves on this one. I believe that Pan stepped back for a couple of thousand years to allow, as G.K. Chesterton suggested, space for theology to emerge. But Pan wasn't dead. He was resting.

And now he's back. And he's pissed.

* * *

Sometime in the early Eighties, I was browsing the Record and Tape Exchange in Notting Hill, when I came across an album titled *Brian Jones Presents the Pipes of Pan at Jajouka*. Even back then it was pricey, at a time when our weekly social security allowance was twenty-two pounds, I think I paid around fifteen quid for it — more than the price of an eighth of good Moroccan hash. But this was a different Moroccan treasure and I instinctively knew that I *needed* that album.

Then, twenty years later, I titled my second novel *Dreamachine*, set in the Rif Mountains of Northern Morocco. The original dreamachine was a stroboscopic flicker device that produces visual stimuli—the invention of painter, writer, sound poet and performance artist, Brion Gysin.

In 1954, Gysin had opened a restaurant in Tangier called The Thousand and One Nights and he hired Sufi trance drummers, The Master Musicians of Jajouka, as the house band. He had first heard them while with American writer Paul Bowles at a festival in Sidi-Kacem in 1950.

Jajouka is a small, insignificant village of about 500 people. The music of this community is rooted in Sufi mysticism and paganism, involving heathen, rural customs and dance spectacles. Over a ritual sequence of many hours, it develops a hypnotic attraction that puts the musicians and public into a trance-like state.

The music is known to have magical and healing properties, the effect of which became known in the surrounding villages, whereby the crippled, the sick and the insane all made the pilgrimage to Jajouka. And so it was that Gysin first brought Rolling Stone Brian Jones to hear the drummers in 1968.

Captivated by the ritual music, Jones returned to the village high in the Rif Mountains armed with a portable reel-to-reel tape recorder. The resulting album captured music from the festival Aid el Kbir—a pre-Islamic pagan ritual that involved dressing a young boy in the skin of a freshly slaughtered goat, representing the Father of Fear, the Goat God Bou Jeloud, who then ran among the crowd to 'spread panic through the darkened village' as the musicians played with furious abandon.

Pan-ic.

Gysin likened the ritual to the fertility festival of Lupercalia and the ancient Roman rites of Pan. I listened to the album obsessively for decades, but it wasn't until my wife was pregnant with our first daughter that I understood the complex time signatures. When the technician put the microphone against my wife's belly and we heard the foetal heartbeat for the first time, I recognised the rhythm of Jajouka.

The rhythm of Life.

And so, it seems, Pan didn't die. He was hidden away and kept alive by a small tribe of devoted Sufi musicians, who awakened him periodically to bless the harvest and bring fertility to the village maidens, before allowing him to retire undisturbed once again to his annual slumber.

But while he slept all was not well in the world. The slaves of the new god were frightened of Pan; they demonised him, portraying him as a cruel, evil, horned figure, representing darkness, temptation, torment and terror.

And they renamed him Satan.

Soon they forgot about Pan and who he really was, and in doing so they lost touch with the old ways. They polluted and fought over the land, creating great machines to rape the soil and tear down the forests; they sucked the nutrients from the ground and spewed poison into the once clean air.

The new god demanded servitude and blind obedience, and people became docile and ignorant, suspicious and cruel. Others rebelled. They turned to satanism in an attempt to revive and in doing so, thus was created the first ever proto-rock the Great Beast himself... Aleister Crowley.

* * *

Crowley is much misunderstood. Even in introducing him under the bracket of satanism I've bought into a hackneyed idea of him as some kind of evil servant of the Devil. I don't think Crowley was the servant of anyone and it would be perhaps more accurate if he were remembered for being instrumental in introducing yoga to the West, the mainstay of North London yummy mummies. Hardly a *dark art*.

Born in 1875 at the height of the Victorian era and ultimately denounced in the popular press as 'the wickedest man in the world', Crowley was a libertine in a time of great repression: a seasoned user of narcotics and bisexual adventurer; an accomplished mountaineer and traveller; a pioneer of meditation, Hindu yoga and Buddhism; an occultist and master of ceremonial magic, alchemy, astrology, Rosicrucianism, the Kabbalah and Tarot; a poet, painter and novelist; almost certainly a spy for the British Secret Intelligence Service; an esoteric figurehead, a philosopher and founder of his own religion. An impressive resume to say the least.

Crowley is a classic case of too much rigid 'goodness' resulting in an explosion of rebellious, defiant excess. When not at an evangelical boarding school in Hastings, he was at home with his parents, who were members of a Christian fundamentalist group known as the Plymouth Brethren. The young Aleister had God rammed down his throat on a daily basis, but from the age of 11, following the death of his father, he soon went off the rails, turning his back on Christianity and devoting his time to more diverse hobbies such as drinking, smoking, masturbating and having sex with prostitutes.

It was while at Cambridge that Crowley was probably recruited as a spy and also where he became interested in the occult. Some biographers have suggested that it was the British Secret Service that had him initiated into the Hermetic Order of the Golden Dawn in order to spy on their activities. Whatever the truth, he soon rose through the ranks, studying ceremonial magic and the ritual use of drugs, and generally upsetting anyone of a straight-laced nature.

In India, he became a devotee of raja yoga, from which he claimed to have achieved the spiritual state of dhyana. Arriving in Paris in 1902, he became the beau of the arts scene, hanging with the likes of Rodin and Somerset Maugham; and then in Cairo two years later while making a study of Islamic mysticism, he channelled his great occult work, *The Book of the Law*, and its infamous invocation: 'Do what thou wilt shall be the whole of the Law.'

Back in the UK, Crowley claimed to have achieved enlightenment through a system of Egyptian magic called the Abramelin rituals that involved the heavy use of hashish, which he proclaimed to be an aid to mysticism. In the years leading up to the Great War, he continued to migrate from country to country, developing his own brand of sex magic and writing prolifically — one of his poems being titled 'Hymn to Pan'.

He spent the war years in the US, writing for *Vanity Fair* and continuing his exploration of sex magic, using masturbation, female prostitutes and the male clients of a Turkish bathhouse, and once again allegedly spying for the British government.

It was while suffering from asthma back in London after the war that he first became addicted to prescription heroin. Soon after, in Sicily, he founded the Abbey of Thelema — an 'anti-monastery' and global centre of magical devotion, where the lives of the inhabitants could be 'spent not in laws, statutes or rules, but according to their own free will and pleasure.'

The point of Thelema was for devotees to be able to discover and manifest their true will, their own grand destiny in life — an action that operates in perfect harmony with Nature.

That didn't go down well with the locals. They didn't like all this same-sex, fag magic and drinking of blood in their village. Then, while Crowley was in Paris seeking treatment for his smack habit, a young Thelemite named Raoul Loveday died from a liver infection. His wife told the story of her husband's demise and the carnal goings-on at the Abbey to the UK press. This, coinciding with Crowley's public criticism of the Dangerous Drugs Act of 1920 and the publication of his novel, *Diary of a Drug Fiend*, earned the magician the title of the *wickedest man in the world*. This resulted in condemnation in the European and UK press, his deportation from Sicily, and the closure of the Abbey.

Crowley went through a large number of lovers over the following years, men and women alike, with whom he experimented in sex magic, all the while dogged by poor health caused by his addiction to heroin and cocaine. That, alongside his lifelong affliction of asthma, contributed to his death from bronchitis in Hastings at the age of 72.

* * *

Crowley, while capable of gross selfishness and cruelty, was clearly an extraordinary and exceptional man—his legacy as an evil black magician is at least in part down to his own PR, playing up to the dark side years before Andrew Oldham took the same stance in marketing the Stones as the bad boys of rock to the cheeky vanilla boys from Liverpool.

But beyond his own spin of wickedness, he denied he was a satanist for the simple reason that he did not accept the Christian view in which Satan was believed to exist. Crowley was a hugely influential figure, helping to shape the twentieth century. It was an era that he believed marked humanity's entry to the Aeon of Horus, in which humans would take increasing control of their destiny.

Now whether that's the case is debatable. I think we still have a long way to go, but it was certainly a dawning, much encouraged by Crowley, who was *way* ahead of his time. What is patently clear is that while mainstream culture was still too frightened of Crowley's radical libertine ideas, they no longer believed in some kind of divine cosmic order. In turn, as Nietzsche had predicted, the new god withered and died.

The people felt lost. They were slaves without a master, no longer believing in an objective and universal moral law that bound them together and made them feel safe. They fell into nihilistic despair and turned to war, materialism and unquenchable, base sexuality to fill the void.

And into this void stepped the Nazi Party.

Nihilistic despair and unquenchable, base sexuality pretty much describes the scene in the Berlin bunker in the last days of the War, by all accounts one of the *greatest* parties ever thrown.

You know that question that sometimes gets bandied around — What would you do if you knew the world was going to end tomorrow?

You got it…

A real feeling of disintegration spread, with heavy drinking and indiscriminate copulation. There was also a good deal of sexual activity between people of various ages in unlit cellars and bunkers — the aphrodisiac effect of mortal danger is hardly an unknown historical phenomenon.

An erotic fever seemed to have taken possession of everybody. Everywhere, even on the dentist's chair, I saw bodies locked in lascivious embraces. The women had discarded all modesty and were freely exposing their private parts.

Storm troopers and terrified, young Aryan vixens rutting like savage beasts, rivers of the finest champagne and century-old cognac, Hitler crazy on bull's semen, pure Columbian flake and crystal meth, heavy pharma jacked straight into the eyeballs, the smell of death and cum and fear and lust and cunt and cordite swirling round the pheromone-infused concrete sarcophagus playpen, as all the while Russian retribution raped its way ever closer through the burning ashes of a shattered dreamscape beyond the wildest imaginings of Bosch's darkest nightmares.

Like The Pistols' first gig at Saint Martin's, or The Smiths' at the Hacienda, I guess you had to be there.

* * *

Hitler was a much lauded and popular world leader at a time when Crowley was being hounded by the press and labelled wicked. Both men were no doubt cruel drug fiends capable of destruction and throwing a great party; but (apart from millions of dead) the main difference could be boiled down to the fact that Hitler drew the world into incomparable darkness while Crowley played an admirable part in shifting human consciousness and therefore, despite his demonic reputation, into the light.

Described both as 'a pioneer of consciousness research' and 'the best-equipped magician to emerge since the seventeenth century', Crowley featured on the cover of *Sgt Pepper*, and both David Bowie and Jimmy Page were devotees. But it was his motto, do what thou wilt, that attracted many and scared even more; and yet, it is no more sinister than Shakespeare's 'to thine own self be true' or Joseph Campbell's 'follow your bliss'.

Aleister Crowley believed that the spiritual quest is to find what you are meant to do... and *do* it. That, to my mind, ought to be one of the Ten Commandments.

Maybe they should go up to eleven.

* * *

Another who was much influenced by Crowley and recognised the PR value of The Devil was *Church of Satan* founder, Anton LaVey, described as, you guessed it, the 'evilest man in the world'.

Like Crowley, LaVey was a consummate showman, not beyond creating pretzels with the truth and manufacturing intrigues to shamelessly promote his image as 'The Black Pope'. Described as 'a colourful figure of considerable personal magnetism', 'the founder of modern Satanism' and 'the most iconic figure in the satanic milieu', LaVey was 'directly responsible for the genesis of Satanism as a serious religious movement'.

To be a member of the Church of Satan costs a one-off

200-dollar joining fee. I'm not tempted, nor would I be to join any other religion or sect, but it seems to me that most of the darkness associated with the satanists is projected onto them through fear and ignorance, in a similar way to the kind of prejudice the pagans receive.

The Satanic Bible, penned by LaVey, has Nine Satanic Statements that are worth a look.

The first one is very much the essence of Left Hand Tantra:

Satan represents indulgence instead of abstinence. Satanism encourages its followers to indulge in their natural desires. Only by doing so can you be a completely satisfied person with no frustrations which can be harmful to yourself and others around you.

Which is a simple, clear explanation as to why Catholic priests and nuns fuck little kids. Repression *doesn't work*. Suppression *doesn't work*. These compressive attitudes create powder kegs of darkness that explode into cruel depravity.

Oh yeah.

I heard about that.

* * *

Number Two: 'Satan represents vital existence instead of spiritual pipe dreams.'

Another hero of mine, the Armenian mystic George Gurdjieff (the Beatle to Crowley's Stone) once stated:

People live in a state of a hypnotic 'waking sleep'. Maleficent events such as wars and so on could not possibly take place if people were more awake. People in their typical state function as unconscious automatons, but one can 'wake up' and become a different sort of human being altogether.

In times of mass sleep such as war, rules change, people's concept of sin is radically altered and morality gets twisted. As Colonel Kurtz observed in *Apocalypse Now*, 'We train young men to drop fire on people, but their commanders won't allow them to write "fuck" on their airplanes because it's obscene.'

Kurtz woke up. He'd seen so much horror and darkness that he couldn't return to society. Why do you think troops returning from war zones like Afghanistan have such a hard time? You can't put someone on a seven-hour plane ride and tell them that they're safe now, that the killing has stopped just because they're 'home'. Home doesn't exist for them any more; they've been trained by their governments to kill.

You can't just switch it off:

WILLARD

When I was home after my first tour, it was worse. I'd wake up
and there'd be nothing. I hardly said a word to my wife until
I said yes to divorce. When I was here, I wanted to be there.
When I was there... all I could think of was getting back into the
jungle.

Then you have the scene in Quentin Tarantino's great gore-fest masterpiece, *Pulp Fiction*, when Jules, played so menacingly by Samuel L. Jackson, has his awakening:

JULES
What's an act of God?

VINCENT

I guess it's when God makes the impossible possible. And I'm
sorry Jules, but I don't think what happened this morning
qualifies.

JULES

Don't you see, Vince? That shit don't matter. You're judging this thing the wrong way. It's not about what. It could be God stopped the bullets, he changed Coke into Pepsi, he found my fuckin' car keys. You don't judge shit like this based on merit. Whether or not what we experienced was an according-to-Hoyle miracle is insignificant. What is significant is I felt God's touch, God got involved.

VINCENT

But why?

JULES

That's what's fuckin' wit' me! I don't know why.
But I can't go back to sleep.

He can't go back to sleep. He can't return to the life of a sleeping assassin.

Osho was, and is, right: 'The only real Sin is that of unconsciousness.'

* * *

Number Three: 'Satan represents undefiled wisdom instead of hypocritical self-deceit.'

I'm not always the best at trying to understand things at face value; unless they're bleedin' obvious, I often need it spelling out. So, I went and got a bit of help on the Internet with this one from a site called About Religion:

True knowledge takes work and strength. It is something one finds rather than what will be handed to you. Doubt everything and avoid dogma. Truth tells of how the world truly is, not of how we would like it to be. Be wary of shallow emotional wants, for they frequently can only be satisfied at the expense of truth.

Let's break that down further: 'True knowledge takes work and strength. It is something one finds rather than what will be handed to you.'

I can't fault that. That's the beauty of ageing, assuming you do it with open eyes. Someone explained to me that the reason that time appears to speed up is because life becomes more and more routine; there are fewer new experiences and so we slip into that waking sleep that Gurdjieff warns against.

For me, the greatest and most valuable knowledge has come from the apparent catastrophes and disasters that I have engineered, the tragedies and losses that I've encountered, the beautiful peak experiences that have visited me in times of deep meditation or psychedelic exploration. Compared with that treasure trove, the exams and qualifications that I studied so hard to achieve don't mean shit.

'Doubt everything and avoid dogma.'

Reminiscent of the last words of Hassan al Sabbah, the Old Man of the Mountain: 'nothing is true, everything is permitted,' an early tattoo of mine. Doubt everything is a wonderful instruction. As Osho said, 'where there is certainty, there is no learning,' and Terence McKenna echoed, 'don't believe anything. If you believe in something, you are automatically precluded from believing its opposite.'

To question is to be alert and therefore alive, especially with oneself. To be full of *self*-doubt—in other words, to always doubt your own persona—can in many ways be the road to enlightenment; not that you should be without confidence or riddled with the anxiety that comes with lack of self-definition. It's more that by adopting an attitude of confident self-enquiry, we can constantly be asking ourselves questions like, Who am I *really*? Do I actually *mean* what I just said? Am I really telling the *truth* here? Once we've slipped quietly into a state of waking sleep, it's amazing just how much shit we can all talk and, more importantly, believe.

Who *are* you?

Answer that—truly answer that—and you are a Buddha.

As for avoiding dogma, I think you know by now where I stand on that one. Dogma is the grey noise that sends us into the zombie coma of living death, the puppetmaster's brain-numbing mantra of deceit and manipulation, by which the State and the Church transform individuals into worker ants who've forgotten how to question anything.

You will be moulded into a state-approved homogeneous drone who cannot think outside the prescribed consensus.

You will learn to repeat information instead of how to think for yourself so that you don't become a threat to the status quo.

When you graduate, you will get a job and pay your taxes in order to perpetuate the corporate system of indentured servitude.

You will stay asleep.

You will obey.

You will obey.

You will obey.

And thus, Cecil Beaton's clarion call to arms was never more so pertinent than now:

Be daring, be different, be impractical, be anything that will assert integrity of purpose and imaginative vision against the play-it-safers, the creatures of the commonplace, the slaves of the ordinary.

* * *

Number Four: 'Satan represents kindness to those who deserve it instead of love wasted on ingrates.'

> There is nothing in Satanism that encourages wanton cruelty or unkindness. There is nothing productive in that, but it is also unproductive to waste your energy on people who will not appreciate or reciprocate it. Treating others as they treat you will form meaningful and productive bonds while letting parasites know that you will not waste your time with them.

I can't find fault with that, nor can I put it any better.

Love is the answer, but there are toxic vampires out there. I'm a hippie at heart, and I believe that everyone is pure and loveable in their essence. But I'll tell you right now, we can all hold hands and pray and send as many good vibes to Trump and Blair as we like, but it won't make any difference. Those motherfuckers will continue to rape and plunder and shit all over the Earth.

* * *

Number Five: 'Satan represents vengeance instead of turning the other cheek.'

Dang! And I was all ready to send my cheque for 200 bucks up until now. Although I do like a good revenge fantasy.

But I don't know, it all seems so post 9/11, so *Bush*. That feeling of, 'I wanna get you back,' always feels so shit. I can't recall a time when I've ever exacted revenge on anyone, but if I had I don't expect it to be all that satisfying.

Then again, the Dalai Lama said:

> We should not seek revenge on those who have committed crimes against us, or reply to their crimes with other crimes. We should reflect that by the law of karma, they are in danger of lowly and miserable lives to come, and that our duty

to them, as to every being, is to help them to rise towards Nirvana, rather than let them sink to lower levels of rebirth.

Middle ground—that's where I always fall down, because my response is: *fuck that*, I'm not going as far as actually helping the bastards.

* * *

Number Six: 'Satan represents responsibility to the responsible.' Huh?

Real leaders are determined by their actions and accomplishments, not their titles, and real power and responsibility should be given to those who can wield it, not to those who simply demand it.

Ah! that'll be the day.

I asked Russell Brand a while ago if he ever worried that he might be assassinated and he got all shifty, like he thought I was suggesting I might do it. Maybe he could see something in me that I wasn't aware of. But what I meant was whether or not he was concerned that he might be taken out by 'The Man' for being all gobby and Essex and asking awkward questions. Because it wouldn't surprise me if he did meet with a mysterious 'accident' sometime. But then maybe 'they' don't give a fuck; 'they' just see him as a lanky ex-junkie with big hair who spouts on about revolution without a plan.

But I'd vote for him. Then again, I'd vote for most people over Trump. Then *again*, I voted for Blair. So don't vote for me.

Someone told me once that political leaders, rock stars and psychopaths have similar personality profiles. I've worked with the second two client groups and I gotta say, the crazies straight out of Broadmoor high-security psychiatric hospital were by far the most charismatic and magnetic people I have ever encountered.

It's that age-old problem, isn't it: those with the ego state who aspire to lead are more often than not the least equipped owing to the very fact they want the gig. Their inherent grandiosity, sociopathy and narcissism tend to blur their ability to govern well, as history has shown time and again. Those with the sensitivity and benevolence that might make them do a better job tend to retire quietly to their books or butterfly collections... or get murdered.

* * *

Number Seven: 'Satan represents man as just another animal.'

How can it be any other way? Our incredible arrogance as a species—indeed, our capacity to feel arrogant—has made us the most dangerous life form ever to have existed. The only life form with the capacity to destroy everything on this planet. The fact that we have denied our animal nature is part of how we have distanced ourselves from nature and therefore from ourselves, believing that we are superior and have rights that other creatures don't.

We are animals. We have animal instincts, traits and needs. If Sin is to behave against God's will, and we accept that God is Nature, then to deny our animal selves...

Is a Sin.

See what I did there?

* * *

Number Eight: 'Satan represents all of the so-called Sins.'

Satan represents all of the so-called Sins, as they all lead to physical, mental, or emotional gratification. In general, the concept of 'Sin' is something that breaks a moral or religious law, and Satanism is strictly against such following of dogma. When a Satanist avoids an action, it is because of concrete reasons, not simply because dogma dictates it or someone has judged it 'bad'. In addition, when a Satanist realizes that he or she has committed an actual wrong, the correct response is to accept it, learn from it, and not do it again, rather than mentally beat himself or herself up for it or begging for forgiveness.

Yeah, I like that one. 'When a Satanist avoids an action, it is because of concrete reasons.' I'd go a step further and say it's because you're awake (I say *you* because I'm assuming you've converted to satanism by now), you're in tune with yourself rather than following orders. I break the law almost daily by consuming, as I just did, minute amounts of psilocybin, which I find enormously beneficial on many levels, both personal and professional. I harm no one and seem to behave in a more productive and compassionate manner in a very broad sense. I certainly find that gratifying, but surely it's 'gratification' that is the contentious word here. It's super-loaded, that one. It almost sounds dirty just to say it. It's so wrong, so Sinful *to fucking enjoy something*. You *perve*. Is that all you care about, gratifying yourself?
And then:

When a Satanist realizes that he or she has committed an actual wrong, the correct response is to accept it, learn from it, and not do it again, rather than mentally beat himself or herself up for it or begging for forgiveness.

I mean, that's just great. It's... *human*. If everyone did that I'd probably be out of business in a week, but it seems a small price to pay for self-compassion. Accept it, learn from it and not do it again…

Evil, Devil-worshipping, sex-mad, menstrual blood-drinking, baby-killing *bastards*.

* * *

Number Nine: 'Satan has been the best friend the Church has ever had.'

True that. I mean, Pan walked right into that one, right? Who better than some lascivious, pissed-up, horny goat-boy who the Christians could use as the bogey man to scare the shit out of good God-fearing folk so that they could be controlled? It's no different than some of those *uber*-scary German fairy tales designed to terrify small children into behaving and going to sleep.

Behaving.

And going to sleep.

Oh, and also to allow people to abdicate responsibility for their actions. 'The Devil *made* me do it.' 'I was *tempted* by Satan.' 'I got the Devil in me.'

What a fantastic construct. He's like the Church's hitman, some shady figure from one of the *Godfather* movies who they can send out to test the resolve of sinners.

Give me a break.

* * *

LaVey also came up with the Eleven Satanic Rules of the Earth, which are as follows:

1. Do not give opinions or advice unless you are asked.

So, that kind of screws this book.

2. Do not tell your troubles to others unless you are sure they want to hear them.

Again, that kind of screws this book.

3. When in another's lair, show him respect or else do not go there.

Lair? Shit, I'm not sure I've ever been in someone's lair. What's wrong with house, home, flat, apartment or pad? However, whatever you call your residence, the principle of respect is a good 'un, so let's go with it.

4. If a guest in your lair annoys you, treat him cruelly and without mercy.

See, there you go again with the lair thing. If a guest annoys you, try telling them before resorting to merciless cruelty, maybe requesting that they don't do whatever it is that's pissing you off, or giving them a gentle but well-constructed complaint with a recommendation for an alternative behaviour?

5. Do not make sexual advances unless you are given the mating signal.

Hmmm, lots of room here for misunderstanding, I fear. Perhaps it should be, Do not make sexual advances unless you are given the mating signal, which is three squawks like a crow. Be specific. Or at least, do not make sexual advances unless you are given the mating signal, which has previously been agreed between you and your prospective lover, and/or in the community or society in which you live. And if there hasn't been any such agreement then just go slow until he or she says something like, 'Do you want to have sex?'

6. Do not take that which does not belong to you unless it is a burden to the other person and he cries out to be relieved.

So, that's a kind of satanic twist on 'Thou shalt not steal.' I'm kind of OK with 'Thou shalt not steal,' actually. The second part seems surplus to requirements. I don't remember crying out to be relieved of my beautiful sky blue-and-silver Toyota Hilux Surf that vanished from outside my front door one night. How about 'Thou shalt not nick my fucking car?'

7. Acknowledge the power of magic if you have employed it successfully to obtain your desires. If you deny the power of magic after having called upon it with success, you will lose all you have obtained.

Fair enough.

8. Do not complain about anything to which you need not subject yourself.

Liking that distinction.

9. Do not harm little children.

Sound advice and myth-busting wisdom.

10. Do not kill non-human animals unless you are attacked or for your food.

Yeah, that means you, Trump spawn, and all you selfie-taking, mega-rich trophy 'hunters', you killers of majestic creatures for the delight of your stunted, spoiled, bloated, poisonous egos.

11. When walking in open territory, bother no one. If someone

bothers you, ask him to stop. If he does not stop, destroy him.

Ah, you had me right up to 'destroy him'. Really you did. My pen was poised, dripping in anticipation over my open chequebook, but you lost me in the very last breath.

* * *

Having busted a few myths about Devil worship and explored a few of my own dark corridors, I'd say that I fall, uncomfortably, somewhere between satanism and Buddhism, with a soupçon of Hindu for extra spice.

So, Namaste motherfuckers, welcome to my lair. Watch your Ps and Qs or I will destroy you with merciless cruelty and furious anger...

You have been warned.

Boom Shankar.

* * *

Satanism, perhaps unsurprisingly, is essentially a child of the Sixties, born out of a time when people began to return to nature, exploring the wilder sides of humanity with free love and increased sexual expression, a rebirth of pagan ideals and Dionysian excesses, albeit psychedelic rather than of the vine. As we've seen, Jimmy Page and David Bowie gave a large nod to Crowley's work, while Mick Jagger asked us to have sympathy for the Devil. And why not?

He's had 'elluva time.

But the bottom line is, the Devil doesn't exist any more than Pan does. The Horney One, like God, is a projection of a side of ourselves that we would, mostly, rather stay asleep to; a side that we describe as baser, more animalistic, more dangerous... more Sinful.

145

The Devil, surely, is our 'Sinful' side out of control, on a bender, off the leash, frenzied, wild, chaotic, destructive, passionate, alive, hungry, libidinous, deranged, angry, crazy, dangerous… authentically *human*. Exactly that which the Church couldn't handle. That's why they put Pan in a cage and made a demon out of Nature.

And *that*… is a Sin.

* * *

An old Cherokee chief was teaching his grandson about life:

'A fight is going on inside me,' he said to the boy. 'It is a terrible fight and it is between two wolves—a dark wolf and a light wolf. One is evil—he is anger, envy, sorrow, regret, greed, arrogance, self-pity, guilt, resentment, inferiority, lies, false pride, superiority, self-doubt and ego. The other is good— he is joy, peace, love, hope, serenity, humility, kindness, benevolence, empathy, generosity, truth, compassion and faith. This same fight is going on inside you—and inside every other person, too.'

The grandson thought about it for a minute and then asked his grandfather, 'Which wolf will win?'

The old chief replied, 'The one you feed.'

* * *

War is a projection of the human condition, our inner conflict with the Devil and God, good and evil, light and shade. And in our sleeping, unconscious state we turn our nightmares into reality, seeing demons in our own brothers and sisters, monsters in our kin.

But all conflicts begin in our hearts, in our souls, and the only way even to contemplate peace on earth is by looking deep within ourselves; until we find harmony with our own spirits, the world will remain a place of conflict and turmoil.

OK, enough of this satanic mischief. Grab your passports and pack your bags…

We're going to France.

* * *

June

Behind every good man there is a woman, and that woman was Martha Washington, man, and everyday George would come home, she would have a big fat bowl waiting for him, man, when he come in the door, man, she was a hip, hip, hip lady, man.

Dazed and Confused

You who live safe
In your warm houses,
You who find, returning in the evening,
Hot food and friendly faces:
Consider if this is a man
Who works in the mud,
Who does not know peace,
Who fights for a scrap of bread,
Who dies because of a yes or a no.
Consider if this is a woman
Without hair and without name,
With no more strength to remember,
Her eyes empty and her womb cold
Like a frog in winter.
Meditate that this came about:
I commend these words to you.
Carve them in your hearts
At home, in the street,
Going to bed, rising;
Repeat them to your children.
Or may your house fall apart,
May illness impede you,
May your children turn their faces from you.

Primo Levi, *If This Is a Man*

The Paris apartment block 17 Rue Beautreillis doesn't look different to any other Haussmannian-style block and that's because it *isn't* different to any other Haussmannian-style Paris apartment block. But the young man found dead in the bathtub of the third-floor flat in the early hours of 3 July 1971 was not your run-of-the-mill, everyday kind of guy.

Standing on the street opposite Jim Morrison's final address, I'm trying to look like neither fan nor burglar. No one gives a shit, anyway. It's a quiet side street in the fourth arrondissement between the Marais and Bastille, and to my surprise I feel *something*. Curiosity brought me, and the notion that it might be a good opener for a section on the glorified Sinners that rock stars are, but I hadn't expected to feel anything, much as I've been a Doors fan since my teens.

There's something about looking up at that third-storey window...

I've seen an out-of-focus shot of Jim looking out of that window, hands in his pockets, pullover, beard and characteristic long hair; and even though the shot is blurry, there's a heaviness to his body language as he gazes into what little future he has left. And now, 50-feet below, I feel as if we are looking at each other over the decades, his energy still there, and I feel the heavy grey hopelessness of death.

I'd like to say these feelings are not mine, that I'm channelling Jim's ghostly angst, the pain that drove him to escape the US with the threat of jail and to take the pure China White heroin that invited death to join him in a bathtub full of regurgitated pineapple chunks; but of course the feelings are all mine, even on this glorious Paris morning, where no one knows who I am and I walk with the carefree abandon that is the preserve and indeed privilege of the anonymous.

An old woman leaves the building and the heavy wooden door remains ajar. I peer through the mesh spyhole to the eerie inner courtyard. Now is my chance to enter Jim's inner sanctum, to get that much closer to the man.

But I don't.

Fear of being caught, of causing offence, of intrusion… even though Jim would have; he'd have been right in there knocking on the door asking to have a go in the tub.

But this is why we need the Jim Morrisons and the Brian Joneses and the Jimi Hendrixes and the Janis Joplins. Like Christ, they died for our Sins, but even *better*, they committed the Sins that we're too scared to. If I had the balls of Jim, I'd be snooping around his flat, not skulking off in search of a croissant.

And the pain I feel even as I walk away is the pain of meeting my own projected Jim, my inner Jim who lives in this apartment still, who bares only a passing resemblance to James Douglas Morrison, the Dionysian poet rock star who died the day before my seventh birthday.

* * *

Much like Faust, the Titans tore Dionysus—the original rock god—to pieces. The effects of fame, the US judicial system and his own demons ripped Jim limb from limb. He couldn't have lived; it would have been too disappointing to watch him grow old. We needed him intact and beautiful, like a virgin sacrifice: pure and untouched by the corruption of age. We like our Sinners to burn fast and bright like ants beneath the laser glare of a magnifying glass. That way we don't get to see them wither on the vine.

As much as young men and not-so-young women the world over still worship Jim Morrison, the wannabe poet and jaded rock star worshipped another fallen idol—Arthur Rimbaud, the nineteenth-century *enfant terrible*, hashish smoker, absinth drinker, child genius and tragic role model for many a lesser bard. Rimbaud unwittingly created the hitchhiker's road map for Jim Morrison when he penned:

I say that one must be a seer, make oneself a seer.

The poet makes himself a seer by a long, prodigious and rational disordering of all the senses. Every form of love, of suffering, of madness; he searches himself, he consumes all the poisons in him, and keeps only their quintessences. This is an unspeakable torture during which he needs all his faith and superhuman strength, and during which he becomes the great patient, the great criminal, the great accursed—and the great learned one—among men. For he arrives at the unknown! Because he has cultivated his own soul—which was rich to begin with—more than any other man! He reaches the unknown; and even if, crazed, he ends up by losing the understanding of his visions, at least he has seen them!

Let him die charging through those unutterable, unnameable things: other horrible workers will come; they will begin from the horizons where he has succumbed...

Rimbaud was not the first pretty face to be worshipped like the member of a boy band and neither was Jim Morrison. There have always been icons and it all started with rock star gods.

There's that iconic Annie Leibovitz photo of an elegantly wasted Keith Richards unconscious in his dressing room, all hair and mascara and rock 'n' roll accoutrements. Why does that photograph work? Because he looks like Jesus on the Cross. Check it out—his head slumped to the right, bare chested, swathed in rags; the look of opiated rapture; the body broken and spent. You take one look at him and you go, 'Jeez...'

With the tantrikas you've got shiva—dancing in fire, smashing shit up; the fuck monster high on bhang and opium.

The Jews have Jehovah. Easy—ZZ Top.

Muhammad? OK, I gotta tread carefully here. They shot artists at *Charlie Hebdo* for drawing a picture of him, so yeah, well done you motherfuckers.

The Sikhs believe God is without gender, so Marilyn Manson?

Boy George? *Bowie*...?

All the Greek and Roman gods were rockers. They made Motley Crew look like pussies. The Egyptians had Horus, whose parents were Isis and Osiris. Osiris was murdered and dismembered by Set, who cut his cock off and threw it into the Nile, where a catfish ate it. Isis collected all the body parts and used her magic powers to resurrect her dead husband, but she couldn't resurrect the cock, so she fashioned a golden dildo to impregnate herself and hence Horus was born.

It doesn't get much more rock 'n' roll than *that*, ladies and gentlemen.

OK, I've probably pissed enough people off by now to get myself whacked, but you get the point. When it comes to chickens and eggs, we definitely had rock stars before we had rock.

Icons fulfil a deep human need: to project our own greatness, as well as our own shadow, onto a hero of godlike proportions. That way we don't have to own our own darkness nor risk inhabiting our own brilliance.

* * *

Jim Morrison, with his perfect mix of angelic looks and bad-boy attitude, was hurriedly interred, with little ceremony and no autopsy (thanks to an exchange of 'baksheesh' with *les flics*), in Père Lachaise Cemetery, in the illustrious *who's who* company of saints and Sinners alike.

There are a million people buried in Père Lachaise, many of whom are household names from theatre, literature and music. The cemetery is worthy of any Gothic horror story with its rotting, broken tombs holding the earthly remains of Chopin, Balzac, Apollinaire, La Fontaine, Héloïse, Abélard, Stéphane Grappelli, Ingres, Henri Barbusse, Marcel Proust, Sarah Bernhardt, Pissarro, Marcel Marceau and Bizet for starters.

Jim's final resting place (assuming Mr Mojo Risin didn't

disappear into the souks and fleshpots of North Africa) has been through several incarnations over the passing years, from an unmarked grave to the vandalised bust that marked the spot when I first visited in 1985, which was stolen soon after. Now it has a simple plaque, touchingly placed there by his estranged father, Rear Admiral George Morrison (commander of the US fleet during the false flag Gulf of Tonkin incident that drew the US deeper into the Vietnam War), with the inscription, KATA TON ΔAIMONA EAYTOY, the literal translation of which means 'according to his own daemon' to convey the sentiment, 'true to himself'.

Nowadays, the grave is fenced off, the railings adorned with tens of thousands of ribbons, hair toggles and friendship bracelets tied like prayer flags in a bizarre display of kitsch colour amongst the predominantly monochrome tombs. As ever, when visiting Jim I feel irritation and awkwardness at the presence of other pilgrims, and long for a moment of intimacy with my projection, but it never comes so I walk away, treading tentatively on the wet path in my ill-gripping Converse.

* * *

The shadow of the Holocaust hangs heavily over the graveyard; indeed, it hangs like a gunmetal smog over Paris, so prevalent are the memorials; particularly, I notice, outside schools, where so many children were spirited away. Clumped together in the north-east part of the cemetery, Père Lachaise has monuments dedicated not only to the victims of Auschwitz-Birkenau, Bergen-Belsen, Ravensbrück, Buchenwald and Dachau, but also of the lesser-known camps—Flossenburg, Mauthausen, Natzweiler-Struthof, Neuengamme, and Sachsenhausen.

In many ways, what I find most chilling is that camps like Auschwitz and Dachau are not household names just because of the horrors perpetrated there, but because enough people actually lived to tell the tale for the camps to seep into our collective consciousness. But of the camps that are *not* so known — it is often because there simply weren't enough people who survived. Who of us has heard of Ebensee, where prisoners were literally worked to death at such a rate that it was considered to be one of the worst concentration camps in the Nazi network?

Or Majdanek, where prisoners were forced to sort the property and valuables taken from the murder victims located at Sobibor, Treblinka and Belzec? Belzec being where half-a-million Jews were murdered but of which little is known, because there are only two known survivors.

Then there's Chelmno, with its innovative use of gas vans in the killing of 150,000. It's possible that you might have heard of Sobibor, where a quarter-of-a-million people met their end at the Polish facility. But you're less likely to be aware of Gross-Rosen, one of the largest and most brutal concentration camps in the Third Reich, where conditions were especially harsh with twelve-hour work days spent excavating granite from the quarry, insufficient food rations, and violent abuse from the SS officers and staff, who were actually awarded military decorations from the Nazi command for inhumane treatment of the prisoners and for the executions.

The Jewish Virtual Library lists approximately *15,000* labour, death and concentration camps. I guess that's a pretty fair indication of the infrastructure required to perpetrate what is almost certainly the most monstrous and significant event in the entire history of our species, which despite our grandiose claims as to being more civilised than our ancestors, happened within living memory.

I'd never heard of Flossenburg, Mauthausen, Natzweiler-Struthof, Neuengamme or Sachsenhausen. The Flossenburg monument is made of granite stone extracted from the camp quarry, where many French deportees were worked to death along with 30,000 Soviet, Czech, Dutch and German political prisoners, criminals, homosexuals and Jehovah's Witnesses. While the bulk of murders were the result of overwork and maltreatment, Flossenburg was also an execution camp. Between April 1944 and April 1945, more than 1500 death sentences were carried out, the condemned being kept alone in dark rooms with no food for days until they were executed. The rate overtook the capacity of the crematorium, to which end the SS began stacking the bodies in piles, drenching them with gasoline and setting them alight.

In early April 1945, as US forces were approaching the camp, the SS began the forced evacuation of 22,000 inmates, leaving behind only those too sick to walk. On the death march to the Dachau, SS guards shot any inmate too sick to keep up and before they reached their destination, more than 7000 had been shot or had collapsed and died.

The death toll at the Austrian slave labour concentration camp Mauthausen-Gusen remains unknown, but it's somewhere between 1 and 320,000. You might think that was uncharacteristically sloppy admin for the Third Reich, but in fact it's because they were aware enough of what they were doing to destroy most of the evidence.

Nicknamed 'the bone grinder', conditions within the camp were considered exceptionally hard to bear, as it was labelled a 'Grade III' camp, which was intended to be the toughest environment for 'incorrigible political enemies of the Reich'. Mauthausen-Gusen was mostly used for extermination through labour of the intelligentsia—educated people and members of the higher social classes in countries subjugated by the Nazi regime.

The rock quarry in Mauthausen was at the base of the infamous 'Stairs of Death', where prisoners were forced to carry blocks of stone weighing as much as 110 pounds up the 186 stairs, one behind another. As a result, many exhausted prisoners collapsed and fell on top of the others like a line of dominos. Survivors of the climb would often be placed at the edge of a cliff known as 'The Parachutists Wall', where they'd have the option of being shot or pushing the person in front of them off the cliff.

Some 3000 inmates died of hypothermia after having been forced to take ice-cold showers and then left outside in cold weather, while other methods of extermination included beating, starvation, hanging, mass shootings, electrocution, drowning, gas and pseudo-scientific experiments.

And yet, had you ever heard of Mauthausen-Gusen?

Not me.

I pause to pay homage at the grave of Henri Barbusse, author of the great anti-war novel *Le Feu*, which I read all those years ago. Yet those brutal mud-stained images are imprinted on my psyche forever. Then I stumble to a heartbroken halt beneath what is, to me, the most impactful memorial in Père Lachaise, to the victims of the Sachsenhausen concentration camp. Sculpted out of hammered copper, it portrays a deportee engulfed in barbed wire and flames; it seems to be clawing its way skyward, arms stretching up through the trees in haunted desperation. At the base, a simple yet awful inscription: 100,000 died in this Nazi concentration camp.

That's 100,000 people—50 per cent of those ever incarcerated there died in this place that I've never heard mention of.

Then 35 kilometres north of Berlin, in the early stages of Sachsenhausen's existence, executions were done in a trench, either by shooting or by hanging. But from 1943, a gas chamber and ovens facilitated the means to kill larger numbers of prisoners.

Inside the camp were workshops in which prisoners were forced to work, primarily on parts for Heinkel bombers, but also for companies who still make many of our household products today. Including AEG and Siemens.

Awkward…

I bet they don't want people to know too much about those

details. So, let's take a closer look, shall we?

In 1933, AEG donated 60,000 Reichsmarks to the Nazi Party. Then, during World War II, the factory near Riga used female slave labour. The company was also contracted to manufacture electrical equipment for Auschwitz. AEG used slave labour in the sub-camp of Auschwitz III, most of whom would die in 1945 during the death marches and finally in Buchenwald.

In the 1930s, like AEG, Siemens helped fund the rise of the Nazi Party and the secret rearmament of Germany. The company backed the Hitler regime in return for lucrative contracts, contributed to the aggressive war effort and participated in the 'Nazification' of the economy.

Siemens took slave labourers during the Holocaust and had them help construct the gas chambers that would kill them and their families. They also owned a plant in Auschwitz, where tens of thousands of prisoners worked to supply the camp with electricity. They supplied electrical parts to many other concentration and death camps, including Ravensbrück, and their factories—which had poor working conditions, where malnutrition and death were common—were created, run and supplied by the SS, in conjunction with company officials.

After the war, Hermann von Siemens, head of the company, was charged with war crimes, but the charges were dropped and he was reinstated by the Anglo-Americans to help rebuild Germany against the Soviet Union.

As recently as 2002, public outrage forced Siemens to abandon a plan to register the trademark Zyklon for a new line of products including gas ovens—the same name as Zyklon B, the poison gas used to exterminate prisoners in concentration camps.

And while we're on the subject, it's also worth noting that during the war Kodak's German branch used slave labourers from concentration camps and several of their European branches did heavy business with the Nazi government.

Ferdinand Porsche met with Hitler in 1934 to discuss the

creation of a people's car. Hitler asked Porsche to make the car with a streamlined shape, 'like a beetle'.

Can you see where this is going?

Four out of every five workers at Volkswagen's plants were slave labourers, Ferdinand Porsche having a direct connection to Heinrich Himmler to directly request workers from Auschwitz.

Bayer, the number-one producer of drugs like aspirin, under the name I.G. Farben, manufactured Zyklon B gas, as well as funding and assisting in Josef Mengele's 'experiments' on concentration camp prisoners. Incidentally, Prescott Sheldon Bush (George W. Bush's grandfather) profited greatly from the slave labour at Auschwitz via a partnership with I.G. Farben.

In 1941, the German branch of Coca-Cola ran out of syrup and couldn't get any from the US because of wartime restrictions, so they invented a new drink... called Fanta.

In 1938, Henry Ford was decorated for his service to Nazism with a medal designed for 'distinguished foreigners', his company profiting heavily from the war by producing vehicles for the Nazis *and* the Allies.

J.D. Rockefeller's Standard Oil, which when it was dissolved as a monopoly morphed into ExxonMobil, Chevron and BP, provided the Luftwaffe with tetraethyl lead gas, without which the German Air Force couldn't have got their planes off the ground. Once again, Prescott Bush was involved, his investment firm brokering the deal.

Chase Bank froze European Jewish customers' accounts and was extremely cooperative in providing banking services to Germany.

IBM custom-made machines for the Nazis to track everything from oil supplies to train schedules into death camps to Jewish bank accounts to individual Holocaust victims themselves.

In September of 1939, *The New York Times* reported that 3 million Jews were going to be 'immediately removed' from Poland and were likely to be exterminated. IBM sent out an internal memo saying that owing to the situation, they really needed to step up production on high-speed alphabetising equipment.

Random House Publishing's parent company, Bertelsmann A.G., produced a book before the war with the catchy title, *Sterilization and Euthanasia: A Contribution to Applied Christian Ethics.*

And while you digest these facts, don't forget what we discovered earlier: US prisoners make 93 per cent of domestically produced paints, 36 per cent of home appliances and 21 per cent of office furniture.

It has been pointed out that none of the artists who created the Holocaust memorials in Père Lachaise Cemetery were Jewish, that there is no mention of the Jewish victims and any national responsibility, and that they primarily represent and memorialise Le Résistance.

Now I must confess to a frisson of excitement as my eyes lap up the plump morsels of betrayal and horror on a web page titled, 'Vichy France, the Nazis and the Holocaust: An introduction...'

Cos I really enjoyed dishing the dirt on Siemens and AEG, and now I can have a really good go at those fucking French Vichy-collaborating Nazi cunts. I'm *really* looking forward to that. I mean, they go on and on and on about the Resistance, but in actual fact there were only about fifty people in the Resistance during the war; the numbers miraculously got magnified once the Germans fucked off and now everyone seems to believe they were part of it.

Balls.

Are you aware that on the nights of 16 and 17 July 1942, *Parisian* police arrested 13,152 Jewish men, women and children? They were deported to Auschwitz and only 811 of them survived the war.

Did you know that?

But what I notice is that the excitement, the fervour, the glee with which I report this information to you is similar to how I feel when reading about Nazi war criminals being hunted down like dogs, of the trial and execution of concentration camp guards, of the collapse of the Third Reich and everything it stood for.

I love it.

I love hating Nazis. I love hating French collaborators.

Much as I enjoy the smug satisfaction of disliking the Polish guys sitting in the playground opposite my home drinking beer or Red Bull at seven o'clock in the morning. Or my disdain at high-waisted, elasticated trouser-wearing, obese US tourists with masticating jaws and dull cow eyes clotting the hostile broken arteries of *my* city. And the Japanese in their droves, blindly proffering their 1000-dollar smartphones to any passing West End tealeaf at the end of a selfie stick.

Then there's the scathing contempt I feel toward the Old Street hipsters, with their skinny legs and tiny feet and baggy jumpers and MacBook Pros and soya lattes and coiffured beards and beany hats and floppy hair and generic homogenised tattoos.

But darkest of all is the broodingly suspicious way that I peer at the Jews of Stanford Hill through my car windscreen as I sweep by on my way to Dalston, with their big hats and buckled shoes and side-lock ringlets and bewigged wives and pale-skinned children…

Best not linger too long on that one.

And so, as I explore the righteous anger and hatred that I have for a particular group of people because of how they look or what they represent, I'm reminded of an impossible question that at times I've asked of myself over the years: If I'd been born in a different time and a different place in the last century whereby I was called upon to participate in the Holocaust… would I have said no?

Would I have had the integrity and courage and self-awareness not only to refuse to 'follow orders', but also to speak out against what was happening all around me?

The darkest and scariest aspect of the Holocaust in many ways is that it was not perpetrated by psychopaths or mass murderers. It was carried out by regular, day-to-day people who went about the task in a practical, enthusiastic and efficient way. Who, as often as not, clocked off and went home after a hard day's work to their wives and children. Where they behaved decently, and with kindness and humanity.

If you can read a statistic like '100,000 dead' and not be moved, you're already on your way to the mindset that allows us to perpetrate genocide. But if you demonise the Nazis, you miss the point and become like them. The Nazis were not demons or monsters.

They were people.

And that's what's so fucked up about it.

The SS were rock stars. Cocaine, meth and the occult. As we've seen earlier, they knew how to party. Cool look too, as Russell Brand pointed out at the GQ Award Ceremony: 'If anyone knows a bit about history and fashion,' he said to a shocked audience, 'you know it was Hugo Boss who made the uniforms for the Nazis, but they looked fucking fantastic, let's face it, while they were killing people on the basis of their religion and sexuality.'

Brand and *GQ* editor, Dylan Jones, exchanged angry words on Twitter afterwards:

'What you did was very offensive to Hugo Boss,' Jones complained.

'What Hugo Boss did was very offensive to the Jews,' Brand replied.

Hugo Boss started making outfits for the Nazis in the 1930s, having himself joined the Nazi Party, which landed him the contract to make costumes for the Hitler Youth, as well as storm trooper and SS uniforms. The business went so well that Boss ended up needing to bring in slave labourers in Poland and

France to help out at the factory.

All this happened just eight years after founding the company, which helped take it to the level that we know and love today.

There are differing levels of fascism at play here.

If we accept that to Sin is to go against God *or* that it is to be unconscious (to be honest I'd say they amount to the same thing, but we're not even halfway yet, so it's too soon for conclusions), then I would argue that uniforms are in fact a fundamental part of the machinery that makes Sin possible.

In other words uniforms, and therefore uniformity, encourage uniform thought. They are the dress code of the mob, of the herd, the pack; and from the minute we knit our babies pink or blue hats, we are destroying their individuality and growing petite storm troopers, whether it be for future armies, neo-fascist far-right paramilitary groups or workers in the city. It makes little difference. The outcome is the same—their identity is compromised and their position as homogenous drones is all but guaranteed.

As Carl Jung pointed out: 'Resistance to the organised mass can be affected only by the man who is as well organised in his individuality as the mass itself.'

* * *

It's quiet in the Holocaust section and strangely cool, despite the sun breaking through the morning's cloud; and whether this is because of the multitude of ghosts that haunt this part of the graveyard or the canopy of trees I don't know, but walking away my T-shirt is soon stuck to my back as I approach the last resting place of lovers, Gertrude Stein and Alice B. Toklas, who lie side by side on the bottom south-west corner of the burial ground.

The two met in Paris in 1907, where they hosted a salon populated by the leading figures of modernism, such as Pablo Picasso, Ernest Hemingway, F. Scott Fitzgerald, Sinclair Lewis,

Ezra Pound and Henri Matisse.

After Stein's death in 1946, Toklas published *The Alice B. Toklas Cookbook*, including the famous recipe for hash fudge contributed by her friend Brion Gysin, who we introduced earlier in relation to the *Master Musicians of Jajouka*.

She was a hip, hip, hip lady, man...

Close by is French chanteuse Édith Piaf, who came from clichéd stock. The daughter of a cabaret-singing gypsy mother and an acrobat cabaret-performing father, she was raised in her grandmother's brothel, her life a set-up for tragedy. In 1935, having already lost a child to meningitis, she was discovered singing on the streets of Pigalle. Her career and fame gained momentum during the German occupation of France, where she was popular in various Parisian brothels reserved for German officers and collaborating Frenchmen. Denounced as a traitor after the liberation, a member of the Resistance spoke in her favour, saying that photos made during Piaf's concerts in POW camps allowed falsifying documents to be used to assist soldiers to escape.

The love of her life, the married boxer Marcel Cerdan, died in a plane crash in October 1949, while flying from Paris to New York City to meet her. In 1951, she was seriously injured in a car crash, and thereafter had serious problems with morphine and alcohol addiction, which contributed to her death, aged 47, weighing just 66 pounds Her last words were, 'every damn thing you do in this life, you have to pay for.'

* * *

Roughly 100 yards east, just off Avenue Pacthod, is apparently where you'll find the painter, sculptor, proto-pot head, cocaine hoover and absinthe spanker Amedeo Modigliani. He is buried alongside his stunningly hot model and common-law wife, Jeanne Hébuterne (who in true bohemian tragic style threw herself from a fifth-floor window the day after his death).

If there is anyone in Père Lachaise cemetery who could match Jim drink for drink, spliff for spliff, line for line, shag for shag, it's Modigliani, the original hellraiser. By the time tuberculosis claimed him at the age of 35, he'd fathered an indeterminate number of illegitimate children by various women, hung with Jacob Epstein, Jean Cocteau, Chaim Soutine and Pablo Picasso, scandalised Paris with his nudes, partied hard, and squandered what little money he earned from his art on his multitude of vices.

In 2015, one of his nudes realised 170,405,000 dollars at Christie's in New York.

That's 170 *million*, 405 *thousand* dollars.

That's as may be, but hard as I try—which isn't *all* that hard, as the first really hot day of the year forces me to strip most of my outer garments, threatening to scorch my recording studio tan—I can't find the crazy artist or his lover in the jumble of near identical rotting masonry. Instead, I head toward perhaps the most famous inhabitant of Père Lachaise Cemetery, even more so than Jim, located halfway down Avenue Transversale No. Three…

Oscar Fingal O'Flahertie Wills Wilde.

Which, despite the hype, I have to say is something of an anticlimax. Sure, the tomb is imposing, the Jacob Epstein sculpture of an Egyptianate winged angel with its balls chopped off makes a striking impression. However, the whole effect is vastly diminished by the glass screen that 'protects' the piece from the thousands of lipstick kisses that used to adorn the monument. But perhaps the biggest insult of all is the big, ugly white *Maire de Paris* stickers on each corner with the immortal words:

INFORMATION AU PUBLIC
PLEASE, RESPECT FOR THIS MEMORIAL.

OUT OF RESPECT FOR THIS GRAVE, PLEASE
DO NOT SULLY BY ANY MARK.
THE CLEANING FEES ARE EXCLUSIVELY
PAID BY THE FAMILY.
Thanks for your visit.

Hardly a fitting testament for a wordsmith of such legendary wit, this Sinful court jester who famously confessed to being able to 'resist anything but temptation'. And who decided that the kisses should be wiped off, anyway? Does lipstick erode Hopton Wood stone? Who in any way associated with the tomb does this offend?

Not Oscar, I'm quite sure.

Our old friend Aleister Crowley reappears at this stage of the story, unsurprisingly in conjunction with the missing angel bollocks. When the monument was finally installed in 1912, French officials took exception to the size of the balls, which they had covered in plaster. Eventually, a compromise was reached and in 1914, a bronze plaque in the shape of a butterfly was placed upon the testicles, which was then duly unveiled by Crowley.

Epstein was furious and refused to attend the unveiling, but a few weeks later, while sitting minding his own business in a Parisian café, Crowley appeared wearing the butterfly around his neck to inform Epstein that the statue had been returned to its natural state.

This wasn't the end of the story, however, because someone nicked the knackers in 1961. It is said that the cemetery manager used them as a paperweight, but whatever the truth, they are now lost, the monument more homogenised than homoerotic behind its kiss-proof screen.

In the centre of Paris, at the crossroads of Rue Montorgueil and Rue Saint-Sauveur, there is a plaque set into the pavement. It bares the inscription:

4 January 1750
Rue Montorgueil
Between Rue Saint-Sauveur
And the ancient Rue Beaurepaire
WERE ARRESTED
BRUNO LENOIR AND JEAN DIOT
CONDEMNED FOR HOMOSEXUALITY
THEY WERE BURNED ALIVE IN LE PLACE DE GREVE
ON JULY 6TH 1750
THIS WAS THE LAST EXECUTION
FOR HOMOSEXUALITY IN FRANCE

Bruno, a cobbler in his twenties, was caught having sex with Jean, a servant in his forties, somewhere around eleven thirty at night at the crossroads, the traditional venue for mischief in a kind of pre-blues tryst that saw them killed in the most horrific manner six months later. Looking at the marker, which bears the footprints of a million tourists and not a few well-heeled Parisians, it seems hard to imagine in this enlightened day and age people being executed for being gay.

Yet, the British lagged behind the French when they executed James Pratt and John Smith for sodomy in November 1835. And while that's shocking, tragically we are not discussing ancient history here.

It is estimated that between 4000 and 6000 gay men and lesbians have been executed in Iran for crimes related to their sexual orientation since 1979.

In Yemen, married men can be sentenced to death by stoning for homosexual intercourse. Unmarried men face whipping or one year in prison. Women face up to seven years in prison.

The law in Iraq does not expressly prohibit homosexual acts, but people have been killed by militias and sentenced to death by judges citing sharia law.

In Mauritania, Muslim gay men can be stoned to death and

lesbians face prison.

Nigerian law classifies homosexuality as punishable by imprisonment, but several states have adopted sharia law and impose the death penalty for men.

In Saudi Arabia, married men engaging in sodomy or any non-Muslim who commits sodomy with a Muslim can be stoned to death, and some southern regions of Somalia have the death penalty for homosexuality.

In Sudan, three-time offenders can be put to death; first and second convictions result in flogging and imprisonment.

Oh, these beastly Muslim countries with their medieval ways.

But yesterday, on 12 June, in Orlando, a lone gunman took it upon himself to single-handedly execute forty-nine gay men in a Florida nightclub. Which makes you wonder if attitudes have really changed all that much since Oscar Wilde, one of the greatest literary figures of all time, was imprisoned in Reading Gaol in 1895 for sodomy and gross indecency. Of his time inside, he said:

> When first I was put into prison some people advised me to try and forget who I was. It was ruinous advice. It is only by realising what I am that I have found comfort of any kind.
>
> To regret one's own experiences is to arrest one's own development. To deny one's own experiences is to put a lie into the lips of one's own life. It is no less than a denial of the soul.

Initially incarcerated in Pentonville Prison in London, a place where prisoners were forbidden the use of pen and paper, or even to talk to one another, this poetic genius spent much of his time walking on a treadmill as decreed by his sentence of hard labour. His health suffered so badly that he was ultimately transferred to Reading, a hostile crowd jeering and spitting at him on the station platform. But the damage was done and

Wilde would never fully recover from the experience, physically or emotionally.

On his release in May 1897, he sailed immediately for France, never to return. He lived out the rest of his short life in abject poverty; a lonely, sickly figure he walked the boulevards in solitude, spending what little funds he had on alcohol, until he finally succumbed to cerebral meningitis, most likely caused by a perforated eardrum that was the result of a collapse while in prison from hunger and exhaustion.

And so died Oscar Wilde, hounded to death for his sexuality. The epitaph—from 'The Ballad of Reading Gaol'—on his grave that on this hot and sunny day is surrounded by US tourists reads:

> And alien tears will fill for him
> Pity's long-broken urn,
> For his mourners will be outcast men,
> And outcasts always mourn.

Whether I'm an outcast or not, I find little comfort in the company of these hushed spectators barred from leaving so much as a kiss. I linger only long enough to watch one of the throng drop her smartphone on the hard, hot tarmac, where it bursts like tantalum fruit shattering the bored silence.

* * *

It strikes me that perhaps this fascination with the dead is a Sin in itself. I've had enough of the heat, the steaming, damp masonry and the ceramic ghosts in this *Who's Who* charnel ground, this *Hello!* magazine boneyard, this A-list theme park where we come to perform fake-blood sacrifice to the cult of celebrity dead brother and bask in the proximity of the immortals who, consigned forevermore now to the Underworld, represent most if not all of the Sins, from genocide (which somehow is conspicuously missing from all the Commandments we have explored to date, unless you take a paranoid view of the Georgia Guidestones): the persecution and horrific murder of people because of their race, belief system, sexual preference or indeed eccentricity— *that* is a Sin; to the Sin of petty-minded, fear-driven bureaucracy and patronising, idiotic censorship; the Sin of exploitation and the turning of a blind eye, of benefitting from other people's suffering and turning mass murder into profit; or *even* the Sin of hero worship, the denial of self through the deification of false idols both in how we disown our own brilliance and in so doing fall ever more deeply asleep; but also in the unbearable pressure and expectations that we project onto these faux gods so that they die in droves, haunted and betrayed, exulted then crucified, just another plume of oily black smoke on the horizon betraying the trajectory of where they flew too close to the sun—it is not just dirty tabloid ink that we must obsessively scrub from our blackened fingers, their blood, too, is on our hands.

* * *

They say Paris is unfriendly.

I don't find it so.

But back in London, the walls are moving in, the pressure is on, the perimeter walls bursting at the seams, tensions perpetually high. House and rental prices rising like tidal waters out of control, threatening to swamp us all, as gouty wine-blushed oligarchs in faraway lands grow fat on the very marrow of our city—this New Dubai, this rotten jewel in a cultural desert that with every passing day looks less and less like the London I once knew and loved.

This week, the gentrification of SoTo pushed my rent up by 250 pounds a month, a grubby slip of paper handed to me by a shamefaced lackey announcing the hike 'owing to unavoidable rising costs'.

And this morning, on 23 June, we awoke to the news that the UK has succumbed to 'Project Fear' and we are to leave the EU, the country divided into a bitter, downtrodden working class and a fat, bloated super elite, and all the while the power-crazed, floppy-haired haters rub their hands in glee.

The smell of Sin hangs heavy like the pall of burning garbage over us all, the stench of racism, of the rise of the far right, of pint-swilling bandersnatch Nazis and Third Reich rhetoric, the blood-spattered steps of small town libraries and slaughtered MPs, of Britain First and truth and freedom and honour and love last.

Hate is in this Land.

It arrived unannounced, and it and it alone is the unwelcome, illegal immigrant. As the grim reality seeps through the gelatinous bubble walls of London Town, I question if perhaps this world is beyond saving.

* * *

And so ends June 2016, which means we're halfway through this ride. Where are we going next? Hard to say, but I've a feeling it's going to be in a corner of a foreign field that if the extreme right had its way would not only remain forever England, but would also be physically dug up and repatriated back to these hallowed, xenophobic shores…

* * *

July

Halted against the shade of a last hill,
They fed, and, lying easy, were at ease
And, finding comfortable chests and knees
Carelessly slept.
But many there stood still
To face the stark, blank sky beyond the ridge,
Knowing their feet had come to the end of the world.
Marvelling they stood, and watched the long grass swirled
By the May breeze, murmurous with wasp and midge,
For though the summer oozed into their veins
Like the injected drug for their bones' pains,
Sharp on their souls hung the imminent line of grass,
Fearfully flashed the sky's mysterious glass.

Hour after hour they ponder the warm field –
And the far valley behind, where the buttercups
Had blessed with gold their slow boots coming up,
Where even the little brambles would not yield,
But clutched and clung to them like sorrowing hands;
They breathe like trees unstirred.
Till like a cold gust thrilled the little word
At which each body and its soul begird
And tighten them for battle. No alarms
Of bugles, no high flags, no clamorous haste
Only a lift and flare of eyes that faced
The sun, like a friend with whom their love is done.
O larger shone that smile against the sun,
Mightier than his whose bounty these have spurned.

So, soon they topped the hill, and raced together
Over an open stretch of herb and heather

171

Exposed. And instantly the whole sky burned
With fury against them; and soft sudden cups
Opened in thousands for their blood; and the green slopes
Chasmed and steepened sheer to infinite space.

Of them who running on that last high place
Leapt to swift unseen bullets, or went up
On the hot blast and fury of hell's upsurge,
Or plunged and fell away past this world's verge,
Some say God caught them even before they fell.
But what say such as from existence' brink
Ventured but drave too swift to sink.
The few who rushed in the body to enter hell,
And there out-fiending all its fiends and flames
With superhuman inhumanities,
Long-famous glories, immemorial shames
And crawling slowly back, have by degrees
Regained cool peaceful air in wonder
Why speak they not of comrades that went under?

Wilfred Owen, 'Spring Offensive'

How will they regard this slaughter, they who live after us...?
How will they regard these exploits, which even we who
perform them don't know whether one should compare them
with those of Plutarch's and Corneille's heroes or with those
of hooligans?

Henri Barbusse, *Le Feu*

July 1st.

Across the room the clock shows 7:20 a.m.

One hundred years ago to the exact minute 40,000 pounds of
high explosive detonated beneath the Hawthorn Ridge Redoubt
at Beaumont Hamel in Northern France, marking the start of the
Battle of the Somme.

Later, I climb into the car beside Noor, my eldest daughter who, at not quite fourteen, is almost the same age as the youngest British soldier killed in the Great War. Her eyes popping at the amount of chocolate I've got stashed in the glove compartment, we head out of town into an early evening rainstorm. Our mission—to make pilgrimage to the old battlefields on this poignant anniversary, ostensibly because she's studying it at school but, more importantly, because I feel duty-bound as a father to take her there, and—perhaps even more so—because I feel duty-bound to those who lie there still.

I was raised on tales of Uncle Bill, who came home from the front with the mud still caked on his kilt until one day he came home no more. The Great War part of the tapestry of every family in the UK, etched into a collective sorrow that goes far deeper than the tunnels my dead uncle used to dig beneath the enemy lines.

Noor chooses the music of Marilyn Manson and we head towards Folkestone in a now heavy downpour through great sweeping, multicoloured radiant archways like I can't remember since I was a child bridging the Kent skyline before us.

The Britannia Grand Burstin Hotel is a foul and desperate tavern. I search for kinder words with which to bless this rotten fuck-hole but find none. The floor of our room immediately above the karaoke bar is pumping like a diseased heart, the chamber infused with *parfum de chien mouillé*, swinger sex and stale, antique human secretions, while the ghosts of the 10-million troops who passed through this fetid port en route to the war to end all wars cast a drab and sorry pallor over the town.

I sleep a fitful sleep and wonder if the car will still be there in the morning. I wake once again before the alarm and soon we're burrowing beneath the channel, bursting out into French countryside, with rainbow spray chasing our tales as we speed towards the Somme.

Mid-morning and we're in the Newfoundland Memorial Park,

with its visitor centre and designated pathways. It was a far cry from my first trip back in the mid-Nineties, when sheep would get caught on the rusty barbed wire and unexploded shells still littered the mostly unvisited battlefield.

> I found myself alone in front of a trench with three Germans firing their rifles. I returned their fire and took what cover was possible, which, at the time, seemed infinitesimal. I saw, some distance away, a young boy from our battalion break cover and run for the German trenches but he was set on by four or five Germans and killed with bayonets.
>
> Pte R. Love, Glasgow Commercials

The park is busy, a light rain sweeping across doing nothing to deter the pilgrims who walk reverently among the preserved trenches and shell holes, one kneeling to touch the inscription on a gravestone, another to place a wreath. I wonder if I will weep. Suddenly, unexpectedly, great waves of emotion wrenched from my throat as they did last night on my way to collect Noor while listening to old soldiers on Radio 4. But no tears come and I do my best to explain to my daughter the sheer extent of the slaughter that happened here on this blood-soaked soil a century ago. However, I fail miserably because...

By 5:00 p.m. on 1 July 1916, this part of no man's land where my girl and I now walk hand in hand was covered with the dead, dying or wounded. Lieutenant F.G. Hornshaw of the West Yorkshires described their cries as being 'like enormous wet fingers screeching across an enormous pane of glass.'

How do I describe that to a girl of thirteen? And should I? This whole remembrance thing confuses me; part of me dislikes all the visitor centres and public toilets and the general prettiness of this site of horror. Beautiful, poignant and poetic as the British and Commonwealth Cemeteries can be with their Kipling quotes and perfectly manicured English country garden visage, I can't help feeling that a truer memorial would have been to leave the bones of the dead where they fell in their hundreds of thousands amongst the barbed wire that ensnared and disembowelled so many. So many *children,* the youngest but a few months older than Noor, so slight, so delicate, so *new*. To gift wrap this mincing machine with such floral charm makes it even harder to match the blind savagery to this soil that but for the absence of sand in the shell holes could so easily be a Surrey golf course.

Then again, when I first came here these sites were all abandoned. Now, coach loads of battlefield tourists and children on school trips populate the killing fields. One can but pray that in the act of remembrance there may lie hope that such insane folly may never be repeated. But then I look around the world and realise that we'll need a lot more visitor centres for that to be the case.

I first went back to the Somme on a motor-bike in 1935. I have been back twelve times since then and I intend to keep going as long as I can; I try to be there on the first of July. I go out and, at seven thirty A.M. I stand at the exact spot where we went over the top in 1916.

Pte H.C. Bloor, Accrington Pals.

* * *

I've been asked when my 'spiritual awakening' was. I usually reply when I first dropped acid in 1982. Or on encountering a particularly carnivorous and grizzly road accident on the New Delhi Agra highroad in 1989.

But the truth?

I believe it was when I first stumbled blindly into the Somme battlefields on my way back from a dopey weekend in Amsterdam in 1995. My heart burst open and my world would never be the same again.

I could *feel* the earth weeping.

Over the years, I returned time and time again, walking the trench lines, the cemeteries, the memorials; exploring woods where the contour of scrub and bramble betrayed the inferno held in frozen embrace more like a turbulent green sea; the undulating waves of shell-cratered earth betraying the horror that once visited these now tranquil glades, so inviting and peaceful in the daytime yet, as dusk fell, always shooing me away with the warning that I was no longer welcome.

Climbing the dirty little road over the steep bank, one immediately entered the land of despair. Bodies, bodies and their useless gear heaped the gross waste ground; the slimy road was soon only a mud track which passed a whitish tumulus of ruin with lurking entrances, some spikes that had been pine-trees, a bricked cellar or two, and died out.

The shell-holes were mostly small lakes of what was no doubt merely rusty water, but had a red and foul semblance of blood. Paths glistened weakly from tenable point to point.

Of the dead, one was conspicuous.

He was a Scottish soldier, and was kneeling, facing east, so that one could scarcely credit death in him; he was seen at some little distance from the usual tracks, and no one had much time in Thiepval just then for sight-seeing, or burying. Death could not kneel so, I thought, and approaching I ascertained with a sudden shrivelling of spirit that Death could and did.

Edmund Blunden, *Undertones of War*

What became clear to me over the years is that we who return, we who are drawn to this place, do it for many reasons: for morbid curiosity, for vicarious excitement, for remembrance, for pilgrimage and homage, much like those of us who walk the celebrity death paths of Père Lachaise in an attempt to... *what*?

Absorb the ghosts of glory? To be touched by the wraiths of heroism, as if by visiting these fields we will somehow absolve ourselves from feeling accurs'd that we were not here? Maybe. But deeper down we are all trying to *understand*, to understand just how our species could behave so badly, that eternal puzzlement. Are we really such beasts? And deeper still, am I, too, that beast?

In recent months, our group has grown enormously, with membership swelling by the thousands. We now have Britain First brigades across the country and it's common knowledge our social media reach is bigger than any other political party.

People can expect a large amount of action for 2016, it's going to be our year. We have so much planned and there are now so many people in our group at an activist level. Our country and Europe is heading for a civil war. Our leaders have sold us out and the way to save us is to head for the streets.

Jayda Fransen, deputy leader of Britain First

The question: Is killing a Sin or an integral part of our *nature*? The hill tribes in Papua New Guinea don't worry about such conundrums. If a member of a neighbouring clan strays into their territory, they just kill them. No fucking around. No debate. No confusion.

It's a matter of survival.

My recent bout of post-Holocaust ranting anti-Semitism that surfaced while driving to Dalston both intrigued and troubled me. But then when I look at the tribal people of Papua New Guinea I wonder, is that what stirred in me? As I moved out of my territory (which let's face it, in Tottenham is about as culturally diverse as you can get) into the terrain of a neighbouring tribe, did some ancestral, warlike spirit emerge to ensure the survival of *my people*? To crush the competition? To feast on the warm kosher brains of my foe?

Or am I just a beast?

Killing—and on a larger scale, war—has a deeper function than just the survival of the fittest or the protection of borders and territory. For men, it gives a sense of purpose second to none. Time and again when reading first-hand accounts of the Great War, among the blood and the horror and the shells, you hear tales of people consumed with a sense of higher being, complete in the knowledge that what they are fighting for is right and worth dying for, that day-to-day problems fade away by comparison, and life suddenly feels complete and whole.

They who march to war like so many sheep do so with their heads held high because they have discovered the Holiest of Grails...

Meaning.

And *that* is a horrible truth. War gives men a sense of meaning. It doesn't just tear through blood and sinew and bone, it annihilates existential doubt, and elevates the spirit to a place of worth and high focus.

Europe has, for the first time in its history, been mostly peaceful these last seven decades, but the 'baby boomer' men have struggled to find value in the void created by peace. In simplistic terms, if I am not needed to hunt to provide food for my family or fight to defend my tribe, what use am I?

Suicide is a bigger killer than cancer or heart disease in this generation of lost boys (although, interestingly, national suicides rates drop significantly during times of war). As I observe the chaos surrounding me in these turbulent Brexit times, I can't help wondering if the xenophobic response to the refugee crisis isn't just the mentality of a playground bully looking for a fight because he's *bored*.

It's always an incredibly powerful experience for me to visit the Somme, even more so to go with my daughter, to teach her what man can do to man when we are unconscious; the terrible poignancy emphasised even more with people on my doorstep attacking their neighbours because of their race and their beliefs. I heard that, since the Brexit result, the Spanish school in Portobello had the slogan 'go home' daubed on the wall; the Polish centre in Hammersmith was attacked; children born here are being taunted in their schoolyards with racial abuse.

Of the graves we visited, few contained the essence of men beyond the age of 25, many much younger. But did they die for a world dominated by Trump or Britain First or Tony Blair? Blair, who with the death of more than 600,000 on the void where his soul is meant to be at an estimated worth of 60 million pounds in the bank, wrings his waxy fingers in gilt-edged faux guilt as the Chilcot enquiry confirms that the war in Iraq was wrong on every possible level.

I guess they didn't really understand what they were dying for, and I'm damned if I can make sense of it.

Lest we forget?

I fear we did.

* * *

The light at Vimy Ridge has a surreal quality, a kind of ever-present electricity like that which follows a storm: clear, clean, trippy but not quite... natural. High on an escarpment above Arras, the Canadian Memorial to yet another bloodbath fought in the spring of 1917 took eleven years to build from a stone so stark and white it can only have been dredged from the deepest and darkest of ocean canyons.

Standing before it with her pale skin and long, teenage legs, Noor could almost be one of the carved figures come to life, reanimated by the sheer power of the grief that clings to this hillside, replenished daily with every tear and wreath laid at the feet of the weeping statues.

The headlines in the British press throughout the Great War were largely positive—old-school Empire bullshit celebrating huge advances and triumph over the Hun, yet all the while clashing horribly with the mile-long casualty lists published daily on the back pages.

Looking around this pockmarked hilltop now, in this Chinese Year of the Monkey—a year of mayhem, madness, mischief and chaos—with Trump and the far right on the ascendant, UK politics in devious disarray, the EU in collapse, war ravaging Chechnya, Dagestan, Ukraine, Nagorno-Karabakh, Iraq, Israel, Syria, Yemen, and a further twenty-nine countries in Africa and sixteen in Asia, plus the war against drugs in Mexico and Columbia, and only eleven countries in the world that are actually free from conflict, with the US involved in a total of 134 wars, and Blair smarming his way out of war crimes, it is hard not to collapse beneath the prevailing negativity.

But there is light.

Of all the memorials on the Western Front, it is the Canadian ones that are arguably the most poignant, the most impressive and the most emotive. The Canadians fought in a war that wasn't theirs to fight, pulled in as a part of the ageing British Empire. 'In those few minutes I witnessed the birth of a nation,' Brigadier General A.E. Ross famously said of the Canadian assault on Vimy Ridge. It is this nation a century later that is now lead by Justin Pierre James Trudeau, the light to Trump's rising darkness, and for once you can't help feeling that he represents something that might have been worth fighting for.

So, what's so special about Trudeau?

Well, let's start with the most important detail in this man's life. Take your copy of The Rolling Stones album *Love You Live* and listen to Side 2, Track 3, recorded at the El Mocambo nightclub in Toronto in 1977. At approximately 4:35, as 'Little Red Rooster' grinds to a halt, you will hear Mick Jagger say, 'Hello Margaret, are you awwwwlright?'

That's Justin Trudeau's *mum*, that is.

Now, you see, to me (and sure, I've been accused of being

a little 'whacky' or 'out there' at times, so feel free to take this with a pinch of salt), when given the choice of electing an alleged rapist who believes US mosques should be kept under surveillance, that all Muslims should be tracked by law enforcement and should not be admitted to the US; who believes in waterboarding and other methods of 'strong interrogation'; who believes in 'bombing the hell out of ISIL'; who has openly denounced Mexicans as 'rapists' and criminals, and that he wants to build a wall to keep both them and Syrian refugees out (which, by the way, Mexico should pay for); who proposes to deport 11 million illegal immigrants from the US; who believes doctors should be punished for administering abortions, as should the women who obtain them; who supports the NRA and the right to bear arms; who believes that climate change is 'just weather' and that global warming is a hoax constructed by the Chinese; who believes that the Black Lives Matter movement is 'trouble'; who is anti-gay marriage; who is a sexist, sociopathic, narcissistic, pathological liar with an itchy trigger finger.

Or...

A happily married man that tokes weed; who marches on Gay Pride; who defines himself as a feminist; whose attitude towards the indigenous people of Canada is that he sees the constitutional guaranteeing of their rights as a 'sacred obligation'; who supports solving climate change; who founded the Trudeau Centre for Peace and Conflict Studies; who ended Canada's airstrike mission against ISIL; who personally went to the airport to greet Syrian refugees; who has some great ink and whose mum is a Buddhist who partied with The Stones...

I think you see my affiliation.

In a world devoid of good male role models and few inspirational leaders, Trudeau is a beacon of light at a time when mass killings are almost daily news (last week, on 14 July, it was Nice; this week Florida and Japan. Oh yeah... I heard about that) and suicide bombs are so prevalent that they don't even make the papers (because most of them happen in countries populated by brown people).

In June this year, Donald Trump took to Facebook and Twitter to congratulate himself just hours after a gunman attacked a gay nightclub in Orlando, Florida, leaving fifty dead and fifty-three injured: 'The bottom line is that the only reason the killer was in America in the first place was because we allowed his family to come here.'

And posting separately he continued: 'While I greatly appreciate everybody congratulating me for being right on radical Islamic terrorism, I don't want congratulations, I want toughness and vigilance.'

Trump regularly incites political violence.

Trudeau is a voice of reason in a world where it was recently announced that 52 per cent of Americans actually believe that 'Trump is running for president for the good of the country rather than personal gain.'

Trudeau has pledged to launch a national public inquiry regarding 1200 missing and murdered Indigenous women and girls in Canada.

In May this year, Trudeau delivered a formal apology in his country's House of Commons for the Komagata Maru incident. The event took place more than a century ago, when in mid-May 1914, a Japanese steamship carrying Sikh migrants was not allowed to dock in Vancouver. Its arrival in Canada was anticipated by doom-mongering local headlines, which warned of an impending 'Hindu invasion'.

Trudeau tweeted: 'No words can fully erase the suffering of Komagata Maru victims. Today, we apologize and recommit to doing better.'

When it comes to racism, however, Trump really excels...

I've got black accountants at Trump Castle and at Trump Plaza. Black guys counting my money! I hate it. The only kind of people I want counting my money are short guys that wear yarmulkes every day.

And it goes way back. In 1973, the US Department of Justice sued the Trump Management Corporation for violating the Fair Housing Act on the grounds that Trump had refused to rent to black tenants and lied to black applicants about whether apartments were available, after which he signed an agreement agreeing not to discriminate to renters of colour.

In 1989, four black teenagers and one Latino teenager who became known as the 'Central Park Five' were falsely accused of attacking and raping a jogger in New York City. Trump immediately took charge in the case, spending 85,000 dollars to run a campaign in local papers demanding, 'BRING BACK THE DEATH PENALTY. BRING BACK OUR POLICE!' After serving time in prison, the teens were found to be innocent, but Trump argued that because they were most likely (according to him) involved in other criminal activity that night, they were treated too well.

In 2000, when the St Regis Mohawk tribe proposed building a casino, Tump opposed it because he felt it threatened his own gambling operations in Atlantic City, running a series of ads suggesting the tribe had a 'record of criminal activity that is well documented'.

In 2011, Trump played a large role in circulating false rumours that President Obama was not born in the US, even sending investigators to Hawaii to look into Obama's birth certificate. He also suggested that Obama wasn't a good enough student to have got into Columbia or Harvard Law School, and demanded the President release his university transcripts. Trump claimed, 'I heard he was a terrible student. Terrible. How does a bad student go to Columbia and then to Harvard?'

During a discussion on gender equality at the UN in New York, Trudeau said, 'I'm going to keep saying loud and clearly that I am a feminist until it is met with a shrug.' He continued:

> There are lots of things you can do to be a better feminist as
> a man, but here's a simple one—don't interrupt women, and
> notice every time women get interrupted in conversation.

Trudeau appointed a gender-balanced cabinet after he became
prime minister, made up of fifteen men and fifteen women,
explaining his decision by saying, 'because it's 2015'. He said:

> Study after study has shown that if you ask a man if he wants
> to run for office, his first question is likely to be, 'Do I have to
> wear a tie every day?' And if you ask a woman if she wants to
> run for office, her first question is usually, 'Really, why me?'
> Let's start rewarding politicians and companies who aren't
> driven by a macho approach.

Trump? 'You know, it doesn't really matter what they write as
long as you've got a young and beautiful piece of ass.'
On the subject of prenuptial agreements:

> There are basically three types of women and reactions. One
> is the good woman who very much loves her future husband,
> solely for himself, but refuses to sign the agreement on
> principle. I fully understand this, but the man should take a
> pass anyway and find someone else.
>
> The other is the calculating woman who refuses to sign
> the prenuptial agreement because she is expecting to take
> advantage of the poor, unsuspecting sucker she's got in her
> grasp.
>
> There is also the woman who will openly and quickly sign
> a prenuptial agreement in order to make a quick hit and take
> the money given to her.

In 2004, he stated that 'All of the women on *The Apprentice* flirted with me, consciously or unconsciously. That's to be expected.'

About his child, he said, 'If Ivanka weren't my daughter, perhaps I'd be dating her.'

About comedian Rosie O'Donnell:

Rosie O'Donnell is disgusting, both inside and out. If you take a look at her, she's a slob. How does she even get on television? If I were running *The View*, I'd fire Rosie. I'd look her right in that fat, ugly face of hers and say, 'Rosie, you're fired.'

We're all a little chubby, but Rosie's just worse than most of us. But it's not the chubbiness, Rosie is a very unattractive person, both inside and out.

Rosie's a person who's very lucky to have her girlfriend. And she better be careful or I'll send one of my friends over to pick up her girlfriend. Why would she stay with Rosie if she had another choice?

In 2012, he attacked *Huffington Post* editor and cofounder, Arianna Huffington, on Twitter saying, '@ariannahuff is unattractive both inside and out. I fully understand why her former husband left her for a man—he made a good decision.'

Of Hillary Clinton, he tweeted, 'If Hillary Clinton can't satisfy her husband what makes her think she can satisfy America?'

And regarding his Republican candidate rival, Carly Fiorina, he said:

Look at that face. Would anyone vote for that? Can you imagine that, the face of our next president? I mean, she's a woman, and I'm not supposed to say bad things, but really, folks, come on. Are we serious?

This is no joke. Trump appeals to Americans for many reasons, one of which is that he represents—to frightened, weakened people—an old-school type of masculinity, a kind of silverback John Wayne, go-get-'em brand of moron who dares to say it like it is.

He's not frightened to upset people.

This is no time for diplomacy, people.

This is *war* and if there was ever a war worth fighting, albeit hopefully a bloodless one, this may well be it.

* * *

The potential Hitlers of this world are legion, but they only rise to prominence when a vacuum presents itself. Such a vacuum exists now. And at the risk of sounding like The Donald, I feel that the social sexual changes that we saw in the last century lost their way. No doubt there was enormous heroism, sacrifice and bravery, which resulted in a partial equalising of gender dynamics, but the work is not done. The job not complete. There is still a long way to go.

As the men marched away en masse and women took to the workplace, the Great War sowed the seeds of the massive changes in gender roles that we witnessed in the last century. Over the course of time, men slowly learned that the John Wayne version of masculinity was no longer relevant or appropriate, that to dominate and crush was no longer acceptable or indeed desirable. With the emergence of rare men like Trudeau there may be some light at the end of the tunnel, but what is really missing, to me, are the powerful *women*. Not female versions of *men* who cut their hair short and don power suits and behave like bullish, aggressive men always have in an attempt to redress the inequality that they experience at every turning, because of course to 'allow' women to be more like men is still in essence misogynistic. No. If we are indeed to save Mother Earth, we need to return to the more pagan attitudes of goddess worship, where women are allowed to be raw and untamed, where their wild, savage nature is celebrated rather than shamed or squashed in a seismic shift in our global attitude toward the Feminine.

Because the Feminine is more powerful than you can possibly imagine.

The Feminine eats Trumps for breakfast.

The Feminine takes absolutely no shit from anyone.

The Feminine is raw, pure, uncontained power.

I do a lot of work with men. One of the images I use is that of the Great Goddess Kali, destroyer of all things evil, Divine Mother and Protector of the Universe. Not a bad title, I think you'll agree.

Kali is usually portrayed wearing a necklace of skulls, holding the severed heads of men, standing on the prostate body of Lord Shiva. I take this image and I ask men what they see. The response is usually something along the lines of a crazy bitch whose pussy whipped and trampled all over the guy.

Which is one way of looking at it.

Another way, the Hindu way (and man, those Hindus knew a thing or two about gender dynamics *thousands* of years before Freud), is that while Kali goes bat-shit in her wild and uncontained Feminine passion...

Shiva is chillin'.

The Masculine is totally cool with the Feminine. Both energies exist in pure harmony. And that, ladies and gentlemen...

Is Tantra.

Not feeding each other chocolate while blindfolded, wearing a sarong listening to sitar music and burning Nag Champa.

Tantra is the Feminine Principle and the Masculine Principle in perfect balance, working together, not in opposition: the wild and the calm, the chaos and the order, the light and the shade, heaven and hell, yin and yang...

A friend of mine who would define herself as a prominent feminist said something that I would never have had the wisdom to figure out or the courage to say. It was, to me, quite radical. She said the problem with women is that they are misogynistic.

What?

She explained that women hate the Feminine Principle as much as men do. That is why women have such contempt for men who exhibit their feminine qualities. Chicks hate pansies.

Fuck.

But it makes sense to me. When I started working with gay men I remember being surprised at how homophobic they were. It's just for them the hatred was directed mostly inward. But then I thought, *Of course. Why not?* They were raised in a homophobic world. Why wouldn't they have ingested those judgements the same as anyone?

The same is true of women. In a misogynistic world, why would they have learned to exalt the Feminine?

And The Donald feeds on the vacuum where men experience themselves as bitter, resentful, emasculated victims.

Time for goddess worship, people.

Time for Tantra.

* * *

August

Run from what's comfortable.
Forget safety.
Live where you fear to live.
Destroy your reputation.
Be notorious.
I have tried prudent planning long enough.
From now on I'll be mad.

Rumi

The only performance that makes it, that really makes it, that makes it all the way, is the one that achieves madness...

Mick Jagger, Performance

Corsica. What better place to begin this month's Sinful reflections? A wild-west island of well-worn denim skies, broken-tooth rock formations and the promise of a jagged, violent death to those who fail to negotiate the heart-in-the-mouth hairpin bends; a place of bandits, separatists, gun-runners, renegades and diminutive dictators.

Corsica.

What better place to pause, lick our wounds and reflect on the journey so far? With little to distract but birdsong, cicadas, and the occasional pack of bloodhounds baying in the distance for fresh blood, bone and sinew...

For flesh.

What, if *anything*, have we learned? And perhaps more importantly — are we any closer to saving the world?

I fear not.

Nevertheless we have voyaged far and wide, been to realms I could never have imagined...

Of the 'Big Seven' — *Lust, Gluttony, Greed, Sloth, Wrath, Envy* and Pride—we have seen but fleeting glimpses; seven Sins and seven months of beard and hair growth. I look like a wan version of a street-dwelling Green Man, but my vanity is no less. I just have a cupboard full of balms, pomades, gels and powders to sculpt the craziness into some kind of order—a biker sans hog, I've managed to adapt it to fit my rock and roll demeanour.

We've tinkered with the Ten Commandments, brushed with Buddhism, rolled with the Georgia Guidestones; we've been to hell and back with Dante; we've met with Osho and Rumi, O'Brien and Perry, Trudeau, Roosh V, Pan, Gurdjieff, Crowley and Hicks, LaVey, Brand, Satan, Morrison and his Père Lachaise compadres; we've explored genocide, concentration camps, racism, warfare and capital punishment; we've done drugs from ayahuasca to psilocybin to MDMA to whisky and weed.

And if I were to summarise at this stage of the game in but one sentence all that we have explored...

I would say that Sin is what happens when we ignore ourselves. *Everything* we need to follow a path that is true to ourselves exists within us at all times, perfectly formed, accurate, precise and definite.

The *only* Sin is that of being unconscious.

So, surely we therefore have to conclude that *that* which encourages us to *deviate* from our own truth is the cause of all Sin: education, religion, government, society, codes of conduct, ethics and morality—*rules*.

The Seven Deadly Sins.

The Ten Commandments.

Ironic, huh?

The true sophisticate is one who has spent enough time first learning the rules, then questioning the rules, and only then abandoning the rules and replacing them with their own. One who abandons rules prematurely is thoughtless, ignorant, reckless and reactive. One who considers and only then replaces is a true sadhu, a Holy person, a being of substance and authentic divinity.

Authentic. There's that word again.

> To be authentic means to be true to oneself. It is a very, very dangerous phenomenon, rare people can do that. But whenever people do it, they achieve. They achieve such beauty, such grace, such contentment that you cannot imagine.

Oh, how I love that Osho equates authenticity to danger, for in the eyes of society it truly is a deviant and threatening behaviour. A good member of any society, corporation, army or religion will obey. But society is only necessary if its members are sleeping. When people awaken there is no threat. They will interact harmoniously because that is their true nature. No one with love in their heart ever hurt another (well, not unless you're a Papua New Guinea tribesman, in which case my hippy idealism goes *right* out of the window and you're tonight's brain soup).

But I'm not talking tribalism or survivalism or cannibalism, people.

I'm talking deviance and Love.

I believe that—despite the millions of dead in warfare and genocide, the ever-present threat of nuclear holocaust, the near total absence of leaders who we can trust or a banking system that isn't wholly corrupt—we as a species are evolving, indeed that we are programmed to evolve, even…

That evolution is the meaning and purpose of *Life*.

Often when there is a seismic shift, the old ways get stronger as they die, like an old king reluctant to abdicate the throne. Observing this world through the lens of Sin as I have these past seven months, it has been hard not to see only Sodom and Gomorrah, conservatism and extreme right-wing thinking closing in.

But on the morning that I write this, a friend of mine on day-three of an ayahuasca retreat emailed me with a simple message. He wrote, 'I am enough.'

And boom! *There* it is, right there, the Holy Grail; and in that moment, in that realisation, the whole world shifted, minutely, imperceptibly but irrevocably on its axis as another cell in the organism awoke and everything changed forever.

You might not have felt it. But trust me.

It did.

* * *

So my friend—let's call him Dave, for that is indeed his name—just realised something that changed the world: principally, that he is *enough*, he is complete, he is whole, he is love and he is loveable.

Which, I'm sure you will agree, is a wonderful thing. There's just one small snag. Several billion other souls haven't made that leap...

Yet.

And until everyone else does, we do have a problem, peeps. You see society, as we understand it, is a system born out of fear *of* the individual, maintained by making the individual full *of* fear. This is different from *community*, which values and *knows* the individual, working together collaboratively in groups of not much more than 150 *individuated* and autonomous people.

To find out what is truly individual in ourselves, profound reflection is needed; and suddenly we realise how uncommonly difficult the discovery of individuality in fact is.

Carl Jung

Individuation is the process of transformation whereby the personal and collective unconscious are brought into consciousness and assimilated into the whole personality.

And when it comes to saving the world individuation is the goal.

The individuated understands their *separateness* and their part of the *whole*.

The individuated is *not* the same as the renegade.

An individual cell in an organism exists in perfect harmony *with* the whole. This is a *healthy* cell. A renegade cell acts separately *against* the whole. This is a *cancerous* cell.

And so, if Justin Trudeau represents the healthy cell, working on *behalf* of or collaborating *with* the whole organism, then Donald John Trump is that lump that you found on your left bollock that you hoped was nothing. That lump that you thought if you ignored it long enough would go away. That lump that your doctor just told you was untreatable.

The analogy of the cell within the body is useful, as it helps us to understand the incredibly complicated and incredibly simple notion of oneness, in that a healthy cell, representing the individuated person, is at the same time both separate and inseparable from the whole.

When we as a species, as a whole, awaken to the fact that we are all part of one greater consciousness (a notion that, let's face it, is no more weird or wacky than the very real fact that we, as individuals, are made up of a mass of cells that in themselves are a collection of subatomic particles that have always been here and will always be here and that therefore the concept of death is an illusion) there will be no more war, no more hate, no more barriers, no more political parties, no more countries, no more racial differences and no more gender divides.

No more Sin.

And the world will be saved.

You may say that I'm a dreamer.

You may say that I've taken too many mushrooms.

And maybe you'd be right.

But you have to ask yourself, are you denouncing my hippy ways because you think they're the ravings of an idiot? Or because to consider them makes you uncomfortable?

And even if I am talking shit, was Rumi? All those years ago? Or was he wise beyond comprehension?

Run from what's comfortable...

Society is predictable, society is order, society is unthreatening, society is a centrally heated three-bedroom house in a cul-de-sac with off-road parking, double garage and a 100-foot rear garden.

Forget safety...

Safety is a legally binding document whereby you swear in the eyes of the law or your god to love, honour and...

Obey.

Live where you fear to live...

This is the zone beyond the edge where fear is your ever-present companion, your guru, your friend who keeps you filled with a sense of aliveness and possibility and expansiveness.

Destroy your reputation...

Reputation is the steel door of the prison of your persona, which keeps you trapped in who you think you are rather than face the reality that you are nothing and you are everything.

Be notorious...

To be notorious you need do no more than to shine with all the brightness that you fear to manifest.

I have tried prudent planning long enough...

To plan is to live with the delusion that we are in control. We are not.

You are going to die.

Get the fuck over it.

From now on I'll be mad.

Hallelujah...

And God bless Jalāl ad-Dīn Muhammad Rūmī.

* * *

But are there any Rumis in the world these days?

I think not. We don't pay that much attention to philosophers or poets any more; songwriters and comedians have superseded them. Not that that's necessarily a bad thing. The likes of Bob Dylan and The Beatles have written poetry worthy of the greats, while Bill Hicks and Russell Brand have philosophised great wisdom to the masses who, as Hicks observed, would not have paid 20 bucks for a babysitter unless they believed in principle that they were going to be entertained with dick jokes, and yet went away with their brains addled with the truth.

In my last book, *Play from Your Fucking Heart*, I quoted Gurdjieff, the mystic who first drew my attention to the fact that I was asleep:

If a man in prison was at any time to have a chance of escape, then he must first of all realise that he is in prison. So long as he fails to realise this, so long as he thinks he is free, he has no chance whatever.

Osho, however, makes it very clear that awakening is no simple feat:

Keep your wristwatch before you, and look at the hand that shows seconds and remember only one thing: 'I am looking at the hand which is showing seconds'.

You will not be able to remember for even three seconds together.

You will forget many times... just a simple thing: 'I am looking and I will remember this; that I am looking'.

You will forget.

Many things will come into your mind. You have made an appointment; just looking at the watch the association will come into the mind: 'I have to go at five o'clock to meet a friend'. Suddenly the thought comes and you have forgotten that you are looking at it. Just by looking at the watch you may start thinking of Switzerland because it is Swiss-made. But you will not be able to remember even for three consecutive seconds that you are looking at the hand showing seconds moving.

If you can attain to one minute's self-remembering, I promise to make you a Buddha.

Of course, Rumi—hundreds of years before Gurdjieff and Osho—had something quite exquisite to say on the matter:

For years, copying other people, I tried to know myself.
From within, I couldn't decide what to do.
Unable to see, I heard my name being called.
Then I walked outside.
The breeze at dawn has secrets to tell you.
Don't go back to sleep.
You must ask for what you really want.
Don't go back to sleep.
People are going back and forth across the doorsill
Where the two worlds touch.
The door is round and open.
Don't go back to sleep.

Don't go back to sleep. And yet so much of our world is constructed so as to encourage somnolence: opiate TV, hypnotic PlayStations, the chloroform of social media...

Close your eyes. Fall in love. Stay there.

Rumi's roadmap to enlightenment.
Close your eyes. Fall in love.

Stay there.
Rumi's roadmap to save the world.

* * *

Before I left town for this dusky criminal kingdom, I decided to consult my neighbour, a man both devout and holy known to all as Mem the Mad Sufi, the inhabitant of a strange and fragrant apothecary in the bowels of my warehouse home.

I figured those Sufis know a thing or two and I wanted to be in on the action.

'Sin? What defines what's acceptable or what's right or wrong? Is it something that's come divinely to human beings, or is it a natural thing in the heart of a person?

'Arguably it's the same thing.

'I have to say at this stage that I believe in something that I don't understand. I say the word Allah. In English, we use the word God.

'Before, we had idolatry. Man would carve stone or wood and say, "This is God, this is the Goddess," so I guess what I'm saying is that before we talk about Sin we have to understand that Sin suggests that you have broken something or impeached something or transgressed a law, or that you've done something that's harmful to yourself or another person, or to the environment... to the planet.

'Sin suggests that something you have done is not correct.

'There is no such word as religion in Sufism. The word they use is an Arabic word, which is *Dīn*. It means "The Way".

'Is someone born immoral? I don't think so. Do people intrinsically know what's right and wrong?

'Essentially, elementally—yes.

'But the river without the riverbed is a flood. And we're the same. I don't think we're any different. A car needs the road, the train needs the track and so, as a society, if we run our track in a particular way, we must not therefore complain if we don't like the destination.'

He goes on with a perspective reminiscent of Shivam O'Brien…

'There is no consequence. People are not held accountable. There is no responsibility or accountability for the people who are our leaders, so when we look at the world we are morally outraged at the injustices that we see.

'Everything is upside down. You have horrible monsters in the political arena who commit genocide and international war crimes, and you have politicians working at grass-roots level who are almost saintly but who we've never heard of. It's almost like if you know their name then they're no good.

'And I'm not sure I understand atheists when they say they don't believe. If someone says, "I don't believe in God, I don't understand God," what are they saying? They're saying, "I don't believe in something that I don't understand." But they acknowledge that there is something to be considered. They've decided they don't understand something and so they don't believe in it.

'That makes less sense than a fool like me who says, "Well, there's something. I'm not sure what it is, but I believe in it even though I don't understand it. And because I don't understand it I don't project onto it what I think it is. And I don't think it's male and I don't think it's female."

'There's something far greater. And it's in the heart of every human being.

'So when we see horrendous things in the world today where human beings are suffering, where the earth is being polluted and where shameful things are happening…

'Does mankind not have enough love, compassion and mercy to overcome all these problems? Do we not have more resources to eradicate poverty and disease?

'Most people today will tell you they're struggling—with their relationships, their children; struggling to pay the mortgage, the rent, etc.

'People are feeling very unfulfilled.

'It's not that they want much more.

'People are not that greedy. They just want a little bit more.'

He pauses a moment to pour tea from a wrought-iron pot.

'We're always told that we have to acquire confidence, and this fits in very nicely with commercialism, capitalism and materialism; that it's something outside that we have to reach for and put inside ourselves—nice clothes, nice perfume, money, power, fame...

'That implies that we must therefore be lacking, which reinforces the feeling, by my very nature, I'm less of a man, less of a woman than I should be.

'All of that is false. You don't need to grab hold of anything. You have to let go; it's the complete opposite. You have to let go of fear.

'In science, when you have a space and you remove something, you create a void. And in that void, when you take away fear in rushes confidence.

'When people have confidence, they're more likely to listen to their heart. Heart is absolute. You love. You like. You're repelled. You're attracted. Whereas the mind creates doubt.

'Because the mind is so magnificent, it can see things in so many colours, it gives you so many options; but we are limited. We can't comprehend all of those possibilities, so while it's great it can also develop doubt. Whereas the heart...

'Is straight.

'You don't consider whether it's peaceful. You feel it. So, there is a time to think and a time to feel. And so to come full circle, as a society we are disconnected from our hearts and our spirituality. We're disconnected from our very essence and our very being. It is no wonder, therefore, that we don't know who we are.

'What the Sufi way teaches me is to focus on myself. As Rumi once said:

Yesterday I was clever; I tried to change the world.
Today I'm wise—I'm just trying to change myself.

'There is great power in that. If you have 100 people who are trying to better themselves, to collaborate and communicate with each other, they are more powerful than a million people who are running around in a wheel as part of the machinery.

'And I think that slowly in society, more and more people are waking to that.'

* * *

Mem the Mad Sufi has confirmed and reaffirmed much of what we have explored, and with the poetry, vision and spirit of one who is seeking with all his beautiful heart, with all his beautiful being and with all his beautiful *Soul*.

In all cultures, societies, countries, tribes and lands, no matter how distant, disparate or different, there is one thing that unites all human beings…

This concept of the Soul.

Inexplicable, indescribable, untouchable, invisible, amorphous, ethereal and existential, this 7-gram notion is shared between all human beings.

And this concept of Soul is inextricably linked with the concept of Sin, for it is when we deviate from our Soul's true path, true intention, true nature, that we enter the realm of what we call Sin.

But this is why codes and rules do not work, because your Soul's true path is *your* Soul's true path and no one else's. And no matter whether it be by religion, meditation, yoga or plant medicine, the job of every human being, your job as a human being, is to connect with your Soul. When you do this, you will experience peace; when you do this, you can do no wrong; all concepts of Sin dissolve; good and bad cease to exist.

If I have any mission in life, in this book, it is to make the apparently complex simple. And these complex and perturbing ideas like enlightenment and Soul are not complicated—they are the essence of simplicity. Indeed, enlightenment is not something we are moving toward, it is something we are returning to, like death. Mark Twain—an incredibly deep thinker—famously pointed out that the fear of death is bizarre given that we all have known the experience of non-existence.

> I do not fear death. I had been dead for billions and billions of years before I was born, and had not suffered the slightest inconvenience from it.

Likewise, we have all known enlightenment. It is how we enter this life. Just watch a newborn and tell me it is not in a state of perpetual *newness*; it's just that we unlearn, mostly by being drawn away from ourselves with notions of right and wrong, good and bad, to appease and calm our more-than-often exhausted parents. And so through the process of learning what we need to do to please and placate those on whom we depend for our very survival, we lose our awakened state.

As a dyslexic, so much seemed unattainably complex to me and in order to comprehend my world I learned the art of simplification. When I read Osho, or any of the acknowledged masters, their wisdom can seem profound but at the same time out of reach, belonging to those who have attained a consciousness way beyond my own evolution. This may be true, but what I'm hoping to present here, as ever, is the notion of the *bleedin' obvious*, the reality that these enormous spiritual concepts are much simpler than they may seem.

Similar to enlightenment, the notion of Soul can seem impenetrable, but once again it is not something as distant as you might imagine. We all encounter our true essence in the most domestic of ways on a daily basis, it just requires a little attention to appreciate — that thoughtless moment when everything connected and the golf ball sailed straight down the centre of the fairway. The poem scribbled in a journal that we have no memory of composing and yet is right there before our eyes in our own handwriting. Doing the washing-up with total focus and suddenly experiencing absolute presence. Taking a corner at speed and feeling at one with the car. That's why Soul music is called exactly that. It comes from spirit, from the source, the centre, the heart, from the other side, from God.

It can't be programmed.

And when you get a glimpse of that Soulfulness, of *your* Soulfulness, it will no longer feel academic, and you will understand what the great teachers mean by 'Oneness', that great soup that connects us all, where your persona dissolves and you understand everything.

I realise, however, that until we can find our own reference points, this is only theoretical, which isn't satisfying at all; which is why I'm suggesting apparently non-mystical moments like the golf course or the kitchen sink. The miraculous is more often found in the minutiae, in the mundane.

Of course, everything becomes much easier once you give up the ideas that you have been taught about God and accept that God is a projection of our own divinity. Even the word divinity can make it seem something distant, unattainable or foreign, but listen to a piece of music that really, really turns you on and you'll be in that place. Music is one of the few universal direct lines to God that we have left.

And so, when working with Sin, if we accept the concept that to Sin is to go against God's will, it helps enormously when we understand that we are God, and therefore Sin is when we go against our own true self, when we are unfaithful to ourselves, when we behave in an unconscious way.

When we are asleep.

And so the irony is that codes, rules, ethics and morality encourage unconsciousness. They encourage a state of sleep. They encourage polarisation, duality, and notions of right and wrong. They discourage self-awareness, curiosity and self-enquiry, the routes to enlightenment.

Any statement that begins with 'Thou shalt not...' closes a door. Prohibition creates shame and therefore distance.

For example: Thou shalt not covet thy neighbour's ox (for ox, read wife/girlfriend/au pair, etc).

Well, that's a problem because I don't half fancy her, but the Good Book says that I mustn't, even though I really do, and so I'd better not look at that part of myself because not only does it make me feel shit, but it also makes me really frightened. Apparently, these dark and dangerous yearnings mean I will fry for all eternity and I don't want that, because I burned my finger on the stove once and it really hurt. So the idea that if I have these feelings means that I'll be roasted for ever is like really, *really* scary.

And boom! There you have it. The rule causes the unconsciousness and unconsciousness is the only Sin.

But what do we do? Because to not follow orders means we have to think and feel for ourselves, and we do *so* like the safety of being told what to do and how to be. Which is kind of strange given how much, in the West anyway, we go on and on about being free and the importance of freedom. But how many people actually have the balls to be truly free? Most people who believe themselves to be free are self-delusional.

You are not free. For as long as you experience fear of consequence, you are not free.

This is not to suggest that the 'right way' is to do whatever we want at any time—rape, murder, steal. It means we need to make conscious decisions as to whether or not we actually want to rape, murder or steal from a place of deep self-awareness, and that requires us to know our own rapist, murderer and thief intimately. And once this personal intimacy is achieved, these behaviours become impossible and so Commandments and Deadly Sins are rendered obsolete.

And you are free.

Osho was notoriously anti-rules and anti-establishment, but he did acquiesce 'as a joke' to a journalist when asked what his own Ten Commandments might be. And so, as guidelines go, these are as good as any I know:

One
Never obey anyone's command unless it is coming from within you also.

Two
There is no God other than life itself.

Three
Truth is within you; do not search for it elsewhere.

Four
Love is prayer.

Five
To become nothingness is the door to truth. Nothingness itself is the means, the goal and attainment.

Six
Life is now and here.

Seven
Live wakefully.

Eight
Do not swim—float.

Nine
Die each moment so that you can be new each moment.

Ten
Do not search. That which is—is. Stop and see.

* * *

So, let's pick that apart.

Never obey anyone's command unless it is coming from within you also.

Surely that' s worthy of getting tattooed on the inside of your eyelids, chiselled above your front door, glazed into your crockery, engraved on your mirrors and windows, and etched into the screen of your TV, laptop and/or smartphone?

Never obey anyone's command.

Obey? To command someone to obey is a Sin in my book. It is an abuse of their nature.

To tell someone what to do comes from a place of fear, power imbalance and a desire to dominate. In Native American culture, they do not command a child not to touch a pot of boiling water. They say, 'That pot is hot.' The child is informed, not crushed. The child is respected, not controlled; its autonomy is cherished and preserved.

But we don't live in a culture where autonomy is valued; we live in a society where automated worker ants, not individuated souls, are prized.

Unless it is coming from within you also.

Ahhh… *Unless*, that's the pivotal word.

So, if I say to you, 'Go and find a place in nature and meditate until you become enlightened…'

Kill me.

Unless you know it is the right thing for you, because it chimes with your own deep, innate sense of your inner truth. In which case, you owe me 700 quid for the spiritual guidance.

* * *

There is no God other than life itself.

That's a beautifully simple way of explaining what I've been labouring to express. Life, soul, presence, God—it's all the same thing, that which connects us all. We may experience ourselves as separate, but that force we call life is universal, regenerative, creative, circular and eternal. We love to overcomplicate things, but be with a tree, a plant, an animal or a person in stillness, in silence, and *feel* their energy. That, simply, is God—not some geezer with a big beard who lives in a cloud.

Energy is God. God is energy.

Again, I'm in danger of writing in such a way as to create a state of intimidating exclusivity with phrases like that, but remember, the point here is to simplify. Watch another person's chest rise and fall as they breathe, and you will see that energy that we call life, that energy that is God, that energy that is both inside and outside. Of course, there is no inside or outside, but let's not complicate things, we were doing so well.

* * *

Truth is within you; do not search for it elsewhere.

Try introducing *that* idea to the Minister of Education.

Imagine a classroom where *that* was the lesson. OK, maths

and science and English literature and all that may be interesting if that's what you're into, but it's always been the *inner* journey that has fascinated me.

Imagine a school where children were taught to meditate, to listen to *themselves*, a school of intuition, a university of instinct, a college of self-connection, an academy of self-reference, a conservatoire of self-knowledge.

Imagine a world populated by adults who had been raised to reflect, to look inwards before they acted, before they reacted, before they spoke, before they responded. Before they even *thought*.

You may say that I'm a dreamer and yeah, I get you. I'm just being wistful. I know it's never going to happen—we need drones not individuals.

* * *

Love is prayer.

So, what did the beardy old bastard mean by that one? If it was the other way around—'prayer is Love'—then it might be easier.

I was understanding it as prayer is Love, but no, the emphasis is on Love. And yeah, I see that now. Love *is* an act of prayer, an act of devotion, an act of focused intent. A place to inhabit perpetually.

I think we kind of lost touch with Love. It became about *the other* rather than a state of existence and a state of mind. It is possible to exist in Love without it being about anyone else, a way of interfacing with your world.

The hill-tribe people of Papua New Guinea love their neighbours, but in their case it's how their neighbours *taste*. What I'm suggesting is loving thy neighbour and all existence with a state of grace, openness, compassion and benevolence, just... without digesting them.

* * *

To become nothingness is the door to truth. Nothingness itself is the means, the goal and attainment.

It strikes me that those of us who have ever been guilty of deciding that we need to find our own true selves have been barking up the wrong tree. Because there is no true self. There is essence, that quality of pure *youness* that you arrived in this incarnation with. Essence is the place that you are operating from when you are being dangerously authentic, unmoulded and real; but *you*, that person who you think of as you, is ultimately no more you than the car that you drive. It is a vehicle that you travel in, just don't mistake it for…

You.

Persona is no more real than a cornflake packet, a construct that identifies the contents in a certain way, with a certain promise, a certain dream.

I was interviewed when my last book came out and the reporter finished up with the question: 'How would you like to be remembered?' He seemed surprised when I said that I did care, that I wouldn't be, that in 100 years' time it was unlikely that anyone would remember me at all. I pointed out that we die twice—the first when we leave our physical bodies, the second when the last person who ever knew us dies. Then you're gone, along with the 120 billion other humans who ever lived. And how many of them can you name? Hitler? Napoleon? Genghis Khan? Fuck that. It seems to me that apart from writing rather good plays or being good at painting ceilings or inventing flying machines that don't work, the only people who get remembered commit genocide. And I have neither the inclination nor the resources at my disposal.

My maternal grandfather was a hero to me. He was the father I wanted and I was the son he never had. When he died, I recall watching the news on TV and being astounded that his death wasn't featured, even though I knew that was crazy. But for me, it was the biggest news event in history. The day Kennedy was shot? I wasn't born. The day Lennon was murdered? December 1981, I think. My grandfather? 6:20 p.m. on Sunday, 22 March 1998, in the back bedroom of his house in Wheeler End.

Pete Muckley. His mum christened him Pete cos she said people would just shorten it to that anyway. He meant everything to me. But soon, he will be forgotten. He was born, lived for eighty-seven years, served in the RAF in World War II without any noticeable distinction, did a bit of farming, grew some nice potatoes and then snuffed it.

He didn't save the world. But he saved *my* world and soon no one will know that he ever existed.

The same will be true of you and me. We are going to be forgotten. Soon. And that's OK. Like the cells in a body, we will be replaced and no one will know we were ever here. And that's cool. As long as you leave the world a better place than the one you arrived in, then you've done your job. Like Pete did.

But nothingness?

It's the key to true freedom. I have no real ambition, apart from to own a hand-built *Lazy J 20* guitar amplifier, but there's a seven-month waiting list for them. I don't really care what happens. I matter and I don't matter, and at the end of the day all I am is matter: I've always been here and I always will for all time.

The day I became enlightened simply means the day I realised that there is nothing to achieve, there is nowhere to go, there is nothing to be done. We are already divine and we are already perfect—as we are. No improvement is needed, no improvement at all. God never creates anybody imperfect. Even if you come across an imperfect man, you will see that his imperfection is perfect. God never creates any imperfect thing.

Osho, *Autobiography of a Spiritually Incorrect Mystic*

* * *

Life is now and here.

Most, if not all, spiritual teachers will have this message at the core of their philosophies, from Eckhart Tolle's *Power of Now* to Maharishi Mahesh Yogi's *Be Here Now* to Sri Nisargadatta Maharaj's *I Am That* to Jiddu Krishnamurti's thoughts on presence…

You can't argue with them, incredibly hard as it is to be in the now.

But it doesn't mean you should trust them. Another teaching common to many of the 'greats' is to question everything, especially gurus; otherwise, there's a danger that they become cult leaders. Osho was a tricky bastard, probably, possibly, quite deliberately; but when it comes to his views on homosexuality, he and I part ways:

Homosexuality has arisen because we have deprived people of heterosexuality.

Homosexuality was born as a religious phenomenon in the monasteries because we forced monks to live together in one place and nuns to live in one place, and we separated them by great walls. Homosexuality is bound to happen. It happens only in monasteries and in the army, because these are the two places where we don't allow men and women to mix. Or it happens in boys' and girls' hostels; there also we don't allow them to mix. The whole phenomenon of homosexuality is a by-product of this whole stupid upbringing. Homosexuality will disappear from the world the day we allow men and women to meet naturally.

That's just bollocks, isn't it.

And sadly, not the first time that I've heard such beliefs from a so-called Master. I was taught much the same by my Tantric teacher in Southern India, part of the reason why I left the course earlier than planned. Personally, I'm not a big fan of the whole gay-straight divide; although, how you identify yourself is of course entirely your choice. I tend to think of us as sexual beings and compartmentalisation is of no interest to me.

Perhaps the most useful way to take this 'teaching' is as a reminder that Osho was a human being—'even if you come across an imperfect man, you will see that his imperfection is perfect'—often brilliant, certainly challenging and controversial, but also flawed and blind and even ignorant at times. It's always disappointing, that moment when you realise that your parents are fallible, not the gods you wished them to be, and the same is true of gurus and leaders. And yet, it is an incredibly healthy moment, a transformative moment, when you remove them from their false pedestal and equalise the relationship.

* * *

There's a pleasant breeze in the office this morning as I write, the office being a deckchair in the grounds of an ancient convent looking across the sea to the hazy outline of Elba; nothing but the smell of warm cedar and the sound of tuned-up Harleys cornering hard and fast on the coast road below to entertain my senses while I contemplate Osho's Seventh Commandment, to 'Live Wakefully'.

Osho was unusual in that he bridged the gap between Eastern and Western thinking, a factor that certainly explains a lot of his appeal and accessibility. He was a fan of the brilliant Georges Gurdjieff, yet another flawed, chain-smoking, Armagnac-swilling, disciple-shagging mystic, compulsive liar, and champion of wakefulness and the digging of unnecessary holes.

It was Gurdjieff's contention, having studied extensively in Tibet or thereabouts (his autobiographical accounts are shady to say the least), that Eastern meditation techniques are terribly hard for the Western mind to master. And so, at his Institute for the Harmonious Development of Man at the Château Le Prieuré outside Paris, he would have devotees dig holes for no reason other than by engaging in repetitive, monotonous manual exertion, it placed the student in a meditative state.

Once the hole was complete, Gurdjieff devised a second phase to the procedure.

Fill it in.

Who said that the road to enlightenment would be glamorous or exotic?

Bombay Airport, 1990, I still remember seeing the book with its bright green cover on the stand in the transit lounge shop: *The Occult* by Colin Wilson. I bought it for two reasons: the first, that I had always had an interest in the esoteric; the second, and this was the clincher, it was the only book they had in English.

It was a hefty tome, lasting me all the way back to the UK via New Delhi and Baghdad, and it was here that I first heard of both Crowley and Gurdjieff, contemporaries who could be described as the light and shade of the same coin.

And it was this idea of Gurdjieff's, that we exist in a state of half-sleep—automatons barely conscious of our own existence—that really got me. That we live life in a dream state, and that it takes great effort to wake up and be conscious. And the realisation that I was asleep. I could feel it, like looking at the world through the cloudy walls of an aquarium. I could detect movement and muffled sounds, but there was no clarity.

It was both exciting and depressing to suddenly notice the walls of my prison.

I've been in Corsica eleven days now. It feels like years. And yet eleven days in Tottenham fly by. This is why life appears to speed up as we get older—time passes quickly the more things become familiar. Routine and habit rush us towards the grave. Change your environment by going on holiday, and the new environment and daily regime slow things down, for a while anyway, until you become accustomed to this new lifestyle, which explains why the second half of a holiday always goes faster.

Industrialisation brought about a need for a much more routine lifestyle for the drones who served in the factories; for example, our eating habits, breakfast, lunch and supper, regulated by the clock rather than by a connection to our own eating habits and needs for sustenance. It's one o'clock, I had better have lunch, regardless of whether my body is sending me signals that it requires nutrition—one of the routine ways that we have, as a culture, fallen asleep.

Sleep and you die, or perhaps more accurately, sleep and you won't know that you have lived. Gurdjieff had people wear their shoes on the wrong feet to live more wakefully. Osho wore his noisy wooden clogs. Do what you need to do to live more lucidly and beware the mind-numbing routines that we all so easily fall into lest you wake up too late.

In about 1988, my band supported a guy called Wilko Johnson at the closing of a grand old rock 'n' roll establishment, The Clarendon in Hammersmith—a beautiful Victorian music hall that had survived the Blitz but was now about to fall victim to modernisation and the need for another shopping centre.

I'd never heard of Wilko, but our agent informed us that this was a great gig, as the dude had been the guitar player in Dr Feelgood, and later with Ian Dury and the Blockheads. I wish he'd told a few more people, because the room was cavernous and almost empty. After our set I stayed for a couple of Wilko's numbers (he had the legendary Norman Watt Roy on bass) and then split.

Fast-forward a couple of decades and Wilko was back in the limelight once again, but this time because he had just been diagnosed with terminal pancreatic cancer. By now, I'd bought a DVD of the *Old Grey Whistle Test* from the Seventies and had fallen in love with Dr Feelgood, only vaguely remembering that we'd been on the same line-up as this bug-eyed speed freak with the electrocuted style of guitar playing.

What stood out and touched people was not Wilko's diagnosis—it was his response. Turning down the option of debilitating chemotherapy, he chose to live out his last few months on the road. A genuine farewell tour. Tickets sold out in minutes. But owing to a great music business connection, I managed to blag the royal box at Koko in Camden—a fantastic venue that had once been the BBC radio theatre—to see Wilko's last ever gig.

There was speculation as to whether or not he would be well enough, but come the day he was on fire, closing the set with a blistering version of Chuck Berry's 'Bye Bye Johnny'.

There wasn't a dry eye in the house.

But then a funny thing happened.

Wilko got better.

He was offered a revolutionary new surgery and it worked.

I felt delighted. And a little bit... cheated. Like going to see a public execution and at the last minute the condemned gets a reprieve.

I'm not proud.

But it was Wilko's account of the moment he received his initial diagnosis that is relevant here:

I felt pure elation. I'd always imagined hearing something like that would bring horror and panic, but I was extremely calm, then I felt this extreme sense of elation that continued throughout my illness. Staring at death gives you profound feelings. Everything seems more vivid. Walking down the street everything seemed sharper, brighter, more in focus.

Wilko had woken up. The depression that had dogged him his entire life lifted and, facing death, he felt the exquisite joy of pure presence. But his recovery came at a cost...

> I wish I could regain it. It's like a powerful dream that has faded. Feeling like that almost made having cancer worth it. I knew I was really getting better when I started getting depressed again.
>
> Jesse Pinkman

Listen, if you've gone crazy or something, I mean, if you... If you've gone crazy, or depressed. I'm... I'm just saying. That... That's something I need to know about. Okay? I mean—that affects me.

Walter H. White

I am awake.

Breaking Bad

* * *

Do not swim—float.

That's not such a tough one. I don't like swimming. I never did. I wasn't quick to learn or particularly good once I did. I wasn't helped when they insisted on breaking the ice in our school pool so we could have a dip. Getting into water that cold is like stepping into fire. I don't think my balls ever fully recovered.

Floating is effortless. What's not to like?

Have you ever had an idea that you thought was great, that you knew was great, but no matter how hard you tried it just didn't seem to work out? You couldn't get anyone else interested, doors wouldn't open and you couldn't generate any momentum.

And then another time you tried something and it just flowed? Nothing got in your way, progress was easy and everything just seemed to click into place.

This is what Joseph Campbell was talking about when he described being 'in flow'—when you follow your bliss. Following your bliss, doing what you really want, what you are most passionate about, isn't that popular as a belief. I mean, it's all very well wanting to be an artist, musician or writer, but let's face it, it's not a real job, is it? It's not going to pay the mortgage.

And so it is that for every shattered dream a drone is born.

Fuck that.

Do what thou wilt shall be the whole of the law.

Crowley was all over that one—follow your bliss, to do otherwise is to break the only law, the law that you be true to yourself, to do what is right for you.

Remember? If to Sin is to go against God, and God is the projection of your own divinity, then Crowley, Campbell, Osho and just about everyone else who was ever worth listening to were all saying the same thing...

To thine own self be true.

Which, by the way, requires zero effort. Going against ourselves, fitting in, conforming, adapting, manipulating, controlling or allowing ourselves to be controlled all takes a whole load of energy—to morph into a different shape, to resist our true nature.

Be you.

Be a floater.

* * *

Die each moment so that you can be new each moment.

I was just watching with fascination death welcoming a dozen or more jellyfish, trapped among the rock pools with no hope of escape, picked at by crabs and circled by fish patiently waiting for their demise. Today's contribution to the food chain, they seemed unperturbed as only a creature with no ears, eyes, nose, brain, heart or bones can be, in what can only be described as less than favourable circumstances.

This is my secret. I don't mind what happens.

Jiddu Krishnamurti

They say if you lock a bunch of monkeys in a room with a typewriter for long enough, they'll come up with the complete works of Shakespeare. Personally, I doubt it. I think they'd just throw poo at each other and masturbate, but what do I know? Maybe I'm being prejudiced and stereotyping monkeys.

But a bunch of jellyfish and a typewriter?

Forget it, you could wait an eternity and you wouldn't get jack.

Jellyfish are as thick as shit.

They don't, however, mind what happens and they fear not death.

Unlike your average human, a species that spends much of its short life pretending that it is immortal and avoiding even the very concept of death, spiriting it away in sleek white vans and enclosing it in nice veneered pine cabinets so as never to have to quite face its creeping presence.

I've written before about how I first met death in the bloody twisted metal of a fogbound Indian highway. I watched it take my grandfather, screwing him up in a ball of pain as the cancer gnawed into his spine, and then, in turn, my grandmother, dissolving the sharpness of her mind, consuming her imperceptibly yet relentlessly as she transformed into a ghost before our eyes, until there was nothing left but translucent skin and rage.

Other friends since have been scared, numb, powerless, full of disbelief, unprepared and broken as the cogs turned regardless and uncompassionate to the desperate weeping of widows and orphaned children.

It has long been recognised that happiness is relative to the awareness of our own mortality. With that in mind, do you think there's a correlation between this obsessive denial of death and the 400 per cent rise in the use of anti-depressants in the US alone since 1988? Yeah? No? I dunno, I'm just *spitballing* here, as they say in the US.

Die each moment so that you can be new each moment.

Has it ever occurred to you that whether you ever considered that statement or not, whether you had even heard of Osho or not, that it's actually happening—whether you like it or know it or not?

Think of yourself when you were a 5 year old. Where is that child? On a faded and yellowing piece of photographic paper, on an old and flickering digital tape perhaps, even a locket of hair; but that's it. That child no longer exists in physical form. You may not have noticed death take it and replace it with an almost identical replica, day after day after day, but that child, that 5-year-old *you*, that child *literally* died years ago. And *you* have died each day in order that you can regenerate, so that you can live each day. It is only when that regeneration process fails that we finally cease to exist in the human form that we recognise.

So, you and I are dying and being reborn on a daily basis. It works, even if it is finite. So what's the big problem?

Ego.

It's our ego that most fears death. 'What? *Me*? I can't die. I'm too special. I'm too important, I'm…

'*Me.*'

And it's true. Your ego should fear death, because it's the only thing that's actually going to die when you finally depart your current mortal form. And so it's like a petulant toddler fucking things up for everybody by screaming and whining for the entire car journey that is your lifetime, because it doesn't like the destination. And thus you live a miserable, fear-driven existence that is often, ironically, cut even shorter by the stress-related diseases that affect more and more of us every year.

Die each moment so that you can be new each moment.

Let go of who you think you are. Remember most events that we call 'life changing' involve the death of who we thought we were, of who we imagined ourselves to be. Once you're rooted in certainty, you have ceased to evolve. The moment you decide that you have found your true, authentic self, you just lost touch with reality and entered a fantasy realm, where you can only stay small and incomplete.

The moment truth is asserted, it becomes false.

Lao Tzu

Die each moment so that you can be new each moment.

There is nothing to be scared of unless you fear tasting every moment, savouring every breath, squeezing every last bastard drop from life itself until the well is as dry as your bones, in which case, turn on the TV and relax.

It will all be over really soon.

There is one simple thing wrong with you—you think you have plenty of time.

Carlos Castaneda

* * *

And so it is that we come to Osho's final Commandment:

Do not search. That which is—is. Stop and see.

Osho always claimed that he became enlightened when he stopped trying to become enlightened.

Similarly, in Taoism you have Wu Wei, the art of 'non-doing', the cultivation of a mental state in which actions are quite effortlessly in alignment with the flow of life. The art of non-doing comes in many forms. For me, it's most noticeable in my guitar playing. I can work and work on a lick, and the harder I try the worse it sounds. Throw my guitar in the corner in disgust and a week later, when I pick it up again, I can play the riff perfectly.

Writing, too. I'm just glad no one knows who I am and thus the luxury of not having to write to a deadline other than that which is self-imposed. I sit. And wait.

For the muse.

But once again, try selling that one to the Minister of Education and see how far you get. It's never gonna happen...

'What class you got next, Jerry?'

'Oh, I'm off to non-doing.'

Nope. Never happen.

You see, it's just not productive. Productivity, the production of slaves to operate the machine—that is what this world is all about. Which never interested me in the slightest. What I respected as real productivity when I was a teenager was the speed-fuelled, proto-psychonaut, libertine beat generation, with their dream machines and single lens reflex cameras and reel-to-reel recorders and Super 8 movie cameras and Ray Bans and espadrilles, their rejection of consumerism, social conventions, racism, homophobia and their fuck the government, fuck the war, fuck the system, fuck the man and fuck just about everyone else who represented authority or the squares or Mr Jones' attitudes, without which the cultural and sexual revolution, and the hippies along with it, would never have existed.

The beats were the first to really fight back against the system—Kerouac with his Dharma bums, Burroughs and Ginsberg with their Yage correspondence, Gysin and Paul Bowles jiving to the master musicians of Joujouka. And all the while there's Cassady at the wheel of the bus, always going further with a jug full of acid and *Kool-Aid*, changing our minds, changing the world, kicking open the door to new ideas and new alternatives, new esoteric explorations and existential possibilities. Much more than just a bunch of tea-toking, bongo-playing poets, the beat generation created the fertile soil in which Osho and his like could grow roots among the underground outsiders, whose attitudes were already ripe for rebellion.

With their diet of whisky, sperm, amphetamines, tobacco, coffee and non-conformist rebellion, the beat generation had a similar appeal to me as Osho—the original beatnik.

And when I consider *On the Road* and Kerouac's 100-metre manuscript, I feel my own savage, mushroom-fuelled compulsion to write. But I realise that it is out of the *stillness* that real productivity emerges, the *in breath* is as important as the *out breath*. And perhaps therein lies the irony:

Do not search. That which is—is. Stop and see.

Not perhaps the most obvious guidelines for productivity, nor indeed for a wild, marijuana-fuelled road trip, or for having sex with teenage boys in Tangier, but as a recipe for saving the world?

It is simple in its brilliance and brilliant in its simplicity.

And so we segue seamlessly into September like a Chevy doing a handbrake turn at 90 miles an hour with the top down, and furious be-bop blowing hot and crazy from the radio, leaving behind the ragged, broken peaks and heart-stopping hairpin turns of Corsica, and plunging instead into the cool, mellow, slow and tranquil world of Shivam O'Brien's pagan kingdom in Wales; and as the end of August comes panting over the horizon, its face contorted with the desperate intestinal cramps of holiday tummy, belly bursting through the buttons of an ill-conceived Hawaiian shirt and droplets of rancid sweat sparkling like zircon blisters across its raging lobster forehead, I realise that we are now two-thirds of the way through our Sinful adventure and I have absolutely no idea ...

What is going to happen next.

* * *

September

We piss anywhere, man.

Brian Jones

You will not be able to stay home, brother.
You will not be able to plug in, turn on and cop out.
You will not be able to lose yourself on skag and
Skip out for beer during commercials,
Because the revolution will not be televised.

Gil Scott-Heron

Never trust a hippie.

Ancient punk saying

As we have noted, according to Dante, there are Nine Circles of Hell, at the centre of which there dwells the Devil, condemned for committing the ultimate Sin: personal treachery against God. The arch-traitor—once held to be the fairest of the angels before *Pride* caused his rebellion and resulted in his expulsion from Heaven—is a terrifying beast with three faces, six wings and one vast, scaly arsehole. A putrid portal through which you, the hapless pilgrim, need to pass in order to reach the deepest, darkest corner of Hell.

Once inside, you will find the large food court, a comfortable, bright and ideal place to relax and enjoy Hell's great facilities, including JD Wetherspoon, McDonald's, Starbucks, Greggs, Nando's, Patisserie Valerie, M&S Simply Food, WH Smith, El Mexicana, Carvery Express, Chozen Noodle, Mint Leaves Indian Food, Top Gifts and KFC.

Should you need to stay for all eternity, there is an Ibis Hotel and if you wish to eat al fresco or take a walk, there is a large terrace by the lake of fire, with paths into the landscaped grounds and preserved woodlands, plus a great play area for children to enjoy. You can also relax over a nice meal while watching your favourite sporting events on a giant-screen TV.

The very centre of the fiery pit boasts award-winning washrooms and WCs, both within the food court and at the (S) Hell filling station, with free parking for all time.

And so it is that I find myself parking my car up Satan's bumhole at Beaconsfield services, the last vestiges of summer haemorrhaging like an embolism across the Western sky, a sky the colour of Afghan Henna, the colour of a bullfighter's cape, the colour of feet cut to ribbons on the serrated slate of a Welsh riverbed.

'Tis as if the very flames of Hell itself have been chasing us down the motorway, an infernal causeway dry with broken promises and the ashes of our past, while the saltwater tears of my firstborn fall fat and heavy into the grey dust. She who even now staggers barefoot through the automatic glass doors as confused and despairing as any wild animal on glimpsing its zoo enclosure for the first time.

This is what we have become—prisoners of our own making, prisoners of our own fear, running scared from our own *wildness*, trapped in compressed concrete and double-glazed coffins, safe in our high-security domiciles, enemies of our own nature.

Upon soil now encased beneath this glazed tile floor once did Muntjac deer frolic among Chiltern glades abundant with wildfowl and badger. Where there was dappled light there is now neon, the birdsong swapped for piped music, the copses for car parks, the butterflies and rabbit warrens for a globally branded business centre, providing a full range of business facilities and different sizes of meeting rooms.

And yet, though we may have travelled unnaturally far in these short few hours, on our bodies we carry the dirt, the sweat, the cuts, the bruises, the abrasions, the very proof that we do not belong here, that we never belonged here and in our hearts we never will.

No.

We belong to the wild.

* * *

The Spirit Horse Valley, the Pennant Valley, or just *The Valley* —
as those familiar more commonly call it — is not your average
holiday destination.

Hidden away in a secluded, magical corner of Mid Wales,
the Spirit Horse Foundation is a pagan community dedicated
to the practice of ritual, ceremony and nature worship. A living
experiment where a disparate band of people converge for a few
months each year to live as a village.

You will find no last-minute deals or package tours to this
destination; the Spirit Horse Valley has no coach parking, no
hospitality suite and no visitor centre or tourist information.
At Spirit Horse, you will find no designated pathways, no hot
shower blocks nor running water save for the two rivers that
converge in holy union just behind the single, long-suffering
compost toilet that somehow serves the whole tribe without
complaint.

There are no signposts to the Spirit Horse Valley and no
welcoming banner announcing that you have arrived at Spirit
Horse™ sponsored by T Mobile, Budweiser or Wetherspoons.
The long, hard motorways, the farm tracks and the mud, the rain
and the wind act as a natural filtration system, so that by the time
you make it to The Valley you will already have passed through
a natural selection process that weeds out right-wing fascists,
hippie-haters, neo-Nazis, Trump voters, Brexit supporters, fair-
weather campers and weekend warriors.

It is on one cold, dark, rain-swept night that my lover,
Madame Hua, arrives for the first time in the midst of a raging
tempest, small, bewildered children in tow, to a scene of gas-lit

medieval madness, of buccaneers and faeiries prancing barefoot in the mud, perfume of incense, tobacco, firewood and roasted meat wafting on the damp air held tight within walls of aged sepia canvas.

Madame Hua is very refined.

Madame Hua is a well-known and much-loved Parisian blogger.

Madame Hua makes films, and writes about culture and beauty.

Madame Hua has never seen people such as these.

And Madame Hua…

Has never been to a place such as this.

Like the Hole-in-the-Wall Gang, these characters wouldn't seem out of place in a folk tale from the Old West, but instead of *'Flat Nose' Curry* or *'News' Carver*, there's Joe with the drumstick fingers and the musical Midas touch; Alex, his queen, sweetly cursed not to walk but to dance with abandon in her every movement; their man-child, Jake the Mad Hatter, born of the woods, compelled to sing and play from his first waking breath until the small hours of the night, when he finally collapses spent over a drum, lute, guitar or mandolin.

The wise crones rule the roost: Sue the Angel, Lady Bard, Helen on the fiddle, Mia the Pirate smoking cones of raspberry leaf and ganja, and all the while her fresh-faced young husband looks on like an adoring Jesus as Simon, the ragged tent-maker, sits alone in the corner beneath a ragged Afghan hat, providing the heartbeat for the valley on his equally ragged djembe.

My daughters sit unfazed and glowing alongside their mother — newly arrived bearing fine wines — picking delicately at plates of hot cabbage and sweet potato; they have grown radiant in this Mystical Kingdom, raised on a diet of pagan wisdom, toasted marshmallows, magic spells and sacred offerings to the wood sprites, who in return ensure their wellbeing at all times.

Roberto strides into the tent, steam rising from his wet back and broad shoulders, hungry from a day's hard grafting in the impossibly vast Celtic roundhouse that emerges from the dirt high above us on the hill like some insane wooden cathedral; he, too, looks like he has been hewn from the rock, his skin coarse as bark, his rich Elizabethan voice as deep as the wind that howls through the canyon, providing the bass note to Erik's nasal laugh as he sits at the long table, shaven head shining in the candlelight, blue smoke from a roll-up smouldering in his Walter Raleigh beard. And now the door bursts open and in blows Shivam, all long, matted hair, wild eyes, wet fur and bottle of Chilean red clasped close to his heart; he takes up court in the corner presiding over a scene that quite simply *does not exist* anywhere else...

In this, or any other world.

Of course, all this combines to spin Madame Hua right out. She turns pale and retreats to her bug-infested bed, overwhelmed by the mud and the mayhem. I takes her several days until, slowly but surely, the transformation begins and before I know it her high heels are but a memory. She walks barefoot through the glades, delighting in the wet soil that oozes between her toes, a garland of wild flowers crowning her head. Her children are skimming stones and climbing trees, their faces painted with clay from the riverbed as—much as it did to me and my kin years before—the Valley works its seductive magic on them.

* * *

There are many outlaws in the Spirit Horse Valley, maybe even some brigands. There are definitely those who flout the law, felons and footpads aplenty, deviants, outsiders, exiles, weirdos, freaks, heretics, nudists, desperados and nut-jobs, a fair few delinquents, a couple of old lags, a brace of miscreants, numerous untouchables and one lone pariah, but, interestingly...

Little or no Sin.

Perhaps this is because the tribe is primarily pagan, with heavy doses of Buddhism and Tantra in the mix, leaving little room for rigid ruling systems; indeed, Spirit Horse is essentially *without* rules other than common sense, common decency and common respect for nature and humanity. But beyond that, it is effectively a lawless culture, which makes it rather hard to be transgressive. People are accepted as they are.

The tribe rarely exceeds the magic 150 mark and so everyone knows everyone. There is a sense of natural responsibility, care and accountability. There are no locks anywhere. Food, tobacco and wine are shared freely, and I have never once heard of any theft.

Of Lust, there is an ever-present sense of juicy, sexual aliveness throughout the camp, perhaps represented most by the 6-foot-high carved penis that stands proudly outside the men's lodge tipi, around which children and adults alike play without embarrassment or titillation.

It's just a big wooden cock on the village green. A maypole with a helmet.

The spirit of Tantra pervades the fertile Valley, of yonis and lingams and wild nature fruiting among the babbling brooks, the red kites and buzzards, the dragonflies and mysterious caves beneath waterfalls that allow us to penetrate Mother Earth, but a noticeable absence of dark innuendo, of dangerously implicit subtext, lascivious, wandering hands or leering, bloodshot eyes.

Sexuality of all kinds is *welcomed* with open arms, hearts and legs, honoured, embraced and celebrated, allowed to dance and fawn on the mossy banks and in the pastures, to tease and tumble in the woodlands, and to roar and scream in the storms and gales.

Sex is revered, but not in an adolescent, overexcited, tabloid, in your face sex sells frivolity sense. And it is no more and no less important than the rain or the wind or the snow. It's safe sex of the truest kind. The kind of sex that is acknowledged, seen, heard and, perhaps most importantly, never shamed.

Gluttony is not apparent—just an abundance of hot, thoughtful, healthy and diverse food that pours from the kitchen tent's ever-busy production line, served by beaming people catering to all diets and preferences, without complaint or refrigeration or electricity. And it's only the Food Hygiene Rating Agency that seems to think *urgent improvement* might well be necessary.

Gluttony comes when a culture believes (and even ensures) that there is not enough to go around. A culture that paradoxically cannot handle abundance, a culture where competition and winning are given great value and importance, a culture constructed on fear.

At Spirit Horse, there is rarely an abundance of anything apart from goodwill—something has usually run out or gone off or been eaten by squirrels. And with a forty-minute drive to the nearest shop and bugger-all phone signal, it's never a simple thing to rustle up provisions without considerable planning. But there is always *enough* and no one ever goes hungry, because as with all hunter-gatherer tribes, everything that is there is shared within the community, and in that climate Gluttony simply does not exist.

The attempt to satisfy greed is like drinking salty water when thirsty.

When lost in greed we look outward rather than inward for satisfaction, yet we never find enough to fill the emptiness we wish to escape.

The real hunger we feel is for knowledge of our true nature.

Tenzin Wangyal Rinpoche

Greed. How can there be Greed in a community that shares and that has enough? In a society where a neighbour goes next door just to see if the other would like to share a glass of wine or whisky or a joint or some fine locally grown magic mushrooms or a cup of tea or coffee brewed over an open fire or a back rub to soothe an aching shoulder after a hard day's work building an unnecessary wilderness temple.

How can there be Greed where there is little ownership beyond an ancient ragged bell tent or a tattered tipi, a sheepskin or two, a tin of rolling tobacco or a bottle of ale, where the whole tribe owns the land in the understanding that no one can ever *really* own the land?

What place has Greed where there is no financial system beyond a loose agreement that the people will put whatever they can into a collective pot and all will be fed equally without judgement?

Then we have Sloth, which can only exist in a society that has an expectation of a certain amount or division of labour. Spirit Horse has no such rule. Many labour in the rain and the sun and the wind day and night, lifting whole trees skyward in godlike feats of construction. Others awaken at the crack of dawn to make porridge, eggs, pancakes, bacon, toast and hot tea for the multitude of hungry villagers.

And some people just stay in bed.

The ethos within the Spirit Horse community is that all are welcome. If you wish to work on the land, so be it. If you want to peel potatoes and shell peas, so be it. If you want to be a sacred temple painter, so be it. If you want to sit and watch the clouds and the birds and the trees all day... so be it. You will not be judged. While those who devote themselves to the maintenance and expansion of the community are highly respected and valued, they are not seen as being better than the others for their endeavours.

It's just what they do.

And those who choose to sit and smile and speak poetry or words of wisdom or just talk mad shit by the fire or doze in the sun or drink too much gin are highly respected and valued.

They are not seen as being lesser than the others for their lack of visible endeavour.

It's just what they do.

All are welcome — the mad, the bad, the brave and the scared, old and young alike, strong and muscular, weak and infirm.

It is not...

A competition.

It is a tribe.

And so, having waxed lyrical and eulogised at length about the many wonders of this pagan clan that exists in the middle of nowhere in a Celtic crevice in Cymru, I guess you're expecting me to tell you how Wrath has no place at the long communal table there?

Nah.

Believe me, these lenses through which I view this disparate band of transient desperadoes are not tinted with rose; these are not gods nor superhumans, despite their divinity. These people are people with the worldly flaws and faults of *people*, to the point that I've often had the thought, *Anywhere else other than here and you'd be locked up, wouldn't you?*

Spirit Horse has perhaps more than its fair share of Heyókȟas or sacred clowns; but once again, that is the beauty of community. There is room for all, and *normal* is not a prerequisite for membership of this tribe. It's more like, OK, so you're bat-shit crazy, almost completely incomprehensible and naturally synesthetic, meaning that you see rainbows of colour whenever anyone speaks. So, do we:

Option a) Remand you to the nearest correctional institution and deaden your soul with powerful mood-altering pharmaceuticals?

Option b) Give you the task of painting complex Tibetan deities and magic symbols on the wall of the Sacred Temple in the woods by the waterfall, and therefore make you a valued member of our small tribe?

Sure, there are plenty of big egos in the Valley, toes that get trodden on, disputes and disagreements that break out, and there is as much bitching and gossip as with any grouping of human beings bigger than two in number. But when conflict does occur, it is quickly resolved without the need for committees, procedures, protocols, forms, customer helplines, courtrooms, advice bureaus, duals at dawn, humiliation or punishment.

People...

Just talk.

Envy? Envy what? I *guess* you could say that I envy the sharpness of the lines on Roberto's bell tent, the tautness of his hemp guy ropes, the palatial comfort of the interior... but I could do all that if I could be *bothered*. Sloth prevents me. And it's not really envy that I'm experiencing, it's admiration. Like I admire Shivam's crazy vision and his refusal to bow to fear; Joe and Simon and Boris and Matthew and Jake and all those blindingly talented teenagers for their musical abilities; Ian for his fire-lighting talent born out of 1000 hours of practice and dedication; Anthony for his beautiful, resonant singing voice; Fiachna for his genius who forever tiptoes the borders of madness, for that is the only way.

But Envy? No, Envy comes from separateness, from garden fences and divisive borders; it comes from 'mine' and 'yours', from 'bigger' and 'smaller', from 'better' and 'worse'.

But never from 'ours'.

Pride is defined as:

The perversion of the faculties that make humans more like God — dignity and holiness; dangerously corrupt selfishness, the putting of one's own desires, urges, wants and whims before the welfare of people.

Spirit Horse is an ongoing living experiment, twenty-five years in the making—as Shivam describes it, 'reinventing culture'. It is an attempt to return to an older way of existence, in a small, humble way, an almost insignificant way, to create and maintain a free community of people, who can come together at certain times of the year for celebration and sacred ritual to honour life in all forms, animate and inanimate, and which in its essence is the very opposite of corrupt selfishness and where the welfare of the people is paramount at all times.

As a tribe, community and ideal, it is here now and one day it will be gone. The temples and roundhouses and tipis collapsing into dust, reclaimed by the unforgivingly savage weather. No sign that a tribe once lived and loved and danced here in this place of light and laughter and mud and health and safety concerns.

Perhaps our children, who I watch blossom and flourish like no others in this age, will carry the torch forwards. Perhaps they will return each year to continue the ceremonies, the pageants, the festivals and the thanksgivings. Or maybe the Valley will live on in their hearts, shaping the way they see the world as it does my own daughter's, with their increasingly urgent questions about social inequity and ecological destruction.

Who knows?

What I do know is that in eighty years' time there will be crag-faced old men and grey-haired old women who will regale their great-grandchildren with tales of a far-off magical Valley. A place almost beyond imagination, full of faeries and pirates and wood spirits and outlaws. A place of waterfalls and tipis and rock pools and temples. Where people were free and wild, where music played day and night, where food and wine was abundant, where the villagers carried themselves with dignity, and Love ruled supreme throughout the kingdom.

* * *

OK, let's just snuff out one idea to save ourselves some time in this world-saving business, shall we?

Utopia.

It doesn't exist. Not even at Spirit Horse.

For example, The Harmony Society, a celibate Christian commune formed in Pennsylvania in 1805, died out because...

Everyone was celibate.

Fruitlands, founded in Harvard, Massachusetts in 1843, collapsed within a year owing to their extreme vegetarianism. Its residents were not allowed to use animal products, employ animals for labour or plant vegetables because it might upset the worms, the result being mass starvation.

In 1856, the Vegetarian Kansas Emigration Company founded Octagon City near Humboldt, Kansas, which failed owing to mosquitoes, disease and a lack of water.

Fordlandia, the 1930s Amazonian rubber plantation city, went shit-shaped when the inhabitants of Nazi beneficiary Henry Ford's visionary capital rioted against worker conditions, exacerbated by Ford's complete and utter lack of knowledge about how to farm rubber trees.

They had a fair stab at it in India with Auroville, started in the utopian Sixties by a disciple of the philosopher Shri Aurobindo as a place with no rules, no leaders and no money. But in recent years, its perfect veneer has been tarnished by allegations of crime, corruption, murder and paedophilia.

Pretty much like any normal town, then.

Arcosanti, the beautiful Seventies utopian town built by Italian architect Paolo Soleri in central Arizona didn't work out because it's in central Arizona.

The problem with the whole utopian thing — as is highlighted here with Fordlandia — is it tends to drift into demented messianic ego territory. In fact, generally I would say that it is better not to name a city after oneself. It has a tendency to bring out the cult leader, dictator or psychopath in a person, the worst example being Jonestown—Jim Jones' cyanide knees-up.

I think the real clue as to why utopian cities don't work is in the title—*city*. In a *small* community like Spirit Horse, which has no written manifesto as such, the simple fact that it attracts like-minded people ensures a degree of functionality in its own crazy way. But if it grew much beyond the magic '150', I am convinced that you would soon witness all of the Sins enacted sooner rather than later.

So, having doomed utopia, what does that leave us with?

Well, at the risk of repeating myself like a broken record, at the risk of repeating myself like a broken record, at the risk of repeating myself like a broken record…

We need a global expansion of consciousness.

Oh yeah… yawn… I heard about that.

There may well be a revolution, nuclear holocaust or climatic disaster that fast-tracks that shift (human beings who exist in comfort tend to be unmotivated when it comes to spiritual evolution and crisis don't 'alf speed things up; perhaps one of the reasons that Spirit Horse works is that very absence of comfort that heightens the consciousness of its community. It's like a large, damp bed of nails), but ultimately it has to happen on a personal, individual level.

Yeah, yeah, I hear your distain. I know it reads like a lame-ass cop-out ersatz repeat of every spiritual master who ever lived and breathed, and I hear you. I mean, with all of Osho's 300 or so books, it's not like they made any kind of tangible difference; nor did the combined works of Gurdjieff, Sai Baba, Carl Jung, Crowley, the Dalai Lama, Maharishi Mahesh Yogi, The Beatles, Nisargadatta Maharaj, Eckhart Tolle, J. Krishnamurti and all the faux and not-so-faux gurus who've come before or since. Otherwise, why is the world in such a shit state right now?

I've got some more bad news for you: this shift is unlikely to occur in our lifetime.

Evolution is slow. Painfully slow.

'Just like this fucking book,' I hear you say.

And I know, all this talk of saving the world is all very well, but what can we do?

Well, I'll tell you two immediate, practical things that we could *actually* campaign for right now that would make a *profound* difference.

You might want to pay attention for this bit.

First, and most importantly, a total, complete and almost unthinkable attitudinal shift in the way we educate our children (what with them being the future and all that).

And second, the end of the war against drugs and a further radical programme to make *all* psychedelic, consciousness-shifting substances available to the masses, with the appropriate infrastructure implemented to educate people to ensure their safe, risk-free usage.

Or we all die.

Oh, hold on—*three* things:

Stop arming the world. Drop acid, not bombs.

There's me sitting on the fence again.

* * *

Madame Hua remarked how I hate authority. But, I explained, I don't *hate* authority. I simply don't *recognise* it. How can I hate something I don't believe in? And this is the root problem with our education system, in that it's hierarchical.

Remember how the Inuit believe their children are the reincarnation of their elders?

I'm reading Blondie bass player Gary Lachman's biography of Colin Wilson, *Beyond the Robot*. You'll recall that Wilson was the author of *The Occult*, the book that I stumbled upon in Bombay Airport that first turned me on to Gurdjieff.

Lachman says:

Wilson recognized that although adults seem to be reasonable and fair, this is an illusion, and that most disagreements among them are settled through sheer self-assertion ('Now,  The adolescent Wilson concluded that if en there is no objective right or wrong— t adults used to control children.

seems to be one of the primary driving of our children. To tame their wildness ful and compliant units of productivity. that? you might ask.

the individual.

consideration whether or not that is in s.

ows interest in the banking system, then e them to study those things required to world. But a blanket education for all, 's interests or needs, only works if you on wealth, greed and dominance by a e.

at I call for the legalisation of psychedelics I call for massive education reform is ionship here. Governments don't want aking drugs. Just look what happened in ted smoking pot and dropping acid, and next thing you knew they were complaining about the Vietnam War, campaigning for civil rights and feminism, with gays marching in the streets…

You start educating the individual to evolve and expand to their maximum potential, and same thing's gonna happen— you're gonna lose control of them. And *then* what'll happen?

It'll be *mayhem*.

The ruling elite does not want this.

And before you go, 'So what do *you* know about the ruling elite?'

That famous photo of the Bullingdon Club featuring Boris Johnson and David Cameron? The guy in the shades next to Cameron? He was in my class at school. I've still got his copy of *Let It Bleed*.

The Bullingdon Club—an exclusive 200-year-old Oxford dining club and farm for the UK political system—is notorious for the hilarious japes of its members, such as destroying local restaurants and having sex with dead pigs.

The Bullingdon is perhaps more often populated by Old Etonians and Harrovians. I went to a relatively liberal, modern public school called Bryanston, more famous for expelling the artist Lucian Freud, along with other notables such as Howard 'I hate painting' Hodgkin, pop impresario Simon 'the man who brought us Wham!' Napier-Bell, and Terence 'tactless, abrasive, bullying, misogynistic, ambitious and egotistical' Conran.

Oh, and UKIP MEP David Bannerman.

I could write an entire book on my experience of school. But I'll spare you that. And I could let the bitter chippiness that resulted from my schooling dictate my opinions and ideas about how we should rethink our education system. But I'll try not to.

Probably the best thing I can say is that as I've grown older, I've found more to appreciate about my education than when I was actually there. Up to the age of 13, it was unrelenting misery. Brutal, cruel, harsh, bullying and abusive.

From thirteen onwards, as a boarder, I was terribly homesick and lonely, medicated, depressed and always in trouble. It wasn't until my last year, when my artistic abilities blossomed, and I discovered sex and drugs, that I began to enjoy myself— certainly helped by the light at the end of the tunnel.

I had a pretty hefty ayahuasca trip about a year ago, in which I spent a night being shown the terrible damage that school had done to me and explaining that the last thirty years had mostly been taken up with recovery from those experiences. It showed me who I had been before I went into the system and I also had a vision of the kind of learning situation that might have worked for me, which was mostly experiential and outdoors.

So, it is hard for me to be entirely objective. What I do truly appreciate about my secondary school is that it's where I met most of the people still closest to me in my life, including my ex-wife and the mother of my two children, plus an eclectic mix of boho-type artists and musicians.

Bryanston was founded in 1928, with the intention to 'bring out the best in each individual'. Of course, what they actually *meant* was that they wanted to bring out the *best* in the individual, as long as that *best* meant they played rugby for England and went to Oxford or Cambridge. If the *best* happened to be at rolling joints, climbing up drainpipes in the middle of the night to the girls' dormitories, smoking fags, drawing, painting, getting into shit, setting fire to shit, blowing up shit and running away... they weren't too thrilled.

Fickle, that's what I call it.

In fact, there were two qualities deeply and repeatedly instilled in us, as in any conventional school: competition and comparison — two of the most destructive aspects to any society.

Through sports and games, tests and exams, pupils are taught to compare themselves to, and ideally be *better* than, their peers. This feeds how we interface with the world, with catastrophic results — assuming you want a harmonious and abundant sense of community, that is. If you want a warmongering, wealth-accumulating, suspicious, selfish and ruthless people...

It works a treat.

A common way that institutions steal people's identities is by making everyone dress the same, limiting self-expression and creating a herd mentality. The minute you put small people into an outfit or costume that's identical to everyone else, you begin the brainwashing homogenisation required to manufacture drones. Worker ants for the system programmed to function without individual thought.

Think for a moment of a man's tie—such a common, everyday article of clothing. It suggests smartness, style and success. And yet, in reality, it's a useless, strangling, uncomfortable phallic yoke that serves no purpose other than to restrict breathing, with the consequence that the wearer is less alert and easier to *control*.

It's called a tie for a reason.

To be with the others, you have to have your hair short and wear ties. So, we're trying to make a third world happen, you know what I mean?

Jimi Hendrix

It's similar with soldiers. Have you ever thought why they get them to stand to attention? It's because the effect on the inner organs and especially the lungs is to *compress*, to stiffen and to tighten the torso in such a way as to diminish breathing and compact the viscera; the result of which is to significantly *reduce* all feeling, especially *fear*. Kind of useful when you're trying to persuade a mob of men wearing bright red, target-coloured costumes to march toward another mob of men baring muskets and cannons, or Zulu hoards brandishing pointy sticks. It inhibits the natural, *sensible* response to run away and makes them easier to...

Control.

* * *

Of course, the origins of the UK boarding-school system— an anathema to many other cultures that, quite rightly, can't understand why you would want to *have* children if you're going to pay someone else to raise them—are rooted in Empire. Take boys at an early age, preferably six or seven, remove them from their family unit, institutionalise and regiment them with often brutal methods designed to shut down their feelings and, in not much more than ten years you have cold, emotionless machines ready to be sent off to the colonies to manage and/or slaughter the natives. Should they not be army material, not to worry because you have perfect, ruthless and obedient drones for the banking system or politics.

'But Jerry, are you suggesting that we give our children acid and let them run naked and free in the woods and forests? Children need discipline.'

Well...

Let's put this in context. Many Amazonian tribes give their children ayahuasca and other psychotropic medicines from birth, and as part of their teenage initiation rites. These children grow up in touch with nature, with their ancestry and with a strong connection to the spirit world.

In Western culture, we give our children refined sugar and processed, genetically modified foods laced with any number of additives; and when they become hyperactive as a result, we medicate them with hard-core branded drugs worth millions of dollars to the pharmaceutical industry.

Of course, if you start giving Western kids crazy-arse plant medicine, you'll most likely fuck them up and:

a) Go to prison, and
b) Go to prison.

It's not part of our culture and would be potentially dangerous to their forming psyches given that they don't have the communal infrastructure to help them assimilate such experiences, but it *is* interesting to look at these things from a different perspective. Not everything is universal and while the idea of giving trips to babies is horrifying to most people, I imagine the Kaxinawá tribe of Peru might have something to say about our liberal use of money-spinning narcotics like Ritalin. And I challenge anyone to look an Amazonian in the eye while explaining why we give our children selective serotonin reuptake inhibitors.

If you change the way we educate children, you immediately change the future. You immediately make the world a better place.

Now it's probably worth pointing out, or even *admitting*, that my own two children are in mainstream education. Yeah, I don't home educate them in a yurt. They don't go to Steiner or Montessori schools. They wear uniforms and you could say that makes me a hypocrite. It's a long story and had I not divorced I like to imagine they may have been educated in a much more alternative way. But the fact is, seeing their experience of school has made me even *more* aware of the problem.

My eldest daughter and her stepbrother go to a state grammar school, my youngest to a private performing arts school, so not quite mainstream but pretty conventional in terms of what they're taught.

None of them like going to school.

They dread going back after the holidays.

Which is a pretty *normal* reaction from most kids, right? Nothing unusual there.

But when did we decide that was OK? When did it become acceptable to fill their childhoods with occupations and activities that they dislike?

The answer to that is the mid to late nineteenth century. Before that, school was not mandatory. So, for about 2.5 million years, kids didn't have to go to school.

And the world kept turning.

In the 150 years since education became compulsory, you could argue that incredible advances have taken place in medicine, science, industry and technology. And of course there is a correlation there. Maybe it's brought about incredible positive change.

Nothing is black and white.

But my point is not about material success or technological advances. My angle is less easy to quantify. My question would be: Is the world a happier place? But even that wouldn't be an easy question to answer; in truth, it would probably be in some ways yes, in others no.

Really, though, it's not about harping back to some halcyon time, when childhood was bathed in golden sunlight and laughter filled the air. It's about taking what we have and improving it. Rather than just accepting that (a lot of) kids hate school.

For those that don't (and I'm assuming there are some), then cool—the current system works for them. But for the ones that don't like it or don't function so well, let's give them alternatives that they can enjoy and thrive on.

It already happens to a degree in the way kids are now statemented if they exhibit learning difficulties. *That* is progress. When I was at school, if you had learning difficulties you were thick. I was medicated with Ritalin, not in the way it's used these days with ADHD children; for me, it was simply for the stimulant properties. They gave me speed to 'perk me up', because they mistook my undiagnosed dyslexia for laziness.

They were advanced enough to recognise there was a problem—in the old days I'd just have been beaten or sent to the back of the class—and so they had me tested. But when I came back with a high IQ, they just couldn't understand why I was struggling, hence the pills.

But we need to take it further than just those with learning difficulties. We need a super-flexible and hugely diverse range of entire schools—academic and vocational—with less emphasis on training the mind alone, but incorporating the body and spirit also. And I'm not talking about PE and going to chapel.

Someone, I forget who, made the point that if you look at modes of transport in Victorian times, you had a horse and cart. Now you have space shuttles and electric cars—the progress has been phenomenal. If you look at a Victorian classroom, you have rows of children being force-fed data that they learn to regurgitate in order to become white- or blue-collar workers. Look at a modern-day school and you have rows of children being force fed-data that they learn to regurgitate in order to become white- or blue-collar workers.

But even if the school system doesn't change as radically or in the timeframe that I'd like, the syllabus needs to. Let's get real, while I now have a better understanding of why Latin was taught at school (no one explained it at the time), with divorce rates endemic and rising, don't you think it's high time we taught some basic, fundamental relationship skills before we begin conjugating the verb *amo*?

* * *

There are schools out there trying a different approach. Summerhill School in Suffolk, England, dubbed 'the school with no rules', is a heroic example. Founded in 1921 by A.S. Neill, to 'give children back their childhoods', it promotes the philosophy of 'freedom for children and the importance of living in a community'.

Am I too old to sign up now?

With the lack of emphasis on academia, up to two-thirds of Summerhill's pupils leave without any qualifications, but as headmistress Zoe Readhead says:

If you look at a league table we're always at the bottom, but who gives a shit? What the kids learn here is so much more important—things like independence and taking responsibility.

What an absolute hero.

Students at Summerhill continue to exercise a degree of pupil power not seen anywhere else in the world.

At the heart of the system are the thrice-weekly school meetings, where the children decide how to run the community. Rules are proposed, problems aired, and kids and staff vote for appropriate action alike; and as the teachers are outnumbered five to one, the children are essentially in charge. Every few years, the slate is wiped clean, with all rules being abolished, to allow the next generation of pupils to define how the school functions.

Summerhill is not for every child, but then no school is. But it has been shown to be especially effective with dyslexia and for those who have been bullied, and has spawned numerous other schools globally that have developed similar approaches.

Opposition to the school has been huge, with Ofsted trying to close it down in the late Nineties because of its policy not to make classes compulsory.

Readhead is quoted as saying:

We feel constantly under invasion from the outside by people who don't seem to take that step to understand what Summerhill is about, because it challenges almost everything that people learn about children and childhood. Summerhill lets children take emotional and physical risks. It trusts children to make decisions. It gives children the right to talk to adults in the way they want. And that, I'm afraid, is frightening because people know that children should be seen and not heard.

There is an expectation that children will follow a certain course, learn a set number of things, and will achieve academically and therefore be happy. Even though we know that that's not true, we stick with it because we believe there are no alternatives—you may not want to send your child here but we should be able to continue what we're doing.

Even if we are a bit loopy.

* * *

Homeschooling held great appeal to me when I was considering my kids' education, and now that they have to get up at 6:45 in the morning and sit in a classroom all day, it has considerable appeal to *them*.

At the time of writing, 3 per cent of US kids are homeschooled, that's about 1.5 million. In the UK, it's around 50,000. The old concerns around socialisation have been eradicated by the invention of the Internet, which has created a network where parents can arrange meet-ups for play and sport. What's more, homeschooled kids are seen to really benefit from mixing with multiple age groups rather than being streamed together in same age classes. And they're excelling academically as they get much more one-on-one focused tuition, while spending no more than two or three hours a day in study to cover the syllabus.

Looking at Wikipedia, it notes that:

The earliest public schools in modern Western culture were established in the early 16th century in the German states of Gotha and Thuringia. However, even in the 18th century, the majority of people in Europe lacked formal schooling, meaning they were home schooled, tutored, or received no education at all.

Formal schooling in a classroom setting has been the most common means of schooling throughout the world, especially in developed countries, since the early- and mid-19th century. Native Americans, who traditionally used home schooling and apprenticeship, vigorously resisted compulsory education in the United States.

Keep coming back to those pesky redskins, don't we? And I like that word *apprenticeship* a lot. I think we lost something when that went out of the window and no, your ten-pound-a-day intern is *not* an apprentice, it's a slave.

Dyslexia didn't exist before schools—it's the *system* that decided if you don't fit, whether or not you have a problem with your brain. But back in the days of apprenticeship, if you weren't academic rather than being medicated, you were likely to be apprenticed into a trade where you used your hands, because dyslexics are notoriously good three-dimensional thinkers.

Remember craftsmanship?

That's the pre-Ikea thing, where human beings *made* things. Beautiful, hand-made, exquisite one-off pieces. Of course, nowadays we have a lot of artisans. Everything is artisanal— coffee, bread, beer, cheese... I myself make *artisanal* magic mushrooms, but I've got some bad news for you.

That's *marketing*.

It's not the same as a craftsman who's studied and trained and sweated in his master's workshop since the age of 14.

I'm sitting on a couch made by my grandfather about ninety years ago. My mother had her nappies changed on it in the 1930s, as did I when I was a baby, and my children when they were born. It's threadbare, it creaks and its horsehair stuffing wouldn't pass fire standards, but it's solid and comfy, and I'm guessing my grandchildren will have their nappies changed on it at some point.

Can you say that about your Ikea sofa?

I'm also guessing that if you stuck my grandfather in a state school these days, he'd be statemented within a week. He wasn't a *model* student.

He left at fourteen and went to work as an apprentice in one of the many furniture factories in the local town of High Wycombe. He soon got what was called 'the furniture maker's salute'—in other words, he chopped two of his fingers off in an accident—and so was moved into the upholstery department, where all you needed was one finger and a thumb.

It probably saved his life, as one of the digits was his trigger finger, so he was rejected when he volunteered for rear gunner on bombers when the war came. Instead, he became one of the guys who scraped their bloody remains into sandbags when they got killed.

The point being, no matter how much of an attitude he had, or how disabled he became, at all times he was seen as useful.

That matters to a man. And he always had a sense of his own value and a deep, soft, warm masculine confidence.

When I left school, I was written off.

The meds hadn't helped, unsurprisingly, and I was told I was unemployable. And even though my status as a rebel was firmly established by then, I still believed 'grown-ups' and so when they said I was unemployable, I didn't question it. And to be totally honest, it kind of suited me. I had as much interest in their world of offices and suits as I'd had in their classrooms and exams.

But had there been the possibility of apprenticeship, I imagine I might have taken it. These days, when I look at how psychotherapy trainings are structured it makes me shudder—there's no way I could complete that kind of academic programme. When I did mine, it was almost entirely experiential. I learned through *doing*, not reading. And for the first time in my life, I excelled as a student.

I'd found my way.

Native Americans didn't have any sort of official education, but the children were expected to learn. The boys followed the men around, and were taught how to hunt and do men's chores. Young girls followed the women around and learned to do traditional women's work like making baskets, working the fields and cooking.

I like that. Following people around; that's a great way to learn. I always said my real education happened in my grandfather's shed, a far greater seat of learning than public school.

For the Algonquian-speaking Indians of Virginia, it was the

storytellers who had a big part to play in the education of the children, by sharing the myths and legends of the tribal ancestors.

The mother's job was to teach her son to hunt. The child would not be allowed to eat in the morning until he had hit the target his mother threw for him.

From the age of 10 to 15, boys were initiated into manhood through a ritual called the *huskanaw*. This lasted for nine months and was a time of physical hardship, isolation in the forest, fasting and psychedelic medicine that would cause hallucinations or visions.

The boys were ceremonially taken from the village and returned to the village as men.

Now *that's* what I call home education.

How many of us can say that we ever went through a process that initiated us into adulthood? What do we have? Puberty? Your first period? *Bar mitzvah* if you're Jewish?

Hardly the same, is it?

I remember expecting manhood to kind of *happen* when I was eighteen. But I woke up on my birthday and nothing had changed. So, I waited until I was twenty-one—had fish and chips for supper, threw up later, but still... no manhood.

It finally crept up on me through a series of vision quests that I did in my forties; but had I not gone out into the wilderness, and starved in the sun and the rain and the wind, maybe I'd still be waiting now.

Education isn't just about reading, writing and arithmetic.

* * *

Is change possible? Sometimes it's hard to believe that it is and yet, when I look back over the last 100 years and observe just how radically things have evolved socially, sexually and culturally, it's extraordinary. It's fantastic, inspiring and heroic. And even among the darkness that surrounds us all in these turbulent

times, I see hope and light and possibility.
   Real possibility.

* * *

I guess we better talk some more about drugs next, then...

* * *

October

Get lost freaks—be wise not weird!

1950s anti-drugs propaganda

Choose Life. Choose a job. Choose a career. Choose a family. Choose a fucking big television, choose washing machines, cars, compact disc players and electrical tin openers. Choose good health, low cholesterol, and dental insurance. Choose fixed interest mortgage repayments. Choose a starter home. Choose your friends. Choose leisurewear and matching luggage. Choose a three-piece suite on hire purchase in a range of fucking fabrics. Choose DIY and wondering who the fuck you are on Sunday morning. Choose sitting on that couch watching mind-numbing, spirit-crushing game shows, stuffing fucking junk food into your mouth. Choose rotting away at the end of it all, pissing your last in a miserable home, nothing more than an embarrassment to the selfish, fucked up brats you spawned to replace yourselves. Choose your future. Choose life... But why would I want to do a thing like that? I chose not to choose life. I chose somethin' else. And the reasons?

There are no reasons.

Who needs reasons when you've got heroin?

Irvine Welsh, Trainspotting

With the ominous shadows of US politics looming malevolent and stark, we could all be forgiven for running to the medicine cabinet or to the dealer, seeking sedation and oblivion from the malevolent hoards that gather like clouds of grey piss over our fair isle. And yet, over yonder, a glimmer of light in this darkest of dark times, of all places, on the cover of *The Times*: MAKE ALL DRUG USE LEGAL, SAY EXPERTS.

Well, I'm no expert, but I could have told you that. And no, I'm not pro-drugs, I'm pro the choice to do whatever you want with your body and your psyche. I'm pro-safety, I'm pro-education and I'm pro-information. Jim Morrison, for all his beauty, for all his endeavours to prodigiously and rationally disorder his senses, became just another putrefied corpse in a French graveyard owing to the fact that he had no idea what he was sticking up his nose. He wasn't trying to kill himself; he didn't want to die, he wanted to push the edge and like so many others, ignorance and bad luck put him in the ground.

What a shame.

My friend Kevin Barron, the 70-year-old silver-haired, dapper, ex-blotter acid logo designer extraordinaire, was fortunate enough to see The Doors at their peak:

Saw them twice, two nights at the Roundhouse in London with The Jefferson Airplane, and still to this day, he was the most charismatic singer I have ever seen, Morrison, nobody to touch him, you can talk about Jagger or whoever—nobody touched this guy.

Amazing.

And if it weren't for the prohibition of drugs, we could speculate that not only might Jim have lived, but also Jimi, Janis, Keith Moon, Lester Bangs, River Phoenix, John Belushi, Philip Seymour Hoffman, Coco Chanel, Tim Buckley, John Entwistle, Mike Bloomfield, Mitch Hedberg, Chet Baker, Phil Lynott, Paul Butterfield, Gram Parsons, Dee Dee Ramone, Johnny Thunders, Hank Williams, Jesse Ed Davis, Lenny Bruce, Billie Holiday, Jerry Garcia, Charlie Parker and Amy Winehouse, to name a mere few whose raw talent was wiped out forever through their use of drugs.

And we can only wring our hands and guess at what they might have produced had they lived.

None of these deaths was deliberately or consciously self-inflicted, and I'd suggest that most if not all could have been prevented (well, maybe not Amy, she was hell-bent) had they lived in a society that recognised their struggle as that of a health problem rather than a criminal issue.

And before you go, '*fuck 'em, junkie skuzbags*', I'd like to point out that you, too...

Are a junkie scuzzbag.

If...

When asked how you're doing, you've *ever* replied, 'Oh yeah, really busy.'

Remember the days when the normal, insipid, homogenous reply when asked how you are was, 'Yeah, fine'?

When did you last hear that? It kind of vanished from our language and now we're all just so super-busy, like mega rushed off our feet, y'know man, totally full on, it's crazy.

Cos no one ever wants to say, 'Hmmm... nah, been really quiet, not much happening.'

Do yah?

And that is why you (and I) are junkie skuzbags, because we're all addicted to being busy, desperately mainlining our laptops and smartphones and tablets and conference calls and extra-shot soya lattes like blood bags straight into our bulging eyeballs in a desperate attempt to feel important or not feel at all.

In my case there's guitar addiction, which is a powerful thing, hard to understand maybe for those not afflicted. It's the eternal quest for the perfect tone. It's intangible—impossible to convey, but you know if you just keep searching you're gonna find *the one*. She's out there somewhere, the *one* just for you, the *one* with the feel, that unique feel like she's been tailor-made just for your hands; the way you caress her neck, the curves of her body; the way she moans at the touch of your fingers, screams as you tease sounds wilder than hell from her taut strings.

And with every new guitar, there's the hope, the desperate,

hungry hope, the promise that this time she might deliver, this time it might just work out.

But like every cheating husband, no sooner do you have her than your eye begins to rove, your ears pricking at the sound of another. Just the fleeting hint of a power chord caught on the breeze and wafted through your window on a balmy summer evening is all it takes to feed those cells hungry for wood and lacquer, taking you unawares like some dark and sultry temptress in the night.

And so it begins again.

Unless...

You're Portuguese.

Last time I went to Portugal was in the early Nineties. I struggled to find even the smallest blim of hash, with the threat of prison if apprehended.

Oh! how times have changed.

In 2001, Portugal took the incredible decision to decriminalise the possession of *all* drugs for personal use.

In the preceding years, the number of drug-related deaths had soared and rates of HIV, AIDS, Tuberculosis, and Hepatitis B and C among people who injected drugs was rapidly increasing. However, since the reform, HIV infections and drug-related deaths have *decreased*, while the dramatic rise in use feared by some has failed to materialise.

Among Portuguese adults, there are three drug overdose deaths for every 1 million citizens, compared to 10.2 per million in the Netherlands, to 44.6 per million in the UK, all the way up to 126.8 per million in Estonia. The EU average is 17.3 per million.

The very simple, undeniable truth is that Portugal recognised drug abuse as a health problem rather than a criminal one. They changed their stance and now very few people die from narcotics in their country.

Fewer people...

Die.

Do the fucking *maths*.

* * *

Drugs are here, drugs have always been here, and drugs are here to stay, whether it be in the mushroom-infused, cow-shit rich pastures of Avalon or the unforgiving streets of London, where drug-fucked ayahuasqueros stumble dazed and confused on the back of sacred tea ceremonies or the school gates of Crouch End, where weekend, dead-end yummy mummies on low-grade cocaine hide their ruined eyes behind designer shades, or the suburban tipis where sensitive new-age guys inject frog venom into their tattooed flesh, or Stoke Newington where tripping techies microdose LSD with their granola…

Drugs are here to stay.

Again, my friend Kevin Barron was in the right place at the right time:

My first drug experience was in 1964 at a psychiatric hospital in Portsmouth. This nurse and I became 'close' friends, and she broached the subject that there was some ground-breaking psychological treatment that was going on at the hospital. It didn't take too long to persuade me. She kept saying, you're about to go to art school, you might find it interesting from a creative standpoint, it might unlock something.

I was coming from a fairly strict academic background at this point, but with a great interest in art and painting and drawing, and she said, 'y'know, look, I'll be with you every moment of the experience.'

So, I took the ampoule, snapped it open and took the liquid with a soft drink or something and it took about half-an-hour or so, and then things seriously started to change. We were out in the gardens where there were manicured lawns and flowerbeds, and I was soon into the flowerbeds, into this microscopic world where I got lost in this whole new world, this magic city, and I felt more comfortable with the insects and the flowers than I did with her.

There were a few moments when I felt anxious, and it's that moment that you get to when the ego says, 'no, I'm not letting go.' Which of course is what it's all about. The whole experience of an acid trip is letting go of your ego, because all the time you're resisting it for whatever reason, you're diluting the experience.

Time wise—six or seven hours? Pretty intense stuff, brightness and contrast of colour and a greater three-dimensionality to some of the things I was looking at like the bud of a tulip; but most of it was spent in this bizarre world of the plant bed.

In case you haven't worked it out for yourself or in case I'm not making myself clear, drugs are dangerous. But more dangerous is ignorance. I like to think that we're entering a new era where wisdom governs our psychonautical explorations and, dare I say it, a more *responsible* attitude toward getting shit-faced. This is no time for idle escapism; this is the time for heroic adventures and courageous, outrageous journeys to the dark side of the soul and beyond; a time to tear down the walls of prohibition and fear, and break free of the divisive delusions of duality, race, national identity and separateness.

If it were down to me, I'd flood the reservoirs with ayahuasca and turn you all on, but it tastes so fucking horrible I reckon you'd notice.

So, I've made a fairly bold, albeit not unique, statement there—to change the world to a better place we need to end the war against drugs and make all psychedelic consciousness-shifting substances available to the masses, with the appropriate infrastructure implemented to educate people to ensure their safe, risk-free usage.

Kevin Barron, who lived with The Jefferson Airplane in San Francisco in the Sixties and later went to prison for his part in designing blotter acid art, unsurprisingly has a deep inside knowledge of the drug world, but that doesn't make him optimistic about the possibility of change:

> The CIA needed finances to carry out various covert activities that they deemed necessary, 'cos they're a law unto their own, so they got into cocaine and heroin. And so anyone who thinks that the post 9/11 attacks on Afghanistan was anything to do with rounding up a bunch of Jihadists, the reality is it's all about the heroin. Because the Taliban virtually eradicated heroin production. Then you had Gary Webb, the investigative journalist from California, who revealed the CIA's involvement in the supply of cocaine from Nicaragua and the CIA being responsible for the outbreak of crack cocaine breaking out in central Los Angeles. He was 'suicided'.
>
> He shot himself.
>
> *Twice*.
>
> So, maybe some soft drugs like marijuana will be legalised, but all the time heroin and cocaine are in the hands of the intelligence agencies nothing will ever be legalised.

And I'm a realist. I understand that even if my proposals do eventually come about, as they have in Portugal, I know it's unlikely to happen in my lifetime and so I'm just sowing seeds. But for now, I guess I'd better qualify what I'm suggesting and better still, explain why I believe it belongs in a book about Sin.

I want to reiterate something I've said on many occasions: I am not anti-drugs, I am anti-drug *abuse*.

I'm not pro-drugs, I'm pro-freedom and education.

I'm not pro-drugs, I'm pro-quality control, so people don't

overdose on poison. I'm pro-ending the black market so that tens of thousands don't die every year in the war against drugs. I'm pro-streaming the money spent on that phony war into drug education. I'm pro-treating addiction as an illness rather than a crime.

Ultimately, whether drugs are dangerous or problematic is entirely to do with people's attitude, understanding and use of these substances.

Drugs of unknown origin and quality, bought from a stranger and taken in an environment where prohibition encourages secrecy, are fraught with pitfalls and genuine dangers. Ultimately, it's a game of Russian roulette that you are destined to lose.

Drugs of a known source taken under the tutelage of an experienced shaman or psychedelic teacher can still be problematic, dangerous and deeply challenging, given what might inhabit the dark recesses of your psyche. But with the right support, they can be both healing and transformative, and this is how it has been for millennia.

Drugs belong in this book for two main reasons. First, if we equate the law with Sin, in that it's the modern way that we judge what we see to be right and wrong, then to take certain substances deemed by those in authority to be unlawful is therefore deemed Sinful.

Secondly, they belong here because some drugs (and they are certainly in the minority) have the capacity to help certain people to evolve and awaken, and therefore...

Are not Sinful.

Confusing, isn't it?

Part of what taints drugs is the way that they have become synonymous with addiction. And this is a problem, because if we are ever going to take down the hysteria, be objective and turn what is a very real problem into a potential solution, then we need to differentiate.

Of course, it's very important not to glamorise drugs, especially as so many cult heroes have been associated with their use. Kevin Barron knew two of my biggest idols personally, Hunter S. Thompson and Keith Richards:

I knew Hunter Thompson very well, but for different reasons. Hunter used to write a weekly column for *The San Francisco Examiner*, and once a month he'd come from Colorado to pick up his pay check, and we'd get a call saying Hunter was coming to town and we'd go out binge drinking for two or three days. We'd all go berserk.

We'd start out at an Irish bar in the Mission District. We'd meet up at the bar and there were always these heavy duty Irish Republicans. They'd go around with a tray for donations before you sat down for a drink, and fortunately my name was Kevin so it was always, 'ah Kevin, nice to meetcha, Kevin.' Mostly drinking sessions with Hunter, not heavy drug use; although we did do some stuff here and there, and then when he'd blown his pay check for the month he'd go back home. Quite fun times.

With The Rolling Stones, my job was to look after all the hotels, flights and plane tickets 'cos everything in those days was still tickets, y'know? Was a fucking nightmare.

On the Australian tour, everyone had more or less gone, but Keith was still there. Mick had gone, Charlie had gone, so I had to take Keith out to Sydney airport. Keith never knew where he was, didn't know what country he was in, didn't know what town he was in but…

Plug him in for two hours on stage?

Amazing.

So, we get to the airport and I say, 'stay here, I'm gonna go check you in.' So, I went over to the counter, passport, ticket, boarding pass, came back and he's standing there. 'Alright Keith. Here's the ticket, here's the boarding pass, there's your passport, there's immigration. Have a safe flight. See you when you get back to London. Bye.'

I stood there and off he goes. It was maybe 30-metres to the immigration desk. So, I'm just stood there and off he toddles, shuffling more than anything else. And he got halfway and stopped.

I'm like, *what the fuck?*

And it must have been 20 seconds he was just standing there, then he turned round and shuffled back to me, and he said, 'here's the heroin, the coke's good and there's some acid if you want,' and I'm standing there and he's unloading the drugs on me. Then he turns round, and off he goes.

I went straight to the toilet and got rid of everything, flushed it. I kept the acid.

We had a tour doctor which was very useful 'cos he'd give you uppers and downers. Little Chinese guy, and wherever you went there was the drug dealer, all arranged in advance — mostly pot, coke and heroin, although with Keith you never knew what he was doing, never asked. But like I say, that's what amazed me. He'd walk around in this fucking haze, but then you'd plug him in and away he'd go.

Exciting and entertaining tales, but it's worth noting that Hunter ended up shitting himself as a result of the horrendous abuse that he put his body through. While Keith may have coined the term 'elegantly wasted', he hasn't produced anything for over forty years that comes even close to the iconic work he did before heroin wrecked his creative core.

* * *

Being an addict isn't unusual any more. It's like tattoos, suddenly everyone's doing it.

Addiction…

Is the new black.

It used to be that the extreme rich and the extreme poor were addicts. You were either a claret-swilling laudanum junky or a pissed-up gin head. But these days, we're all hooked on something, whether it's gadgets or porn or shopping or substances; and perhaps most of all... consumerism.

The advertising industry realised long ago that the trick is to harness our pleasure-seeking lizard brains, to promote and exploit addictive behaviour, with the ethos, 'create an obsession, then exploit it.'

Companies used to use customer surveys and focus groups. Now it's all neuroscience to figure what triggers obsessive-compulsive brain responses, selling us digital heroin in the form of smartphones and iPads.

Take a look around next time you're on a train or in a bar and see how many people are lost in the glow of a phone. We thought these things were going to make life easier, but they just put people to sleep.

It's a dream-zone, where nothing really matters and no one really cares who's President of the US or what's going on in Syria or how many bodies of toddlers are washed up on Greek beaches.

Now tell me that's not a Sin, a Sin sprung upon us like a bear trap, a Sin that we've welcomed with the open-armed, wide-eyed excitement of children being offered poisoned candy by dirty old marketing men rubbing their greedy, fat hands together with the zeal of hunters shooting rats in a barrel.

The addictive pattern is part of what makes us human, what has made us so successful as a species. Is it not compulsive behaviour that drives us to explore, create and study? Even this book is born of obsession.

But it is also what has driven us to the brink of implosion—an insatiable species out of control, driven mad with desire and hunger for *more*, it doesn't matter what of, just *more* will do.

Dispassionate education is essential. Infantilising people, deciding what they can and can't ingest, is both immoral and impractical to enforce. The war against drugs has created a monstrous and evil black market, where many more people die within that conflict than they do from substance use.

Some drugs really are shit—cocaine and many of its derivatives are among the worst in terms of how they turn people into greedy, grandiose, paranoid, selfish bastards. As a friend of mine said, 'No one ever woke up in the morning after a night on coke and said, "Wow, I'm really glad I did that."'. But no one is going to argue that if you need a hole drilled in your tooth, cocaine has its uses.

Ecstasy has a very dark side; although it did single-handedly eradicate football hooliganism from UK culture once it hit the terraces and fans began hugging each other rather than hitting each other.

But we've all seen the tragic headlines of yet another young person who has died in the dark recesses of a nightclub from poisoned pills and dehydration, where the desire just to have a good time has turned into a lifetime of misery for the bereaved families. Again, I would lay the blame firmly at the feet of prohibition and lack of education, a situation that drug dealers exploit for huge profit given the lack of quality control and advice. The general attitude still pervades that it's tough—you knew it was against the law, so you shouldn't have done it.

That's a Sin. The Sin of blind, irresponsible leadership, fascism and stupidity.

But now *Ecstasy*, in its pure form MDMA, is being tested on combat veterans suffering post-traumatic stress disorder with great results, in programmes approved by the US, Canadian and Israeli governments.

In the UK, psilocybin has recently been shown to be highly effective in the treatment of trauma, anxiety and acute depression in patients who have previously been unresponsive to conventional drugs; although, it took many years and a huge amount of money owing to the red tape that the researchers had to wade through.

The senior author of the study, Professor David Nutt, said, 'It cost £1,500 to dose each person, when in a sane world it might cost £30.'

But we do not live in a sane world.

Amanda Feilding, aristocratic, amateur trepanning enthusiast and codirector of the trial programme, said:

> The results from our research are helping us to understand how psychedelics change consciousness, and how this information can be used to find breakthrough treatments for many of humanity's most intractable psychiatric disorders, such as depression, addiction and obsessive compulsive disorder.

Meanwhile, marijuana (the deadly scourge that drags our children into the quagmires of degradation) has been proven in numerous clinical trials to:

Be an effective treatment for glaucoma.
Help reverse the carcinogenic effects of tobacco and improve lung health.
Help control epileptic seizures.
Stop cancer from spreading.
Slow the progression of Alzheimer's disease.
Ease the pain of multiple sclerosis.
Lessen the side effects from treating hepatitis C and increase treatment effectiveness.
Treat inflammatory bowel diseases.
Relieve arthritis discomfort.
Improve the symptoms of the autoimmune disorder lupus.
Spur creativity in the brain.

Soothe tremors for people with Parkinson's disease.

Protect the brain after a stroke.

Reduce some of the awful pain and nausea from chemo, and stimulate appetite.

Praise the Lord that it's illegal.

I don't smoke dope any more. It tends to make me paranoid and slows my brain down, but how can its use, at least medically, be banned in the face of such overwhelming evidence? Might it possibly be anything to do with the wizards of Satan, Big Pharma?

Wikipedia seems a bit sniffy on the subject, saying: 'According to the Big Pharma conspiracy theory, the medical establishment in general, and pharmaceutical companies in particular, operate for sinister purposes and against the public good.'

I hadn't realised that it was a theory, any more than I thought that 9/11 being an inside job was a theory, or that Princess Diana wasn't murdered was a theory.

I had come to believe that there was a horrible kind of inevitability to the corruption of the pharmaceutical industry owing to the simple fact that they make so much *money* from people's illness. And despite their demonisation, they are merely human—a species notorious for fucking over its own brothers and sisters in the name of profit and power.

In 2013, worldwide pharmaceutical companies made 95 billion dollars in revenue. Big Pharma's top eleven corporations generated net profits between 2003 and 2012 of nearly three quarters of a *trillion* dollars.

That's a lot of pills.

What's more, not all of those pills are entirely good for you.

A recent *British Medical Journal* report concluded that antidepressant drugs actually increase the risk of aggressive behaviour and suicide, especially in users under the age of 18.

Common cold and heartburn medications have been found

to shrink the brain and slow thinking, while also increasing the risk of kidney failure.

Each year 46,000 Americans die from drug overdoses of FDA-approved opioids (while marijuana-based cures that render many painkillers obsolete remain illegal).

* * *

Terence McKenna—ethnobotanist, author, heroic consumer of all things mind altering and psychonautical explorer extraordinaire—made a very convincing argument in his book, *Food of the Gods: The Search for the Original Tree of Knowledge: A Radical History of Plants, Drugs and Human Evolution*, that our brain's development was accelerated by psilocybin mushrooms.

He stated that somewhere around 100,000 years ago in Africa, as humans were forced from the increasingly shrinking tropical canopy in search of new food sources, they began following herds of wild cattle, whose dung harboured the insects that were part of their new diet and would have started eating the dung-loving mushrooms often found growing on cow shit.

And so, according to McKenna, microdosing began and alongside it, the expansion of our brains… and at an extraordinary rate:

> Evolution in higher animals takes a long time to occur, operating in time spans of rarely less than a million years and more often in tens of millions of years. But the emergence of modern humans from the higher primates—with the enormous changes effected in brain size and behaviour—transpired in fewer than three million years. Physically, in the last one hundred thousand years, we have apparently changed very little. But the amazing proliferation of cultures, social institutions, and linguistic systems has come so quickly that modern evolutionary biologists can scarcely account for

it.

Most do not even attempt an explanation.

Food of the Gods: The Search for the Original Tree of
Knowledge: A Radical History of Plants, Drugs and
Human Evolution

McKenna hypothesised that low doses of psilocybin improve eyesight, meaning that early pack-hunting primates on 'shrooms were better hunters than those who were not, resulting in more food and therefore more sex and higher levels of reproduction, with the resulting natural selection ensuring the survival of the trippiest.

At slightly higher doses, mushrooms give you more energy and have a tendency to make you horny, resulting in higher levels of reproduction. With higher, more 'heroic' doses, McKenna stated, 'mushrooms dissolve boundaries, promoting community bonding and group sexual activities.'

Resulting in...

Yeah. Higher levels of reproduction, with an increased mixing of genes, a greater genetic diversity and a communal sense of responsibility for the group offspring.

Some of the key qualities that we've observed lead to a 'low Sin' situation.

Terence McKenna believed that psilocybin mushrooms were the 'evolutionary catalyst' from which language, projective imagination, the arts, religion, philosophy, science and all of human culture sprang.

And so do I.

Part of the plan for this book, you might remember, is that I would microdose psilocybin mushrooms for the duration of the project and I have to say that I have absolutely no intention of stopping when the work is done.

My creativity has exploded, as can be evidenced by the sheer bulk of writing that's gone into this book without the slightest hint of writer's block, plus a noticeable improvement in my musicianship over the year.

My therapeutic work has been enhanced with my concentration and focus being noticeably improved, plus a deepening of my capacity for complex reflective thinking.

I find that my patience with and compassion for people has been expanded, and my own emotional wave pattern has become gentler, with no dulling of my range but a noticeable absence of panic, depression, anxiety or compulsive negative thinking.

And my addictive tendencies have shrunk to almost insignificant proportions. I can now have an occasional joint or cigarette without immediately becoming a thirty-a-day smoker. I'm selling guitars rather than buying and I can't remember when I last purchased a pair of heavyweight Japanese selvedge jeans.

And when you start to use psilocybin in this way, you have to distance yourself from the normal association with drugs that you're doing it to get *high*. That's no longer the point.

You're doing it to evolve.

British writer and journalist Graham Hancock—in his banned TED Talk, the aptly titled, 'The War on Consciousness'—went as far as to say that the prohibition of mind-expanding medicines is inhibiting our very evolution:

> There's a war on consciousness in our society and if we as adults are not allowed to make sovereign decisions about what to experience with our own consciousness while doing no harm to others, including the decisions to use responsibly ancient and sacred visionary plants, then we cannot claim to be free in any way, and it's useless for our society to go around the world imposing our form of democracy on others while we nourish this rot at the heart of society, and we do not allow individual freedom over consciousness.

It may even be that we're denying ourselves the next vital

step in our own evolution by allowing this state of affairs to continue, and who knows, perhaps our immortal destiny as well.

* * *

Some psychedelics can be fun, all can be beautiful, many can be challenging ordeals and all are powerful teachers. Potentially. They can also destroy minds and lives. All psychedelic exponents agree on one thing: set and setting; in other words, state of mind and environment. As The Beatles' publicist, Derek Taylor, said, 'You wouldn't want to take LSD on Reading Station with a bunch of squaddies…'

Kevin Barron saw the two sides of LSD:

Some people were being inspired creatively from doing acid, and I can tell you that there were a bunch of people who never came back; people like Peter Green, for example, had serious problems, and Sid Barrett out of Pink Floyd. So, there have been victims, and I think that's because there wasn't a full understanding. Everyone thought it was this wonderful drug, but you could see there were casualties. Some people were doing it too much. Maybe that was right for them, but over my life I would do it twice a year and that was enough. It became a sacrament for me.

To me it was a tool. That's how I see psychedelics, they're tools. If you wanna get off your face and go dancing all night, that's all well and good, but for me it's a tool and maybe a lot of that was lost once it became illegal or demonised in the late Sixties, and so maybe the negative side was the abuse of acid, and you mustn't forget that it was in certain people's interest to demonise it, and we know the CIA were using it, possibly as a truth serum, and let's not forget how acid came out… it was from the CIA.

But once white middleclass parents heard what was going on, it became a propaganda thing with classic stories like, *seven students go out in the desert and stare at the sun and all go blind!* Or, *young man thinks he can fly and takes off from the roof of a building and kills himself!* None of these stories are true; the only case of a man who died on acid (and it was a very heavy dose) was a guy who worked for the CIA who was dosed and he jumped out of a window and killed himself, but that was very convenient because he was about to spill the beans about a bunch of stuff.

But let's not forget that without LSD, Bill Gates and Steve Jobs wouldn't be who they are and we wouldn't have home computers. I met Steve Jobs two or three times, his big thing was DMT.

DMT has this slang term where it's called the 'Businessman's Lunch', and he used to say to his engineers or his designers, 'look, you've got a problem, you can't seem to solve it. Go out at lunchtime and do a twenty minute DMT trip, come back and see if that helps.'

I'm so, so glad I had the opportunity to take LSD, but it always had a somewhat chemical edge to it and took me more outside myself than in. Mushrooms were harder to predict, more organic and personal, and with a whole different visual landscape.

When I first started taking these powerful psychoactive substances, I was in my late teens and way off the maturity necessary to be able to process the information that I was receiving. But they acted as an appetiser for a meal, which I would return to over twenty-five years later.

Aged 50, I did ayahuasca first—a foul-tasting brew that spun me around in a multicoloured psychedelic washing machine that rinsed away all my pain and left me bright-eyed and free.

Next I took iboga. I'd heard it said that while with some psychedelics you *hoped* you wouldn't have a bad trip, with iboga you *will* have a bad trip.

What's more, it can kill you; so, I had to have a series of medical tests before I could even take the stuff, which always gives a trip a certain edge.

It wasn't pleasant.

Alone in a cabin in the woods with a stranger, who put me into a state close to coma with spoons of acrid, bitter sawdust that tasted of ammonia and bile, which kept me vomiting and immobile for the best part of thirty-six hours.

Unlike ayahuasca, which is pretty trippy, iboga is something that for me I felt the benefits from *after* rather than during. For months, I had a very audible voice in my head that gave me the most amazingly clear guidance in everything that I did. While ayahuasca is the mother plant, iboga is described as being akin to meeting your stern father, and neither plant disappointed.

But, ultimately, if you want my advice?

Don't go near any of them without *really* doing your research.

Ask around, find out via word of mouth from people you trust—who they have been to and what their experience was like.

I'd suggest going somewhere local before you trek deep into the heart of some far-off rainforest. Romantic and mystical as it may sound, until you know how you'll be affected, it's better to play it safe—psychosis and heart failure are horrible at the best of times, but always made better by the proximity of medical support.

Make sure the practitioners have a high level of expertise, not just in preparing the medicine, but also in holding the space. Just because you can cook up some vines safely doesn't mean you have the experience to manage a situation once you have fifteen people tripping their tits off and something goes wrong.

Never do plant medicine on an impulse. I know a girl who took ayahuasca in a car park in Amsterdam. That's just fucked. Take your time to prepare emotionally, spiritually and physically.

Ayahuasca, in particular, requires that you stick to a very strict diet for some time beforehand. You hear from a mate in a pub that there's a ceremony going on in Dalston later in the evening and you decide to pop by the local balti house for a lamb curry on your way there, and I really wouldn't want to be picking up the pieces. Or chunks.

When you decide on a ceremony that feels right to you—and your instinct is going to have to play a big part in this—don't be afraid to ask them as many questions as you like. For instance, how long have they been facilitating ceremonies? Where and how did they train? What is the procedure if something should go wrong? Be on the alert for any defensiveness and don't be embarrassed to walk away if it doesn't feel right.

It's your psyche, after all.

With any mind-altering, consciousness-expanding substance that you decide to play with, seek out the best support that you can to guide you in and out of the experience. Don't go solo.

Until we teach our children from an early age the *pros* as well as the *cons* of drug use, what to expect from different drugs and, if they so choose, how to *take* different drugs, there will continue to be a stream of casualties. Until we have licenced, regulated centres where you can go and safely take drugs, there will continue to be a stream of casualties.

Ibogaine treatment clinics already exist in Mexico, Canada, the Netherlands, South Africa, New Zealand and Costa Rica, mostly offering very effective treatment for opiate and cocaine addiction.

Prohibition never did anything but increase the fatality list and create a black market. Drug reform is on the agenda now and things are changing, but whether I'll be able to go and take ayahuasca at a treatment centre in my lifetime... I don't know.

Time will tell.

You are an explorer, and you represent our species, and the

greatest good you can do is to bring back a new idea, because our world is endangered by the absence of good ideas. Our world is in crisis because of the absence of consciousness.

Terence McKenna

* * *

Don't *do* drugs. Don't *not* do drugs. Do what is *good* for you. Do that which does you *good* and harms no other.

And campaign for the right to be able to decide that for yourself.

Rather than prohibiting drugs, let the scientists find out better drugs which give deeper and more psychedelic, more colourful, more ecstatic experiences and without any side effects, and without any addiction. And these should be available in the universities, in the colleges, in the hospitals — wherever some kind of guidance is possible, that the person is not prohibited, is allowed total freedom to use anything that he wants. And we use his experience to help him grow towards some authentic process so that he can start experiencing something far greater than any drug can give.

Osho

* * *

I asked Kevin Barron if he were disappointed, having lived through such an extraordinary period, and if there had been a sense of optimism then that hadn't come true:

Well, when you're of that age everybody is revolutionary. Kids are now. But disappointing? Yes, because you realise that you're not as powerful as you thought as an individual or even as a collective consciousness, because probably you'll be supressed or removed.

The Fifties were grey, the Sixties were all about colour, and so it's disappointing to see how we have moved to the right again far more. Fascism in Mussolini's Italy was the joining of the corporate world with politics and nothing's really changed—corporations are the power units of the world, they're the ones who control politicians.

Do I see a way to transform or change?

Yeah...

I think a whole series of drug experiences would make a big fucking difference.

* * *

November

Lolita, light of my life, fire of my loins. My sin, my soul. Lo-lee-ta: the tip of the tongue taking a trip of three steps down the palate to tap, at three, on the teeth. Lo. Lee. Ta. She was Lo, plain Lo, in the morning, standing four feet ten in one sock. She was Lola in slacks. She was Dolly at school. She was Dolores on the dotted line. But in my arms she was always Lolita.

Vladimir Nabokov, Lolita

Rape, murder…
It's just a shot away,
It's just a shot away.

Jagger Richards, 'Gimme Shelter'

We need to have a little chat. About the birds and the bees. You do know about the birds and the bees, don't you? Oh good, I'm glad we dealt with that, then.

* * *

And so, moving swiftly on, let's start with one of the biggest moral dilemmas involving sex…

Faithfulness.

Fidelity, monogamy, whatever names you want to give it. It's an issue that's divided anthropologists for as long as there have *been* anthropologists, with no sign of conclusion on the horizon to that troublesome, tricky question: What is our true nature? To mate for life with one devoted partner or to shag like a nuclear holocaust is just around the corner?

Which it might well be.

It seems that most of the world, or the Church, has given up waiting for the academics to work it out, and has decided that monogamy is good and playing around is bad.

I'm reading *Sapiens: A Brief History of Humankind* by Yuval Noah Harari, and he paints a picture of polyamory that's really quite beautiful and certainly not Sinful. He points out that many hunter-gatherer cultures (who did not yet understand the actual biology of fertilisation) practised multiple-partner relationships because women wanted the sperm of the strongest hunter, the greatest storyteller, the most skilled craftsman, to ensure that their child had the best qualities of the men of the tribe. What's more, because no one actually knew who the father was, all the men parented the child as if it were their own.

Which makes books like *My Two Dads* seem positively vanilla.

Don't ask for faithfulness, ask for freedom. Give freedom, so that you can have freedom. And if out of freedom you go on loving each other, it is beautiful.

Osho

For most of us, myself included, anything other than monogamy is scary and threatening. But if you look into the history of it, as a way of pairing it seems most likely to have become the norm alongside the agricultural revolution 10,000 to 12,000 years ago as a way to ensure that land stayed within a family unit.

The Christian Church, of course, had its mucky little finger in that pie, enforcing monogamy because wealth passed to the closest living, legitimate male relative, but should there be no male heir then the estate would go to…

You guessed it. The Church.

Sex and religion in general are not good bedfellows. The religious ruling classes recognised that you need scared, fearful subjects who imagine that they need Big Daddy to ensure their safety if you want to control the populace.

Healthy, guilt-free sexual expression is therefore *not* to be encouraged, as it has the unfortunate side effect of making the masses…

Happy.

I watched Adam Curtis' documentary *Hyper Normalisation* about the corruption, lies and fakery perpetrated by our leadership, to such a degree that we don't even *question* it—it has become our expectation, our normality.

The same, of course, is true in our relationship to human sexuality; repression, guilt and shame are so ingrained in our culture that we don't question the insanity of a society where our most profound, divine form of creative expression has become demonised and taboo.

A *smutty* secret.

A *dirty* weekend.

A *nasty* girl.

A *filthy* thought.

We have made the sacred…

Profane.

Sex has become the greatest elephant in the room of all time. And, as we have seen, you repress anything and it gets pushed into the darkness of the unconscious, where it grows hideous and fowl and mutated. And therein lays Sin.

There's a gigantic, lumbering *Proboscidea* that crashes around our living rooms and even occasionally our bedrooms, tearing up furniture with its trunk, pulverising our abodes with its enormous feet and depositing great ignored, steaming heaps of shit on our carpets while all the while we carry on as if everything is…

Normal.

But sex is not Sinful.

Butt sex is not Sinful, either, for that matter, but we're not here to talk detail…

I'm not even sure that *Lust* is Sinful, to be honest, unless that Lust leads you to harm yourself or others. The film *Shame*—

about sex addiction—showed the pain of insatiable Lust, that itch that can never be satisfactorily scratched.

But that's not sex, that's compulsion. And human beings have a propensity to become addicted to anything that soothes their pain, especially that which is forbidden. It somehow heightens the buzz.

* * *

Meanwhile, more and more children are mysteriously conceived in the darkness and born apparently immaculate, because no one wants to admit that there's a whole lot of fucking going on...

In our *families*.

Sure, it happens in the movies, in soap operas and in novels, but we don't ever get to see it because it's *rude*. No, that's kept for the Internet, for the pornography that's spiralled out of control and now can be seen appearing on a smartphone in a playground near you.

Then you have app culture—anonymous sex at the click of a button, delivered steaming hot and relatively fresh to your door via the magic of global positioning systems that can track the nearest horny person and beam their cock shot straight to your handset.

Forbidden fruit. Original Sin.

Y'know, the apple that Eve picked?

That's a *symbol*.

Duh.

OK, sorry. I know you probably know that already, but let's spell it out.

It wasn't a piece of fruit. It was a piece of ass.

* * *

In 1795, in the Herculaneum Museum, they opened room number

XVIII, a room that contained 202 'abominable monuments to human licentiousness', including the statue of Pan, the horny goat god...

At it.

In 1865, the British Museum founded its 'Secretum' or 'secret museum', a vault containing objects considered too obscene for the public eye. Remember, this was an era that not only entered the word pornography into the Oxford English Dictionary for the first time (1857), but also dressed piano legs in lace skirts because the bare wood was deemed too sexually suggestive.

The Secretum remained locked—save for the occasional private visit afforded to the rich, famous and influential—up until the 1960s, but even today a few items remain under key in cupboards 54 and 55 in the department of Medieval and Later Antiquities.

But as with the rise of plant medicine in the time of Trump, for every shadow there is a light. The era of Victoria (the unbelievably uptight queen who refused to allow her government to legislate against lesbianism, not because she approved of it, but because she regarded it as a physical *impossibility*, and who wasn't beyond toking a bit of weed when she had her period, or a cheeky line or two of nose-up, not to mention being a monster for the laudanum) was a time that, for all its puritanism, also gave us...

Sir Richard Burton.

Born in 1821, two years before the future queen, Burton was one of the most diversely colourful, contentious, cavalier and curious figures of his day. An explorer, geographer, translator, writer, soldier, orientalist, cartographer, ethnologist, spy, linguist, poet, fencer and diplomat, he was famed for his travels and explorations in Asia, Africa and the Americas, as well as his extraordinary knowledge of languages and cultures; according to one description, he spoke twenty-nine European, Asian and African languages.

There are many different accounts of Burton and his adventures. A figure straight out of any *Boy's Own* novel, he was both Biggles and Bond. A chameleon-like Lothario who was famed for making the pilgrimage to Mecca disguised as a tribesman at a time when it was forbidden to any non-Muslim on pain of death to make hajj. (Burton went as far as being circumcised, to ensure that he wouldn't be detected.)

Next, he famously sought out the source of the Nile, discovering the Great Lakes with John Hanning Speke, at times disguised as an Arab merchant, but nevertheless managing to get speared through both cheeks by an attacking horde of 200 Somali warriors.

These exploits alone would be enough to make Burton a legendary figure of *Kiplingesque* proportions, along with his activities as a spy in India and Afghanistan (where he disappeared for long periods of time and was labelled by his peers as a 'White Nigger' for having 'gone native'), his army service in the Crimean War, his diplomatic service in the Congo, Equatorial Guinea and Damascus, his founding of the Anthropological Society of London, and the publication of numerous travel books.

Burton is perhaps most famous for translating and introducing to the West a number of books considered risqué or even pornographic at the time. For instance, the *Kama Sutra* (an ancient Indian-Hindu text that describes the sixty-four arts of love-passion-pleasure), all ten volumes of *The Book of the Thousand Nights and a Night* (better known as *The Arabian Nights*), and a further six volumes titled *The Supplemental Nights to the Thousand Nights and a Night*, and *The Perfumed Garden of the Shaykh Nefzawi*.

The *Kama Sutra*, which details ways in which partners should pleasure each other within a marital relationship, is widely considered to be the standard work on human sexual behaviour in Sanskrit literature.

Modern-day India is as repressive, if not more so, than anywhere on the planet, but the ancients had a much freer and easier attitude toward sex. I've studied Tantra in India, where it is now treated with great suspicion and considered akin to black magic or the dark arts. But it is the Indians of old who pioneered the expression of sexuality through Tantric practice, art and literature, with not just the *Kama Sutra*, but also the tradition of erotic temple carvings, most famously in Khajuraho, as well as many other states throughout the subcontinent.

Perhaps the oldest surviving literature in the world, the *Vedas* reveals moral perspectives on sexuality and marriage, with the description of fertility rituals, prayers and sex magic practices from thousands of years ago (many of which were later adopted by Aleister Crowley). These texts, along with the *Kama Sutra*, show us that in ancient India, sex was not only considered a mutual duty, where husband and wife pleasured each other equally, but also as a path to enlightenment—the roots of what became Tantric practice are at least 25,000 years old.

And so sex was considered a healthy, day-to-day experience not to be hidden away, embarrassed about or tainted with shame. These attitudes played a significant role in establishing India as the seat of spirituality in the world. A creative life force that blossomed and flourished until the arrival of Victorian English culture, with their notions of forbidden fruit and original Sin. This did much to smash the carefree Indian liberalism and the consequent misery that comes with such inhibition of sacred, joyful expression.

Burton's version of *The Arabian Nights*—a collection of Middle Eastern folk tales compiled between the eighth and thirteenth centuries—shocked the piano-leg fearing Victorians, who considered the often-sexual content pornographic. They also judged them for their 'archaic language and extravagant idiom, obsessive focus on sexuality', dismissing the works as an 'eccentric ego-trip' and for being, 'obtrusive, kinky and highly personal'.

* * *

Burton, unsurprisingly, died of a heart attack in 1890, but not before he had scandalised polite society and bequeathed us what might be described as the instruction manuals to what became known as the sexual revolution.

But I have bad news.

The sexual revolution, for all its free-loving, prude-shattering, pill-popping promise...

Failed.

It only *seems* like a revolution when looked at relative to what came before. Yes, much has changed: barriers were shattered, norms reinvented, attitudes relaxed.

But are we shame-free as a society? Comfortable in our own skin? Able to express our needs without embarrassment? Do we even have a sexual vocabulary?

No.

We are still as frightened to really get into those dark, damp, murky corners as we ever were.

We are ashamed of our very nature.

We are ashamed of our own divinity.

And you know what that means, don't you?

It means we are Sinners. Which, quite frankly, is fucking ironic.

Along with ending the war on drugs, demilitarisation and education reform, perhaps I should also have said that to save the world we need to radically alter our attitude towards sex. Or perhaps we can squeeze that in under the umbrella of education. Who cares? Free ourselves from sexual repression and you free the world. Maybe even save the world.

Sex is life force. It's *that* simple. It's what powers us, not just to procreate, but also to overcome obstacles, to expand and grow, to explore; it's the root of our curiosity as a species, and that curiosity is what makes us so unique, so adaptable, so destructive and so creative.

It is the energy of the Universe from where *all* life sprang. It's not called the Big Bang for nothing.

In India, Hinduism accepted an open attitude toward sex as an art, science and spiritual practice, and was perhaps the only religion that recognised the essential electric charge that we called sexual energy as our mainline to the god-force that exists within, not without, us all.

Trouble is, the minute you use the word spiritual, let alone god-force, you begin to distance people. But forget all that language—that's why I call it life-force, and electric charge is the description that fits my experience of the charge that not only makes me a sexual person, but also gets me out of bed in the morning and brings me here to this computer to write. Writing is a sexual act of creation, as was the process that drove the people to create this computer (along with acid); it is the fruit of their creative seed. Every cup of tea that you brew, every email you write, every plant that you water, every meal that you make—you are fucking.

However…

Nowadays, tea is almost always the product of a bag squashed in a cup rather than the prolonged infusion of carefully selected leaves.

Mail used to require hand-pressed parchment, ink and quill.

Plants used to surround us naturally as part of our habitat before they were tamed, poisoned and imprisoned in pots.

Meals used to require the cultivation of vegetables and the hunting of wild beasts rather than the piercing of cellophane.

And as these old ways have all but vanished, as so is it reflected in our sexuality. What fertility rituals we used to have are almost entirely forgotten, save for the occasional comical raising of a maypole (it's a cock) on a village green.

Sex has become plastic-wrapped and instant. Few people even recognise its potential beyond a moment of clumsy pleasure. The culture of fuck-buddy websites and hook-up apps does nothing to encourage intimacy or the time it takes to develop all sexual expression as the art form that it can be.

Sure, if we are just talking the sexual act, some of us men know where and what a clitoris is, a few women really know how to caress a penis. We may have ventured beyond the missionary position and some of us may even talk to our partners about what they *like*.

But compared to the time and commitment that we may give to learning the button configuration necessary to play the latest Xbox game, or the focus required to navigate a new smartphone upgrade, can you really say that you've dedicated yourself to your lover's pleasure in the same way?

Really?

Maybe you've been lucky enough to meet someone with such chemistry that drives your interest for a few months at least, but can any of you even compete with the amours of the erotic sculptures of India?

They're not just titillating sculptures, you know; they are depictions, in a pre-printing, pre-*Joy of Sex* world, of how to pleasure your partner *and raise your consciousness.*

And even if you *have* tried a few risqué positions, did you raise your consciousness last time you came home from the pub after six pints and had Viking sex dressed in that Odin fancy dress costume from last year's office Christmas party?

I think not.

* * *

I'm not big into what passes as Tantra. I think a lot of modern neo-Tantra is bollocks, using sex to sell weekend workshops. But proper, no holds barred Tantra has never left me in any state other than shaken to my core.

When you encounter your deeper sexuality, you encounter *all* that you are. And most people don't like that. They want to stay on the surface with who they think they are. They don't want to risk finding out that their persona is prefabricated.

And this is why, above all else, being sexual, having sex, growing and exploring your sexual energy is the most powerful anti-Sin measure any of us can take. You can only know yourself as well as you know your sexuality.

I'm going to say that again.

You can only know yourself as well as you know your sexuality.

That's kind of an important statement. Do you think Trump knows himself sexually?

That motherfucker has as much understanding of himself as I have of the *Teichmuller theory*.

You can only know yourself as well as you know your own sexuality. Your capacity to really know *who* you are, to have self-awareness and consciousness and therefore true freedom, is relative to how well you know yourself as a sexual being. And I promise you, if you have the guts to make that exploration, what you will discover will not be entirely...

Nice.

Alongside your free spirit, your wild abandon, the *you* who was born to dance, your joyful, uninhibited goddess or warrior, you will also have to encounter your predator, your whore, your player, your slut, your rapist, your abuser, your greed, your selfishness, your insatiability, your fear...

Your shadow.

Sometimes I feel we should rebrand the shadow to something more palatable, cos if you called it the treasure chest people might be more inclined to go nosing around in there, but we're stuck with it now. And the very real truth, as Joseph Campbell said, is that, 'It is by going down into the abyss that we recover the treasures of life. Where you stumble, there lies your treasure.'

Some 2000 years of sexual repression have brought humanity to the brink of auto-destruction. It may be too late. It is one of the single greatest causes of the collective narcolepsy that affects us all, creating an environment where our species has switched off from nature with calamitous results. It's no coincidence that pagan cultures celebrated sexuality and nature as one and the same, with a multitude of fertility rites and ceremonies that were ultimately absorbed or stamped out by Christianity – the subservient religion terrified of its own shadow.

And scared you should be. Sex at its best should never be entirely comfortable: it's raw and visceral, and treads a fine line between what is permitted and what is dangerous. Should you let yourself go completely, who knows what might happen...

You might actually enjoy yourself.

But sex repressed so quickly turns to perversion and never more so has demeaning, exploitative pornography been so in demand; never more so has paedophilia been so rampant and organised; never more so has sex been commoditised and monetised to promote everything from chocolate to cars to soap to cigarettes and just about everything else that you can put a sales tag on.

Take it back. It's yours and always has been.

* * *

Sex is not *wrong*. Sex is not dirty. And for most of us, an orgasm is as close as we're going to get to an experience of the pure egoless state.

Why do you think it feels *so* good?

For a moment, your mind switches off, your sense of self dissolves and you enter into that bliss state that happens when ego is transcended. For a moment, you taste *la petite mort*, as the French call it, a glimpse of *samadhi*, a brush with enlightenment, *kundalini* consciousness that shatters our sense of the 'normal state' and tantalises us with that which could be if we only knew how to regain our birth right.

When the self dissolves, what happens is what people most commonly describe as a feeling of oneness, and that word that is so hard to really describe that it's become something of a New Age cliché. Similarly, enlightened masters have always struggled to describe the experience of transcendence of the ego simply because there are *no words*.

It's not such a distant, supernatural encounter reserved only for sadhus; anyone who has experienced orgasm has touched the mystic. But try really describing the experience of orgasm and see how you get on. You may get close, but it will always be approximate, you will always fall short, because the mystic is beyond description.

Oneness is a place without boundaries, without borders, without life or death, without perimeters or limits; it is a place where everything is interwoven and connected, a place without division, where warfare and conflict simply cannot exist.

* * *

If you want to prevent wars, genocide, rape, murder, sexual abuse, all crime, all social unrest and disharmony, and *all* that we call Sin, we need to become conscious. And as the Hindu *tantrikas* have known for millennia, by opening to our sexuality, our sexual nature, and by following the Left Hand Path, we can accelerate this process to awakening.

We've been taught that sex is a Sin, that sex is Lust and that sex is forbidden. We've been taught that sex will cause us to go blind, that we will be cast into the pit and exiled from paradise. We have been controlled by the shaming of our true nature. And yet, as ever—even though it is our religious leaders who mostly have been responsible for this indoctrination—we have to move away from 'blaming our parents' and take responsibility for what is now ours…

The fear of loss of control.

This is part of our cultural malaise. We have all become control freaks, self-medicating with TV, technology, tobacco, alcohol, pornography, sugar and prescription drugs so as not to feel any discomfort, but most of all, to stay in control at all times.

This is at the root of the war on drugs and the unspoken, invisible yet very real war on sex; the dominator culture does not want the masses to freak out and to engage in the wild, rutting Dionysian fertility rites of old; it doesn't want the revolting peasants getting high on ergot or hippies dancing naked in the fields or marching on Wall Street. And mostly we have succumbed to our masters and learned to obey, and in time we have learned that to go crazy is…

To go crazy.

We have forgotten what it is to lose control of our senses, to surrender to pleasure, to abandon ourselves to the mystic, to *let go* and trust that we will be OK. We have become tight and rigid and fearful of our own animal nature. We spend our lives terrified of what might happen if we let Mr Hyde (that's me) out of the box.

And sure—we might wake up the next morning covered in blood and semen, surrounded by small scraps of human flesh, empty Jack Daniels bottles and broken furniture.

We've all been there.

But few of us know what we are capable of and the tiny glimpses we have had prove that it's really best not to *go there*. Which is why we all need to venture past those boundaries, to poke our noses into the forbidden places, to explore the darker recesses of our consciousness in order to truly gain control of our wildness, by riding it all the way to oblivion with the reins held tight in our teeth rather than nailing the doors to the stable shut.

* * *

So, what do we do? Once again, it's fine for me, the author, to rant on about how we all need to smash through 2000 years of religious indoctrination and complete the stalled sexual revolution, to free our creative sexual cores and save this beautiful world. But how?

Ummm...

OK, for starters we need to take ownership of our projections. A great many of our cultural heroes are what we call 'sex symbols', including Trump; for even though you and I know him to be the Devil incarnate, to a large swathe of Americans he is a heroic figure who represents raw, unashamed sexuality as a real 'man's man'.

But it's interesting to me that we do so love a bad boy, from Jagger to Morrison and beyond, as much as we've always loved a naughty but nice girl like Marilyn Monroe or Elizabeth Taylor.

These smouldering icons often engage on- and off-screen in the kind of sexual behaviour that a great many of us quietly admire or long for, while living a mostly safe and largely sexless life. I've stated this before: most people I know are not having very much sex and this is one of the great secrets of our society, because no one wants to admit it. Surrounded by sex symbols and sexualised marketing, most people imagine that everyone else is fucking like mad hyenas and yet so many aren't having sex at all.

This needs to be broached and, once again, it has to start in schools. Sex needs to be taken beyond the biology class, and the *Joy of Sex* or the like needs to be introduced very early on—not only will this step away from prudishness and give children a much more sophisticated sexual language (which is the real answer to changing *all* of this—teaching people to talk), but they would also be much more aware of what sex is and therefore protected from paedophiles through their own knowledge.

Tantra weekends and psychosexual trainings have their place for adults, but by then it's almost too late. We don't wait until we are grown up to learn about mathematics, science and literature, so why wait to learn about sex? Tantra should be taught in primary school. And by Tantra I still mean the recognition of the goddess and god within us all. Teach children the sacredness of sex, the attitudes of worship and devotion. Help them reclaim it from the realms of instant disposability and surface titillation.

Sex is holy. It requires reverence and respect, practice and study, curiosity and perseverance. Teach children this attitude and you will change the world for the better forever.

It's that simple.

* * *

It's raining and grey as only an English November dawn can be. I've been awake since 5:30 a.m., glued to the news, glued to Facebook, where I posted the simple statement: No words.

No words to describe the horror.

The breathless, heart-stopping, frozen response to the simply unfathomable news that Darth Vader has vanquished Luke, the Wicked Witch of the West has killed Dorothy and her little dog, Toto, The Joker has killed Batman and...

Donald Trump has won the US presidential election.

And so history is made, 2016, the Year of the Monkey, the year of the Trump, the year of Sin and for all our efforts, the world has not...

Been saved.

I saw a photograph on Facebook that somehow seemed to fit the mood of the day—an image that sickened and disturbed me to my core. And no, it wasn't of The Donald, all swollen and bloated and flushed with victory and power; it was an image of a cow in China, a live cow, its legs cut off at the knees so that it could not move, standing on its stumps while it was being skinned alive for its leather.

It was being skinned alive...

For its leather.

That is the world we live in, a world where Donald Trump can be elected as leader, while our vanity has driven us to mutilate and butcher noble beasts to make nice soft jackets and handbags.

Fuck you, Middle America.

This was a campaign of hatred, a campaign that harnessed and exploited poor, uneducated white Americans with the promise of a return to some kind of mythical greatness. This was Roosh V rhetoric—a small, indignant, frightened man all puffed up with an overblown sense of righteousness gathering up all the other small, indignant, frightened men labouring beneath a notion that they have somehow been marginalised by feminism, all ripe and ready for Big Daddy to come and save them from the wicked Hillary.

This was an election where a woman stood against a man, a rich, powerful, white man, a man who no matter what he did or said was always going to have the upper hand...

Because he was a man.

A man who won...

Because he was a man.

When you become frightened of your own true nature, when you become ashamed of your own animal, primordial sexual drive, you become detached from your wild, chaotic, passionate feminine essence, then masculine energy dominates. It crushes and oppresses and constrains and restricts through violence and force.

What this election proves, if anything, is that now more than ever, we as a species are internally out of balance, while the external social revolutions of the twentieth century have failed or at best been incomplete. This is not about feminism or girl power or pussy riots. This is not about men and women. This is about the human race. Our masculine essence is still grossly out of control; we erase nature and drop high-explosive penises on brown people; we subjugate and crush with a swaggering sense of entitlement.

We are the white men and we don't care what happens as long as we are in power. We have been here for a very long time now, doing exactly what we want to whoever we want and crushing all who stand in our path.

But there is an energy that can stop us, an energy that we fear more than anything, externally and perhaps even more so within, and that energy is what we call the Feminine.

The Feminine is not nice. The Feminine is not girly. The Feminine is not weak.

The enemy has shown its face.

Time to go Kali on its arse.

* * *

Just a simple choice, right now, between fear and love...

Bill Hicks

* * *

December

Hitler had great stage presence.

Keith Richards

The interesting adults are always the school failures, the weird ones, the losers, the malcontents. This isn't wishful thinking. It's the rule.

A.A. Gill

My fingers are long and beautiful, as, it has been well documented, are various other parts of my body.

Donald Trump

White men! White women! The swastika is calling you! The sacred and ancient symbol of your race since the beginning of time! The Jew is using the black as muscle against you! And you are left there, helpless. Well? What are you gonna do about it, whitey? Just sit there? Of course not! You are going to join with us! The members of the American Socialist White People's Party. An organization of decent law-abiding white folk, just like you.

Illinois Nazis

It's not the end of the world, OK? It's not World War III. It's not a time to be frightened. It's a time to get off your arse, speak out, wake up and stay awake.

Me. I said that.

I murdered my first client today.

Fuck it. I just ran out of steam. Needed somewhere to put all that pent-up frustration.

I don't mean it was my *first* client, I mean it's the first time

I *murdered* a client. It was a lot easier than I had anticipated. I spiked his tea with a generous dose of butabarbital that I bought on Silk Road and then suggested we did a guided visualisation. Once he was out, I taped a bag over his head. No mess.

Twat had one of those long, sorry faces you just wanna stab. And I say murdered, but it was more of a mercy killing, really. I mean, he was *never* gonna get better, no one was ever gonna love him or even *like* him. He existed without friends or family in some shitty Kilburn bedsit that by all accounts was so crowded with garbage and junk that you had to work your way through a maze to reach his sordid bed, sheets brittle with months of ejaculate and sweat. That's no way to live.

He would've gone on like that another thirty or forty years and then died alone, buttocks like pickled walnuts from years of sitting in his own piss in some municipal care home being abused by minimum-wage Eastern European sadists.

So, the way I see it I was doing him, and society as a whole, a favour.

All part of the service.

People imagine it's easy being a shrink. Just sitting there getting paid for chatting, right?

You try it.

Listening to people's misery, day in, day out. I earn my money. I knew I was gonna do John sooner or later. I could feel it building up for months. I'd begun to dread each session, his fucking mealy-mouthed apologetic smile and dead cow eyes behind those Coke-bottle glasses that he wore, looking at me like some kind of bloater fish from the bottom of the mid-Atlantic whenever I opened the door. You know the look, the kind that says, 'kick me'.

He was so asleep he didn't even know he was alive, so it's hardly a loss.

But I feel much better now. All that tension's gone. I feel lighter and in a way his death has a kind of *poetry* to it, as if he were a sacrificial lamb. He died so that I might be more chilled and in a better mood, and therefore be of greater service to others.

Maybe he'd have found some peace in that. The peace he could never afford himself owing to the fact that he was all twisted up with retroflected guilt from his uncontrollable compulsion to grope women on crowded tube trains. Dirty fucker. Technically, I should've shopped him to the cops, but I thought it better just to kill him and be done with it.

So John—may he rest in piss (or, to be more accurate, in three rolls of cling film, gaffer tape and bin liners at the bottom of the River Lea)—was the first.

Kind of...

OK, there were those two who got swept away in that flash flood on the vision-quest retreat in Tasmania, but that wasn't my fault and the inquest proved that. There was nothing to suggest I'd cut the rope and anyway, it was like that film about those two mountaineers. What was it called? *Touching the Void.* Touching cloth, more like. Anyway, if I hadn't done it I'd have gone too, *and* the others, so I saved lives. Then there was that old bitch who fell off the cliff in Snowdonia. How was I to know she had dodgy knees?

No, John was the first proper one.

And it's not like they should be surprised, right? I mean, I give enough hints. The door to my office has a brass plaque on it that says: Mr Hyde. Psycho Therapist. And my doormat says: Fuck Off.

Do I need to spell it out clearer than that?

I'm a professional. I mean business. I get results.

My name is Jerry Hyde and I help people...

Even if it means killing them.

* * *

Donald Trump stands for something universal, something right before our eyes. It's an aspect of the human psyche that we feel embarrassed and ashamed of, which makes it our collective secret. Going back a century in the field of depth psychology, the secret side of human nature acquired a special name: the shadow.

The shadow compounds all the dark impulses—hatred, aggression, sadism, selfishness, jealousy, resentment, sexual transgression—that are hidden out of sight.

When the shadow breaks out, what's wrong is right. Being transgressive feels like a relief, because suddenly the collective psyche can gambol in forbidden fields. When Trump indulges in rampant bad behaviour and at the same time says to his riotous audiences, 'this is fun, isn't it?' he's expressing in public our ashamed impulse to stop obeying the rules.

Deepak Chopra, *America's Shadow: The Real Secret of Donald J. Trump*

Before Jung, the Shadow had another name. It was known as...
The Devil.

This has been the human dilemma, the inner battle between light and darkness, right and wrong, good and bad, the white wolf and the dark, the Sinner and the saint, the Devil and God, since our dualistic minds were formed.

Donald Trump is the Devil, in as much as the Devil is a construct, a bogeyman built from all of our disowned dark projections.

I have absolutely no memory of what inspired me to write this book, but one thing I can say for sure is that at the beginning of this year I had no idea that by December the Antichrist would not only be walking among us, but would also have been elected to be the next US president.

Kind of makes the subject of Sin all the more pertinent.

'When the shadow breaks out, what's wrong is right.' Deepak has made a strong point there: The *Donald* is not the problem. It is all the sleeping, unconscious, hate-filled souls whose collective fear has been pooled together to make this beast. Remember Gurdjieff?

People live in a state of a hypnotic 'waking sleep'. Maleficent events such as wars and so on could not possibly take place if people were more awake.

Well, I'm no soothsayer, but I'll tell you something: this shit is going to wake a lot of people up.

* * *

I wrote about killing my clients back in May. I'd had an idea about injecting a subplot into this book. I was looking for a vehicle to break the normal flow, and it struck me that if *you*, the reader, began this book in the belief that it were a work of conventional non-fiction and I then started to introduce the notion that I was a serial killer, driven to murder by the *subject matter of this work*, that it might confuse, disturb or alarm you into an awakened state.

Of course, I *am* a serial killer, a rapist, a paedophile, a dictator, a fraud, a predator... a savage. We all are. That wild, untamed, headhunting tribesperson sleeps within us all as we grapple to keep the lizard brain from regaining control, and exploding with terrible violence and base, uncontained indulgence, sexual deviance, gross survival behaviours and the sweet relief of the transgressive.

Relief, relief, relief... Whole worlds have collapsed, empires have crumbled and nations have disintegrated on the back of one of those *fuck-it* moments when the Shadow has broken through, because the effort to keep it at bay any longer was just too great and the relief of letting the Devil loose just too tempting.

You and I know the Devil doesn't *really* exist. The Donald is just a man—true, a very wealthy, powerful, psychopathic man—but he *embodies* so much of The Prince of Sin that it makes it easy to project the Horned One onto him.

Kevin Barron met the bastard:

Yeah, this girl I was dating in '89, her dad was CEO of Kimberly Clark, the people who made Kleenex, and he knew Trump through something or other, and so we got this invitation to go up to his hideous gaudy palace with these metallic windows. It was a hideous place.

These are scary times, although I have to be honest with you, I think Hillary Clinton was a greater danger to the world than Trump because she's a warmonger. What a terrible choice you had to make if you were American. So, very difficult times, and I'm frightened and scared because there is a lunatic in the White House.

The real challenge perhaps is to not demonise Trump, but to really embrace what Chopra is saying and see that we are *all* Donald, much as I felt my inner-Nazi rise toward the freaky Jews of Stanford Hill on the back of documenting the horrors of the Holocaust—he's within me. It's almost like some kind of horror movie—correction, it *is* some kind of horror movie—where all of our collective hatred has pooled into *matter*, creating the great, bloated mass that is Big Daddy T, and now he struts around grabbing pussy as he goes with all his vile little wizards in tow.

All the little men, the ball-less, whining, fearful little men whose mummies never loved them, and who feel bitter and disempowered by feminism—the Roosh Vs and the neo-masculinists—they voted for Trump. They voted for his misogyny, for his old-school swaggering, John Wayne-style masculinity; for his promise to make America great again and the subtext that what that really means is making *men* great again.

But darker still perhaps, what is now emerging is that 53 per cent of white *women* voted for him, this man with his rape rhetoric, who calls women pigs and has a string of sexual assault claims still outstanding. But, nevertheless, they voted—and suddenly the shocking truth became apparent...

Not *all* women are feminists.

I remember my friend, women's activist Samantha Roddick, blowing my mind with the statement that women are misogynistic, in that they hate the feminine in men, which is why they can have such contempt for our 'weakness'. How else to explain that percentage other than by looking at women's misogyny, their secret craving for a *real* man to step in and take control of the situation? To take power.

As the US satirist H.L. Mencken defined it, a misogynist is 'a man who hates women as much as women hate one another.'

When I was younger, I learned that 'all men are potential rapists'. This burden weighed heavily on my new manly shoulders. I felt that I carried the shame of an infinite number of generations of men who had come before me. It made me apologetic and afraid to inhabit my own raw, animal masculinity.

But, strangely, despite years of inwardly and outwardly pleading that I wasn't like the others, it was the admission of the truth that set me free.

I realised that yes, I was indeed a potential rapist. I just wasn't...

Practising.

Of course, I have the potential. I'm a predatory male with perhaps more than the average capacity to objectify and use women, but my desire not to rape is stronger than any wild, untamed *pussy grabber* that may lay dormant within my darker corners.

It's worth pointing out, however, that through my many

discussions with women, I've become aware that most have had some kind of sexual encounter that they didn't actually want, from rape and abuse to agreeing to have sex with their lover just to avoid *a scene*.

Meanwhile, last week an anonymous woman filed a federal lawsuit against Trump, accusing him of raping her in 1994 when she was 13 years old. This was the same week that Obama welcomed him into the White House with words of conciliation, while the rest of the world's leaders sent simpering letters of congratulation, whimpering like frightened dogs going belly up before the new alpha male on the block.

Also, in the last seven days there have been at least 700 race-related incidents reported across the US, which we can assume is sadly the tip of the iceberg in terms of what is to come. And all the while The Donald refuses to denounce the Ku Klux Klan, while in Washington DC alt-right white nationalists hail him with enthusiastic Nazi salutes and cries of 'Hail Trump, hail our people, hail victory!'

Richard B. Spencer is the leader of the National Policy Institute: 'an independent organization dedicated to the heritage, identity, and future of people of European descent in the United States, and around the world.'

I dunno, maybe I'm being oversensitive, but any white supremacist organisation that uses the word *national* gives me the chills.

'America was until this past generation a white country designed for ourselves and our posterity,' says Dick, obviously not a history major. 'It is our creation, it is our inheritance, and it belongs to us.'

And all this makes me wonder what kind of strange undercurrent I picked up on that made me decide to embark on this work at this point in time, to explore a subject that up until now I'd had absolutely no interest in.

So, anyway... What have we learned?

* * *

To be honest, Grayson Perry nailed it when he said that Sin was out of date, that Sin 'has lost its teeth.'

And I think he's right. There's not much about the Seven Deadly Sins that really intrigued me, it was where it *took* me that captivated my interest. We've covered a lot of rambling ground over the course of this road trip, way beyond the sex and the drugs and the rock 'n' roll. What about the Georgia Guidestones? That was a cool discovery. You can bet your arse that Trump either built them or is going to have them torn down, and in terms of instruction on how to save the world I think they come pretty close.

We've done the Ten Commandments, Dante's twisted levels of Hell. We looked at Aleister Crowley, Jim Morrison, the Nazis and the Holocaust, Oscar Wilde and a few other luvvies buried in Père Lachaise.

Oh, and we discovered that satanism is really cool.

We've had Brexit.

We've lost David Bowie and Prince and George Martin and George Michael and Leon Russell (fuck, I loved Leon with his top hat and junkie eyes) and Leonard Cohen and Gene 'But I Shoot With This Hand' Wilder and Alan Rickman and *The Magnificent Seven*'s very own drunkard Robert Vaughan and R2-D2 and Muhammad Ali and The Eagles' Glen Frey and The Jefferson Airplane's Paul Kantner and Harper Lee and Burt 'You Little Yellow Swine' Kwouk and *Fawlty Towers*' Manuel Sachs and Michael Herr and A.A. Gill (his death hit me harder than most) and Funkadelic's Bernie Worrell and Michael Cimino (shit, I didn't know he'd died) and Scotty Moore (shit, I didn't know he was still *alive*… and now he isn't) and many, *many* more.

We frolicked with hippies in the mud at the Spirit Horse community in Wales, and Madame Hua lost her shit and then found it again among the rock pools and the faeries.

We discovered that 150 is optimum when it comes to community and effective tribal culture, and noted the disastrous consequences since we've largely extended beyond that magic number.

And let's not forget my rather rash promises, whereby not only did I commit to exploring the subject of Sin for an entire *year*, while not shaving or cutting my hair and thus looking like some kind of scary mountain man who'd done too much bad brown acid, but also to meditate often and attend the gym three times a week and write each and every day apart from the days that I didn't and curtail my overspending on unnecessary shit on eBay and buy no more guitars and avoid excessive masturbation and avoid tobacco and avoid dairy produce and avoid refined sugar wherever possible and behave with love and compassion towards my fellow man at all times...

So, let's look at the results:

Meditation:

Hyde's attendance this year has been very shabby indeed. I suspect that if he had dedicated as much time to meditation as he did masturbation, he could well be enlightened by now, but as it stands he risks blindness if he doesn't buck up his ideas.

Must try harder.

Physical Education:

Hyde has not been seen at the gym since January.

When questioned as to why his attendance was so criminally poor, he cited dyslexia as the reason.

Fail.

Writing:

Hyde seems to believe that *quantity* is preferable to *quality*. His grammar is dreadful and his spelling atrocious; he veered wildly off the subject and on occasion appeared quite incoherent, while at times his pupils looked suspiciously dilated.

See Matron.

Purchases:

Hyde seems to think that because he *sold* a guitar, this somehow created a loophole in the contract whereby he could replace it with another, often of far greater value. What's more, he has squandered vast sums on effects pedals in the belief that this will make him a better player. His practice has been inconsistent, and while he has admittedly shown *some* technical improvement over the year it is far below what he is capable of.

Poor.

Tobacco, Dairy and Sugar:

Giving up *buying* cigarettes is not the same as giving up smoking. Hyde seems to show no sign of curtailing this filthy compulsion, and while his former addiction often manifested in a 30-a-day habit he still keeps the company of other smokers from whom he unashamedly 'bums' cigarettes.

Likewise, Hyde has shown no sign of cutting down on the amount of milk that he adds to his coffee each day, and at times he has done cheese. His relationship to sugar has been inconsistent, although there are signs of minor improvement.

He needs to show much more self-discipline if he is to succeed in the future.

Fail.

Love and Compassion for Others:

While I believe that his intentions are often usually good, Hyde needs to learn to discriminate between love and narcotics. Giving people unregulated psychedelics with the instruction, "'ere, try this. This'll sort you right out' is not the same as compassion, nor is it reliable. Timothy Leary and Ken Kesey were convicted criminals, not gurus of love, and I fear that if he continues to model himself on these 'folk heroes' he too could end up in deep water.

Fail.

* * *

I say you have to be a visionary, make yourself a visionary. A Poet makes himself a visionary through a long, boundless and systematised disorganisation of all the senses. All forms of love, of suffering, of madness; he searches himself, he exhausts within himself all poisons and preserves their quintessence's. Unspeakable torment, where he will need the greatest faith, a superhuman strength, where he becomes among all men the great invalid, the great criminal, the great accursed—and the Supreme Scientist...

Arthur Rimbaud

Oh. And then there was the drugs.

I have, of late, been microdosing psychedelic mushrooms each and every morning to the great enhancement of my spirit and the benefit of my constitution, but I have, *as yet*, seen no giant bats in the skies over Tottenham.

And so it was that a little over a week ago, with almost poetic perfect timing given how close we are to completion, I received a 'Notice of Seizure' from the UK Border Force Post Detection Team, or UKBFPDT as I shall henceforth refer to them for the sake of simplicity, telling me that 830 grams of a 'controlled substance' had been found and confiscated while en route from the Netherlands...

To my address.

UKBFPDT have a lovely simple-yet-powerful logo—a laurel wreath with the slogan: *'INVESTORS IN PEOPLE'* ®

The outcome presumably of numerous countrywide focus groups and high-budget graphic design and PR contracts, and many, many months of behind-closed-doors, in-depth meetings.

The seizure of my magic mushroom grow-kit comes at a time when the Imperial College London's four-year study into the effectiveness of psilocybin in the case of otherwise 'treatment-resistant depression' has observed that 'depression symptoms lifted considerably following just a single treatment dose of psilocybin for every participant in the study.'

'This is the first time that psilocybin has been investigated as a potential treatment for major depression,' says lead study author, Dr Robin Carhart-Harris.

Professor David Nutt, who coauthored the study, has this to say:

Treatment-resistant depression is common, disabling and extremely difficult to treat. New treatments are urgently needed, and our study shows that psilocybin is a promising area of future research.

Previous animal and human brain imaging studies have suggested that psilocybin may have effects similar to other antidepressant treatments. Psilocybin targets the serotonin receptors in the brain, just as most antidepressants do, but it has a very different chemical structure to currently available antidepressants and acts faster than traditional antidepressants.

For a majority of the twelve participants in the study, the antidepressant effects of the mushrooms were still in effect three months after the dosing, while five were in complete remission from depression three months after the study took place, even though they were following no other treatment plan.

And so I must confess to feeling a degree of *Wrath* at UKBFPDT's decision to confiscate my delivery, along with the suggestion that they may prosecute me under Section 170 of the Customs and Excise Management Act of 1979, of which I'm ashamed to admit I am woefully ignorant.

In the eyes of the law, I am a drug abuser.

I had thought that perhaps my experience of microdosing might have featured more in this book, but the clue is in the word micro—the effects, while profound, have been subtle and, in truth… there's not much to tell. I take 0.2 grams of home-grown psilocybin every two or three days, which have confirmed the many reports that microdosing is not only nature's antidepressant, but that it also helps with a multitude of things from enhancing creativity and physical stamina to alleviating anxiety and the symptoms of trauma.

Psilocybin has made me calmer, kinder and more focused in my creativity, and in my work as a therapist, and so, all I conclude is that despite their good intentions, UKBFPDT are in fact not investing in *PEOPLE®*, they are in fact—if you subscribe to Terence McKenna's Stoned Ape Theory—playing a part in inhibiting the evolution of the human race.

I am not a drug dealer.

I am not a menace to society.

I am not even a habitual lawbreaker. I pay my taxes and I have a spotless driving licence, but I *will* break any law that I consider a Sin. And if to Sin is to go against God's will, and God is in real terms *Nature*, then the prohibition of *any* naturally occurring medicinal plant is…

A Sin.

Unless, as Bill Hicks pointed out, God made a mistake.

Ultimately, the very *idea* that anyone can tell me what I can and cannot do to my own body and my own psyche would be comical.

If it were not so sinister.

* * *

I didn't even consider what the outcome might be when I started this trip. I don't know that I was even looking for a result. It was more the following of a compulsion. But I've learned much, much more than I ever anticipated.

I still maintain that the most important thing of all if we are to salvage this planet is to do whatever you can to wake up. And in terms of Sin, I honestly believe that the only one is that of unconsciousness and that all Sins spring from this sleepy well.

But let's face it, we went way beyond Sin and I'm happy to have found some kind of guidelines or direction to a better world, and to me these conclusions have made it all worthwhile.

And so, to recap, we need:

1) A total, complete and almost unthinkable attitudinal shift in the way that we educate our children.
2) To end the war against drugs and make all psychedelic consciousness-shifting substances available to the masses, with the appropriate infrastructure implemented to create safe treatment centres with skilled facilitators and educators to ensure their safe, risk-free usage.
3) To stop arming the world, and redirect much of those funds and resources into the above.
4) A radical shift in our attitudes toward sex and sexuality.

Do all these things and our world will be transformed. Saved, even. Even better still, I'll work on them and you come up with your own list. That'll do it.

Of course, you'd be right in pointing out that since writing most of this book a rather fat, rich, right-wing fly has landed in the ointment of change, evolution and hope in the form of The

Donald.

In both the US and Europe, the rise of the far right threatens much of what many of the heroes of the last century, and especially the 1960s, fought for, from Civil Rights to race relations to abortion; although, as we've observed, attitudes toward drugs really *are* changing and this is no coincidence. The same day Trump was elected, recreational marijuana was legalised in the State of California.

But as Russell Brand so eloquently pointed out within days of the election results:

The conditions existed yesterday (for Donald Trump to become President). They did two days ago, a month ago, a year ago, and for the last 10, 20 years, we've been building towards this moment. For the last 20 or 30 years, we've been creating the conditions where, as we now know, this was inevitable—because it has happened.

Now we have to find alternatives, and I don't think it's going to take place on the superficial administrative level of Washington or Westminster politics. It's going to take place philosophically and deeply. So, if you do feel afraid, or disappointed or angry about it, try not to. Try to feel optimistic because this had to happen. In the end, we had to reach some kind of climax, some kind of crisis, some kind of nadir where it's no longer possible to continue in the way we have been.

If Hillary Clinton had been elected, what I suspect is that we would not have got real change.

With Donald Trump, it's no longer possible to ignore that real change is required.

Under the administrations of Lyndon Johnson and Richard Nixon, we saw more profound change than perhaps in any other era. Trump has brought the darkness *centre stage* and we now have something to rebel against, to speak out against, to take to the streets and make one great big fucking noise about. Now is the time for civil unrest and organised, intelligent disobedience; now is the time to fight against racism, hatred, oppression and injustice. With leaders like Blair, it was underground, shady and hidden; with a thug like Trump it's all super visible and impossible to ignore.

And don't forget John Pilger's point: 'We are *not* the good guys.'

Harder now than ever to deny.

I grew up in the Cold War in a world where the Russians were the bad guys. We were shown films of where to shelter in the event of a nuclear attack. Then the wall came down and there was a bit of a vacuum for a while until 9/11, and suddenly we had The War Against Terror© and it was business as usual. Not that I ever really took that seriously; seemed to me like a bunch of propaganda and spin on behalf of the arms trade, and to make us scared, so that we believed that we needed our governments to protect us.

But now, suddenly, it's Middle America that really seems to be the one to watch. Trump may be the one with his thumb on that big red button, but it's his millions of supporters that have me worried. And they really do believe that God is on their side and that's a mindset that as history has proven leads to a very itchy trigger finger.

We are not the good guys.

Our governments are the ones controlling drones from afar; our governments are the ones building pipelines and committing acts of war against indigenous peoples; our governments are the ones engaged in multiple wars; our governments are the ones who lie to us on a daily basis.

We used to have celebrity chefs, now we have celebrity presidents. We have put a reality show host in charge and he's got the nuclear codes.

What could possibly go wrong?

As I write this, while still under Obama's rule, the biggest gathering of Native Americans for over a century is assembled at the Standing Rock Indian Reservation. This sounds really beautiful and cosmic, until you understand that they are there in their thousands to protest against the Energy Transfer Partners' Dakota Access Pipeline, where they face armed police with attack dogs, tear gas and armoured cars equipped with water cannons. It's proper cowboys and Indians.

It's war.

Fact is, let's face it, although I might have a little moan here in this book, or you might have a dreamcatcher in your bedroom window or even a rather impressive feather tattoo on your arm, few of us give much thought to the extermination of the Native American people. Generally, we kind of go, 'Oh yeah, *Bury My Heart at Wounded Knee*, I read that...'

I remember giving a copy to my grandfather. It upset him deeply. I think he died despairing at what humans can do to humans.

But...

Social media has somehow grabbed the attention of the world (well, my little algorithm world, anyway), and people are protesting against the pipeline and, perhaps even more so, against the treatment of the tribe's people gathered there to protect their ancient, sacred sites.

Now *that's* what I'm talking about.

Whatever you do, whenever you read this book, even if it's fifty years from now, whenever you hear of injustice or inhumanity...

Speak out. Speak out. Speak out.

Remember, for many years after the World War II, it was generally accepted that the bulk of the German population knew nothing about the extermination of millions of people in the Holocaust. Lord Dahrendorf, ex-warden of St Antony's College,

Oxford, stated in his 1966 study into Society and Democracy in Germany: 'It is certainly true that most Germans "did not know" about National Socialist crimes of violence; nothing precise, that is, because they did not ask any questions.'

But in 1995, Daniel Goldhagen's *Hitler's Willing Executioners*, and again in Robert Gellately's 2001 book *Backing Hitler*, came the revelations that most ordinary citizens knew full well the extent of Hitler's atrocities, not only toward the Jews, but also other ethnic groups and minorities, toward all those considered *Untermenschen*—subhuman.

They knew that Hitler had promised the extermination of every Jew on German soil, because the concentration camps had been reported step by step in thousands of officially inspired German media articles and propaganda posters. Gellately states that the only thing many Germans may not have known about was the use of industrial-scale gas chambers because, unusually, no media reports were allowed of this *final solution*.

And so, I would say that the Holocaust was *not* only perpetrated by the Nazis or the SS, or by the camp commandants or the guards or even the regular German soldier recruited into a firing squad; the Holocaust was perpetrated by rosy-faced *housewives* and laughing teenagers and kindly *old men and ladies*; the Holocaust was perpetrated by everyone...

Who remained silent.

And that applies to you and me, perhaps now more than ever. If you stay silent, *you* are a perpetrator, an accessory; you become compliant in the racist attack, the violent incident, the misogynistic joke, the homophobic comment. Challenge your friends, challenge your families, challenge the stranger on the bus or the subway, challenge the politicians, the media, the state and the establishment, challenge Mr Jones...

Don't ask *if* you are racist, homophobic or misogynistic.

Ask yourself *how* you are racist, homophobic or misogynistic.

Dig deep.

* * *

Hey so my name
Is called Disturbance
I'll shout and scream
I'll kill the king, I'll rail at all his servants...
                    Jagger Richards, 'Street Fighting Man'

* * *

And so, out of the four conclusions that I've come to, which do I feel is the *most* important? Which, if I were only allowed to keep one, would I choose?

No question. Number one—a total, complete and almost unthinkable attitudinal shift in the way that we educate our children.

There's an old oak door to a dark closet somewhere in a school in Buckinghamshire, England, that if you open it and look inside, there still will you find the boot marks of the boy who was repeatedly locked in there 100 years ago.

My grandfather didn't like school.

And me, from the first dread-filled day in September 1969 to the last angry, fucked-up rebellious day in July 1982, I hated every tiny second of the whole miserable, dull, frightening, crushing, oppressive, soul-destroying experience.

It *harmed* me.

So yeah, I have a chip on my shoulder, an axe to grind, a grudge that skews my view, a distorted perspective that makes it hard for me to be impartial and dispassionate.

No. Fuck that. I feel too strongly about this subject, and as I've watched my children slowly being moulded from bright, carefree, happy beings into pale, stressed and anxious creatures, the bile of at least 100 years has risen up in my throat. Therefore, it is my sworn contention that if we are to change the world for the better, we must change how we educate our future citizens. To change the world from hate to love, we must change how we educate our future citizens. To rid the planet of racism and cruelty, we must change how we educate our future citizens. If we are to move from war to peace, we must change how we educate our future citizens. And to prevent a global disaster like the election of Donald Trump from *ever* happening again, we must change how we educate our future citizens. And if we are, indeed, to save the world, we must, above all else...

Change how we educate our future citizens.

Of course, the threat is if you don't get your qualifications, you won't get a good job, you won't be able to buy a home and you won't be desirable. In other words, *fear* is used to make people into good little employees, the worker ants of a well-behaved society.

Fuck that.

In the US 100 years ago, one in ten people was employed by another person. The rest worked for themselves. Now it's reversed: one in ten is self-employed. The rest, 90 per cent of the workforce, are told when to come to work, when to go home, when they can go on holiday, how much they can earn and, should they disobey or underachieve, that they are fired.

You know what I hate about working? Bosses. That's what I fucking hate. First of all, let me tell you something real quick. The very idea that anyone could be my boss, well... I think you see the conflict. Not in this lifetime, Charlie. A few more incarnations, we'll sit down and chat...

Bill Hicks

When I was at school, I was told that my exam results were the most important thing imaginable, that if I didn't get certain grades my life would be... actually, I can't quite remember what the consequences were. I just recall the threat and the fear.

I didn't get all my exams, but I did OK. No one ever asked me since then if I have any qualifications.

When I left school, I was told that I was unemployable.

They were right. Apart from a brief, ill-advised period as a runner for a film company, I've been unemployed since 1982. I have never had a job, never had a boss, never had an interview, never had to ask anyone when I should get up or when I should go to bed.

That won't ever happen.

I'm not rich, but according to my own criteria I *am* successful in that I'm happy in what I do and people keep coming back. And while there may be something to reincarnation, given that all we know for *sure* is that we have this one life to live, I'm very fussy about how I spend that precious time. So, considering I enjoy what I do to make a living, it feels like a result to me.

Our schools are mostly farms for blue- or white-collar worker units. I mean no disrespect to the incredible teachers who work long, long hours in stressful jobs because they want to help educate children. I'm not critical of them or even the schools that exist. I'm critical of the system, which feels limited, restricted and one-dimensional. I imagine that they, too, would welcome reform.

On a personal level, the biggest impact of making this study into Sin, and my own immediate contribution to saving the world, is that subsequent to a lengthy three-minute discussion with the mother of my children and her partner, we decided to permanently remove our kids from school in order to take charge of their experience of learning ourselves.

We're springing them.

And that alone makes every second I've sat at this keyboard worthwhile.

I felt deeply uncomfortable while writing the piece on education, and that despite my protestations, criticisms and objections, my kids were in mainstream schools, albeit good ones. It felt a bit like that lying scumbag Tony Blair telling us that the multiple vaccine was safe while making sure his kids didn't get it.

And so, to educate my kids myself feels honest and congruent to who I really am and what I've learned this year. So, I want them out, and I want to take control of *what* they learn and *how* they learn. And that, for me, is how I deal with my sense of powerlessness and take charge of saving my world in my own minute way.

I'm not suggesting that you take your kids out of school or that you start popping psychedelics on a regular basis or that you become vegan or that you buy a hunting rifle from Wal-Mart and blow Trump's brains out... buy a hunting rifle from Wal-Mart and blow Trump's brains out... buy a hunting rifle from Wal-Mart and blow Trump's brains out...

No.

No, I'm not suggesting that.

But I *am* suggesting that you take a long, hard look at how you live life and make any changes, no matter how small...

Right now.

Don't wait. Don't relax. Don't live in hope. Wake the fuck up and do whatever you have to do to save the world you live in and make it a better place.

Now.

* * *

I asked a lot of people to contribute to this book.

Anton Newcombe of the Brian Jonestown Massacre initially said yes, before immediately behaving like... Anton Newcombe of the Brian Jonestown Massacre, and I quickly realised that I'd either have to dedicate an entire book to dealing with his twisted, maniacal ego or back out fast. Which I did.

Grayson Perry was gracious enough to say yes and make

some very good points. My old friend Shivam O'Brien was good value, as ever. As was Mem the Mad Sufi, and I loved talking to Kevin Barron.

Billy Brag came tantalisingly close and would've been great but was ultimately unresponsive. As was British actor Keith Allen, whose views I would love to have had. Bonkers, posh drug campaigner Amanda Fielding promised an interview time and again, but somehow she never quite seemed to be able to organise her diary.

Another who agreed to an interview that never happened was Australian stand-up comic Steve Hughes, who did a wonderful piece on political correctness that went viral on YouTube, some of which, because we never got it together to speak, I'm going to nick and transcribe here:

> Political correctness is the oppression of our intellectual movements so that no one says anything anymore in case someone gets offended. Now you have adults going, 'I was offended, I was offended and I have rights'. Well, so what? Be offended. Nothing happens. You're an adult, grow up, deal with it.
>
> 'I was offended!'
>
> I don't care. Nothing happens when you're offended.
>
> 'I went to the comedy show, and the comedian said something about the lord, and I was offended, and when I woke up in the morning I had leprosy.'
>
> Nothing happens.
>
> 'I live in a democracy, but I never want to be offended again'.
>
> Well, you're an idiot.

He makes a good point, as with health and safety regulations, when you make these laws and guidelines you infantilise people, and then...

They stop thinking for themselves.

They follow orders.

They fall asleep and, as we now know, sleep is the number-one cause of Sin.

Please don't follow orders.

Don't stand by and watch.

Don't ever just say, 'Oh yeah... I heard about that.'

Don't behave.

Don't conform.

Don't fit in.

Don't be frightened of speaking out and stating your truth, *even* if it upsets people. They'll get over it. So will you.

Don't be too cautious. Climb trees, fall in lakes and streams, let your heart be broken, forget safety, question everything, graze your knees even if you are over forty, destroy your reputation, try all of the Seven Deadly Sins at least once, make the sacred profane and the profane sacred, observe angels in demons and demons in angels, run naked in nature whenever possible, sleep out under the stars, walk in the rain, stop being so nice, smoke a cigarette, don't eat for a week, quit your job, tell someone you love them, be notorious, break some fucking rules and, most of all...

Never give up hope that we can save this beautiful world.

* * *

With our love, we could save the world.

George Harrison

Personal transformation can and does have global effects. As we go, so goes the world, for the world is us. The revolution that will save the world is ultimately a personal one.

Marianne Williamson

You begin saving the world by saving one man at a time; all else is grandiose romanticism or politics.

Charles Bukowski

It doesn't matter what the newspapers say or the politicians or the whole world. They don't define who you are. You do. And not by your words, but by your actions. The truth will come out. But until then, I'm going to keep fighting, just like you do.

Captain America

'Cos something is happening and you don't know what it is. Do you, Mr Jones?

Bob Dylan

* * *

Epilogue

> Every line in it is actually the start of a whole new song. But when I wrote it, I thought I wouldn't have enough time alive to write all those songs so I put all I could into this one.
>
> Bob Dylan discussing 'A Hard Rain's Gonna Fall'

New Year's Day 2017.

I sit, or rather, slump at my old oak desk and reflect on the year just passed.

It's late. Outside the rain taps out an executioner's beat on the glass, and the droplets and streetlights are sparkling like fake diamonds, while an icy draft creeps through the plantation shutters, which rattle like dry bones…

Like something out there wants to come in.

The single bulb of a 1940s Herbert Terry Anglepoise lamp struggles to penetrate the smoky gloom; cigarette butts are piled high in a Bates Motel china ashtray. My emphysemic MacBook, with its cataract-clouded screen, returns my gaze with tired resignation; dull eyes staring back at me through a dirty patina of grime, compacted dust and coffee stains, while beyond, the world tosses uncomfortably in a fitful slumber made all the more brutal by the slippery, blood-soaked floors of Ottoman night clubs, the broken bodies of hit-and-run children and infantile Trump tweets, and all the while an apocalyptic dread hangs over the streets, slick with last night's vomit and the ghosts of already-discarded resolutions.

A dream visited me in the dying weeks of 2016, 'the most dreadful year ever' as some have claimed; although those more versed in history have quite reasonably pointed out, 1916 was a fuck-sight worse.

I'm looking out of my bedroom across London. A mile or so away, above Muswell Hill, a huge brown mushroom cloud blossoms, a giant plume of death spiralling upward like a nuclear genie released from its bottle. I don't run; I know there's no point. I stand and watch in horrified fascination, waiting for the blast to return me to a series of subatomic particles, and all I can think is, 'They've done it. They've actually done it.'

Of course, Muswell Hill will be one of the first places taken out in the event of a nuclear strike; it has huge strategic value, given that its elimination will cut of the supply of cocaine to Westminster and the City, thus bringing what's left of the country to its knees. And those of us on its fringes in the leafy burbs of SoTo will be swept away like so many discarded fried-chicken carcases in its fiery wake.

Since that dreadful, one could say with hindsight, *inevitable* day, when the world awoke to the news that Donald John Trump was to be President of the Un-United States, I have been plagued with such visions, day and night. I find my mind randomly drifting off into thoughts of just how long it would take me to walk from London to my kids' house out in the country in the unlikely event that I survived the initial attacks. And would I have to walk at night to avoid military patrols or vigilante gangs or zombies? How would it be to leave my flat with all my worldly possessions, to step out into the rubble and the fire and the shadows of the dead and the acid rain? And if I made it to my daughters' house, what would I find there? Would they have survived? Would the government have put some plan into action to maintain their safety, or would I somehow have to protect them from the threat of a lawless society and all that can befall a beautiful child-woman when darkness prevails?

And what kind of world would we inherit?

I've never harboured these kinds of thoughts before, even though I was born on the back of the Cuban missile crisis into a nation frozen in terror at the prospect of nuclear war. But back then, even though fear was an ever-present factor, it just didn't seem likely that anyone would be crazy enough to actually push the button. That was the whole *point* of a nuclear deterrent, right? You don't nuke us because we'd nuke you and nobody survives. The problem is, I don't think Trump gives a fuck about that. The man is clearly insane.

Check his New Year message to the world. Remember, while blowing tea through your nose or whatever reaction it might engender, this is from the *President Elect*. As I write, this man is set to become the most powerful man in the world in *less* than three weeks.

> Happy New Year to all, including to my many enemies and those who have fought me and lost so badly they just don't know what to do. Love!

Really? I mean, *really*? Does that not just leave you *speechless*? We have a *little boy* in charge of the most powerful military nation in the world. And people say to me, 'Oh! don't worry, he's just a puppet. There's a whole load of people actually running the show. He won't have that much power.'

Well, that may be true, but I'll tell you this, if they can't even stop that fucker from pressing *Send* on his Twitter feed, how are they gonna stop him pushing other buttons?

But...

Despite everything, or maybe *because* of everything, I'm an optimist at heart. Even with the horrors we've explored, the darkness and the prevalence of Sin, I still believe in humanity and our capacity to save the world. I believe in beauty, and I believe in love, and my instinct tells me that the light will prevail; indeed, the shift between darkness and light is an ever-swinging pendulum. The Donald and all his evil little wizard scum merely represent the death struggles of base consumerism and bloated, hate-filled greed. And perhaps Crowley was right—maybe we really are at the dawn of the new age of Horus, in which we will take increasing control of our destiny.

Of course, the darkness won't go gently. It never does. Nor will it die with grace, humility or dignity. But remember, if it comes to a fight between darkness and light, the one that wins...

Is the one that you *feed*.

* * *

Close your eyes.
Fall in love.
Stay there.

* * *

Acknowledgements

Who to acknowledge in a book of Sin?

Well, first off it has to be my co-conspirator **Will Kitson**, whose demonic and fiendish editing of this book went way beyond the call of duty, and without whom it simply would not exist in its present form; instead, it would have been more like Dante's depiction of the Devil, some hugely overblown monster that no one would have wanted dealings with. Thank you, **Will**, for your tireless dedication to the project, the gentle yet clear and intelligent way you sifted through mountains of shit, for your ever-present enthusiasm, care and commitment, and for letting me bum roll-ups off you every time we met.

Next up, I need to thank my wonderful former wife, lifelong companion and devoted mother of my children, **Janan Kubba**, who, when I said to her, 'We need to get these kids the fuck out of school,' just looked at me and went, 'Yeah... let's do it.' And then her partner and equally devoted stepdad to my kids, **Andrew Saffron**, who when we said to him, 'We need to get these kids the fuck out of school,' immediately went, 'What a relief.'

When I'm working with guys who are thinking about ending their marriages, I always say to them, 'Look, I know it's hell right now, but have you thought about how it's gonna feel when another man is parenting your children?'

They don't like that thought.

I'm blessed that **Janan** chose **Andrew** and doubly blessed that we are in the position, albeit not without considerable (First World) sacrifice, to be able to home-educate our children.

Which leads me on to them.

OK, so we all think our kids are special, because they are. But I'm kind of shocked at my kids. **Noor**, **Tara** and their stepbrother, **Sam Nathan Saffron**. I don't really *understand* them. They seem to really *know* themselves. They are strong, independent, confident, creative people. That's not how I remember being when I was a child and I don't remember many other children being like that. I thought children were supposed to be all crushed and subservient. Not these ones. They're really interesting, each very different from the other and, to me, trouble-free. Someone asked me recently how I discipline my kids and I didn't know the answer. It's never been necessary and if I ever needed evidence that our children are the reincarnation of our ancestors, they're it.

My grandparents, **Pete** and **Alice Muckley**, who saved and defined my life, my heroes, role models and the inspiration for just about everything I do. I hope you're resting peacefully in the bottom of the wardrobe in my mum's back room.

When you lose someone you love, don't let anyone ever tell you that you'll get over it. You won't. The very idea is insulting, both to your feelings and to their memory. You'll get used to it, but the pain and the longing will never end.

Sorry about that.

Madame Trúc Mai Hua, who I didn't even know when I set out on this adventure, has been a champion of my work and a creative inspiration throughout; whose love, enthusiasm and artistic expertise helped keep me going at times when it all felt too much. Thank you for your vision, your devotion, for putting up with my cool, English reserve, for trying to keep me from the abyss and, on occasion, joining me there.

Shivam O'Brien, thank you once again for your depth of wisdom, your fearless spiritual energy, your giant heart and the priceless gift of your friendship. Your furious words are burned into the pages of this book and for that I love you.

Thanks to **Grayson Perry** for ranting Sin with me and for giving me some left-field pointers when I first set out, for your acerbic wit, your Sid James laugh and your generous, wounded male spirit. We need people like you now more than ever.

Robert Crumb for taking the time to write me your thoughts on the Big Seven that kicked off this book.

Sufi Mem and **Kevin Barron.** When I began this trip I searched far and wide for colourful, fascinating people to interview and you were right here all along, on my doorstep, infusing our building with your laughter and wisdom. Through your stories, the lives you have lived and continue to live, you make the world a better place through your presence.

Mirana Woska, **Michelle Scott**, **Rory Mcquaid** and everyone in the Norfolk gang, heroes one and all. Keep up your amazing work. You truly are saving the world.

Friends both new and old, those precious gems who enrich our very existence, and without whom life would be a bleak and frozen wasteland. I'm forever amazed at the richness and depth of your characters. Thank you, **Serena Morgan**, **Omolola Awomolo**, **Ian Mackenzie**, **Nick Van Gelder**, **Esther Kwaku**, **Sian O'Gorman**, **Erika Indra**, **Anthony Johnston**, **Paloma Suarez**, **Sue Angel**, **Melissa Unger**, **Sam Yearwood** and **Guy Gladstone**.

Without you I wouldn't get out of bed in the morning, let alone write this book.

And my mum, **Pat**, and sister, **Gerry**, you, too. Even though you'd never know it.

Oh, and **you**, thank you for reading this book. I hope it was of value. I hope it brought you more hope than hopelessness, more smiles than tears, more direction than confusion, more determination than despair. And now you're done with it, please give it to a friend or a charity shop or leave it on a train for a stranger to find rather than abandon it on a dusty bookshelf. Spread the word. Reviews on places like Amazon really help, believe it or not, if you can take a few minutes or feel the inclination. But, better still, let's all band together, everyone who reads this book. Let's start a movement and package up our well-thumbed copies and post them to:

Mr D. Trump
c/o The White House
1600 Pennsylvania Avenue NW
Washington, DC 20500
USA

Not because it'll save the world. But it'll make me smile.

* * *

First time I met **Shivam** he told how there's a Buddhist belief that sometimes it's necessary for a god to return to Earth to perform a certain task. These immortals hate the prospect of having to incarnate in human form and so the deal is always: get in, get the job done and get out as quick as possible.

And so, in closing, I'd like to dedicate this book to the memory of:

Boris Johnston Suárez
12 November 1997—23 February 2017

Spirit Horse Warrior and all-round beautiful soul, who completed his mission and left us as I was finishing the final edit of this book.

If you depart this world, leaving it a more beautiful place than the one you arrived in, then I consider that a life well lived, no matter how short.

Thanks for coming, Boris.

Mission accomplished.

* * *

Soul Rocks

NEW GENERATION

Recent bestsellers from Soul Rocks are:

The Rainbow Way
Cultivating Creativity in the Midst of Motherhood
Lucy H. Pearce
The comprehensive, soulful companion for artist mothers on their
creative journey.
Paperback: 978-1-78279-028-0 ebook: 978-1-78279-027-3

Toxic World, Toxic People
The Essential Guide to Health, Happiness, Parenting and
Conscious Living
Anna Victoria Rodgers
A jam-packed guide book full of researched information to detox
your lifestyle, create happy and healthy children and help tread
lighter on the environment.
Paperback: 978-1-78099-471-0

Play From Your F*****g Heart
A Somewhat Twisted Escape Plan For People Who Usually Hate
Self-Help Books
Jerry Hyde
Taking therapy down to street level, a rock and roll guidebook to
the science of the bleedin' obvious.
Paperback: 978-1-78279-408-0 ebook: 978-1-78279-407-3

How Not to Wear Black
Jules Standish
A guide to showing that the right colors, black, grey, red and blue,
can stimulate, enhance, inspire or calm.
Paperback: 978-1-84694-561-8 ebook: 978-1-78099-000-2

In10tions
A Mindset Reset Guide to Happiness
Melissa Escaro
Discover how to reset your mindset and make positive changes, while creating unlimited possibilities through your unconscious mind.
Paperback: 978-1-78279-602-2 ebook: 978-1-78279-601-5

Living and Coping with Epilepsy, My Way
Cara Coles
We really can have anything we want in life, so let's stop Epilepsy from getting in the way!
Paperback: 978-1-78279-746-3 ebook: 978-1-78279-745-6

The Real Gypsy Guide to Fortune Telling
Deborah Durbin
A concise yet comprehensive guide focusing on different types of fortune-telling and divination techniques.
Paperback: 978-1-78279-452-3 ebook: 978-1-78279-183-6

Soaring
A Teen's Guide to Spirit and Spirituality
Deneen Vukelic
This book, written with teens and young adults in mind, is an introduction to spirituality in the New Age.
Paperback: 978-1-78279-874-3 ebook: 978-1-78279-873-6

Teen Spirit Wicca
David Salisbury
Teen Spirit Wicca will give you exactly what you need to start practicing the craft and living your life as a Wiccan today.
Paperback: 978-1-78279-059-4 ebook: 978-1-78279-058-7

What A Blip
A Breast Cancer Journal of Survival and Finding the Wisdom
Alicia Garey
A look behind the curtain of a devastating diagnosis and finding
the joy of living again.
Paperback: 978-1-78279-225-3 ebook: 978-1-78279-224-6

Readers of ebooks can buy or view any of these bestsellers by
clicking on the live link in the title. Most titles are published in
paperback and as an ebook. Paperbacks are available in traditional
bookshops. Both print and ebook formats are available online.

Find more titles and sign up to our readers' newsletter at
http://www.johnhuntpublishing.com/mind-body-spirit.
Follow us on Facebook at https://www.facebook.com/OBooks
and Twitter at https://twitter.com/obooks.